ROMANTIC DAYS
IN OLD BOSTON

FRANCES ANNE KEMBLE.

From the painting by Thomas Sully, made in 1832, in the possession of the Boston Museum of Fine Arts.

ROMANTIC DAYS IN OLD BOSTON

THE STORY OF THE CITY AND OF ITS PEOPLE DURING THE NINETEENTH CENTURY

BY

MARY CAROLINE CRAWFORD

AUTHOR OF "OLD BOSTON DAYS AND WAYS," "ST. BOTOLPH'S
TOWN," "AMONG OLD NEW ENGLAND INNS," ETC.

With Numerous Illustrations

BOSTON
LITTLE, BROWN, AND COMPANY
1910

Published, October, 1910

Electrotyped and Printed by
THE   COLONIAL   PRESS
C. H. Simonds & Co., Boston, U.S.A.

FOREWORD

WE Americans have a curious habit of dating back our heroes and of refusing the stamp of authentic valor — at least in our histories — to any act of moral or physical courage which has happened since the Revolution. John Hancock we glibly dub " patriot," though he never fought at all, and in many ways is admittedly a man of pretty small calibre. It seems never to have occurred to those in charge of the spiritual sustenance of our youth that, beside William Lloyd Garrison, Hancock shrinks to really pitiful proportions. Webster's " Bunker Hill Oration " we read, to be sure, but the emphasis is always put upon the Bunker Hill rather than upon the Webster. And I never heard the name of Wendell Phillips pronounced during the years in which I prepared, in the Boston public schools, for college. This in spite of the fact that our country cannot present a finer example of moral heroism than Phillips exemplifies; nor has any orator ever given to the world

more stirring appeals to noble action than did
he. Clear-sighted foreigners perceive the truth
of what I am here trying to say — and in
this book endeavor to prove. Fredrika Bremer
observed long ago: " The anti-slavery struggle
will be the romance of American history."

But the youthful enthusiasm of the newly-
made city expressed itself also in literature,
in art and in experiments with life. Steele
said of a certain lady that to have known and
loved her was a liberal education; to have
shared in Boston's life and loved what it st
for during the nineteenth century was a lib
education. I remember once to have felt
with a pang of unmistakable envy at a din
given by the Boston Authors' Club to Mrs.
Julia Ward Howe and Col. Thomas Wentworth
Higginson, president and vice-president of th
club. Norman Hapgood, Clyde Fitch a
Owen Wister, all of whom were just too yo
to have shared in the stirring events of wh
Mrs. Howe and Col. Higginson were importa
parts, referred in their speeches to the wonderf
opportunities those two had enjoyed from the
very fact of living when and where they did
and the rest of us younger folk feelingly echoe
these sentiments. For though the twentiet
century will have its opportunities, also, the
will not be so akin to things literary as were th
opportunities of the nineteenth century. Will

said of London that the cultivated American peculiarly enjoys the place because he there sees whole shelves of his library walking about in coats and gowns, and an age when, as Wister happily put it at that dinner, — in referring to Mrs. Howe and Higginson, — " a lady could turn her pen into a sword and a gentleman his sword into a pen " must of necessity be the Golden Age to literary workers.

Yet other high notes, also, were struck in the nineteenth century, notes upon which we the twentieth century may well work out a symphony. The equality of woman, about which Margaret Fuller wrote an epoch-making book and for which Phillips all his life contended, we have yet to realize; and the fulfilment in some measure of that " sweetest dream ever dreamed in America," the Brook Farm experiment, — of which Hawthorne said towards the end of his life that " posterity may dig it up and profit by it," — remains. Yes! to us, also, are given wrongs to right and shackles to strike from the wrists of slaves. It is my hope, then, that this book, by recalling freshly the heroes of the nineteenth century, may help to hearten heroes for the twentieth.

It but remains to speak with gratitude of the many courtesies and quotation privileges extended to me. Most of these are acknowledged in the text, but I wish here particularly to express my appreciation of the kindness of the Houghton Mifflin Company, who as publishers of the works of the most eminent American authors, at least in the New England group, have necessarily been often appealed to and never in vain; to the invaluable *Memorial History of Boston;* to Mr. Francis Jackson Garrison, who has read my chapter on The Anti-Slavery Movement and given me much-prized help in connection with it; to Mr. John Bouvé Clapp, who placed at my disposal the results of his research in connection with the old Boston Museum; to E. P. Dutton and Co., who brought out *The Recollections of an Old Musician;* and to the Lothrop, Lee and Shepard Company, publishers of Mrs. Ednah Dow Cheney's *Reminiscences* and of Wendell Phillips's *Orations.*

In the matter of illustrations thanks are further due, and are gladly given, to the Massachusetts Historical Society, to the Boston Athenaeum and to the Bostonian Society for permission to reproduce certain valuable pictures in their possession; also to Mr. Frederick P. Vinton, the artist, a number of whose portraits of distinguished Bostonians are here used, and to Mr. Louis A. Holman, who has again given me the benefit of his keen scent in the matter of appropriate contemporary illustrations. To the attendants at the Boston Public Library and to Charles Knowles Bolton of the Boston Athenaeum I feel deep obligation also. How greatly do such courteous custodians of untold treasures lighten an author's labor!

M. C. C.

ARLINGTON HEIGHTS, MASSACHUSETTS, 1910.

CONTENTS

16149

ILLUSTRATIONS

ILLUSTRATIONS

ILLUSTRATIONS

ILLUSTRATIONS

ROMANTIC DAYS IN OLD BOSTON

CHAPTER I

THE MOULDING OF A CITY

IT was a very charming, comfortable old town — this Boston of uncrowded shops and untroubled self-respect which, in 1822, reluctantly allowed itself to be made into a city. For not lightly nor impetuously was the old plan of town government abandoned. Though the venerable John Adams, " the man of the town meeting," had generously set aside his own personal predilections and had cast a ballot (in 1820) for an amendment to the State Constitution that should enable freemen in large municipalities to delegate to representatives " the privileges of voting supplies," many there were — Josiah Quincy among them — who so firmly believed that the town-meeting form was peculiarly suited to the character of the people of New England that they resisted with all the power they possessed the impending change.

Yet the time for this change had certainly come. Quincy himself, in his *Municipal History of The Town and City of Boston* (written after the struggle had long been ended), amply justifies the step: " When a town-meeting," he says, " was held on any exciting subject in Faneuil Hall those only who obtained places near the moderator could even hear the discussion. A few busy or interested individuals easily obtained the management of the most important affairs in an assembly in which the greater number could have neither voice nor hearing. When the subject was not generally exciting town-meetings were usually composed of the selectmen, the town officers and thirty or forty inhabitants. Those who thus came were, for the most part, drawn to it from some official duty or private interest, which when performed or attained, they generally troubled themselves but little or not at all about the other business of the meeting. In assemblies thus composed, by-laws were passed, taxes to the amount of one hundred or one hundred and fifty thousand dollars voted on statements often general in their nature, and on reports, as it respects the majority of voters present, taken upon trust, and which no one had carefully considered except, perhaps, the chairman."

None the less, when the subject of adopting a city charter was brought before a "special meeting of the inhabitants" (in January, 1822), the vote on the test proposition "that the name of 'Town of Boston' should be changed to 'City of Boston'" was very close — only two thousand seven hundred and twenty-seven in the affirmative against two thousand and eighty-seven in the negative. The number of qualified voters at this time was between seven and eight thousand, about one-sixth of the total population, which, according to the national census of 1820, was forty-three thousand two hundred and ninety-eight.

It is interesting just here to observe how slowly Boston had increased in population during the past thirty years and to contrast this with its increase after the city charter was taken out. In 1790 the population of the town, including the people settled on the islands in the harbor, was 18,320. From 1790 to 1800 the increase was 6,617 or 36.11%; from 1800 to 1810, the increase was 8,850 or 35.48%; from 1810 to 1820 the increase was 9,511 or 28.14%. During the decade marked by the change in the form of government, however, the increase was nearly double that of the ten years preceding.

Happily, there was now beginning to be room for an increased population. Nathaniel Inger-

soll Bowditch, who in his *Gleaner* papers
characterizes Mr. Uriah Cotting as the " Chief
Benefactor of Boston," appears to have been
well within the facts of the case.   For Mr.
Cotting, as the projector of the Roxbury Mill
Corporation by whose " gigantic enterprise "
the Mill Dam was built, really made it possible
for Boston to grow.   This undertaking drew
in its train a series of constructions by which
alone the town has been enabled to become a
great city.

The charter which led to this complete change
in the town's physical conformation was passed
in 1814.   In the early summer of 1821 the Mill
Dam was finished and opened for travel.
Upon the granting of the charter the *Daily
Advertiser* printed a communication signed
" Beacon Street " which began as follows:
" Citizens of Boston!   Have you ever visited
the Mall; have you ever inhaled the Western
breeze, fragrant with perfume, refreshing every
sense and invigorating every nerve?   What
think you of converting the beautiful sheet of
water which skirts the Common into an empty
mud-basin, reeking with filth, abhorrent to
the smell, and disgusting to the eye?   By
every god of sea, lake or fountain it is incredible!"   By 1821, however, the same paper
is printing the following praise of this very
project: " The road over the Boston and Rox-

bury Mill-Dam was opened for passengers for the first time yesterday morning when a cavalcade of one hundred citizens and upwards, headed by General Sumner and Major Dean, passed over. . . . General Sumner in a pertinent address took occasion to advert to the magnitude of the undertaking the completion of which they were met to celebrate. . . . He reverted to the position of Boston thirty-four years ago when there was only one passage from the peninsula to the main. ' It was then,' he said, ' our town resembled a hand but it was a closed one. It is now open and well spread. Charlestown, Cambridge, South Boston and Craigie's Bridges have added each a finger, and lately our enterprising citizens have joined the firm and substantial *thumb* over which we now ride."

Thus it was quite a sizable territory over which John Phillips was elected mayor in 1822. Phillips had already served Boston as public prosecutor, as a member of the House and Senate of Massachusetts and as judge of the Court of Common Pleas. But it was to his charm of manner and to his " pliable disposition " rather than to his previous public services that he owed his election as first mayor of Boston. For Harrison Gray Otis and Josiah Quincy had both been in the lists with him and had only withdrawn their names because of the nomination, at the last moment, of a third candidate, Robert C. Winthrop, the presence of whose name on the ticket had made it impossible for either of them to carry the " majority of all votes " necessary for a choice. Phillips, therefore, came in as a compromise candidate; but he offended so few people that he would undoubtedly have been speedily re-elected, upon the expiration of his term, had not ill health made him refuse to run again.

Thus it was that the real task of " moulding the city " fell rather to the second mayor than to the first. Josiah Quincy, who was elected when Mayor Phillips retired, has left such an impress upon the government of Boston that he is generally called the city's *great* mayor. One reason for this is that he did many things during his six years of office. Another is that he had the chance and the ability to let posterity know about his activities. For it rarely happens that a mayor has so good an opportunity to tell just what was accomplished during his administration as Mr. Quincy made and improved when he published in 1852 his *Municipal History of The Town And City of Boston*. More than three-quarters of this book are devoted to an account of what was done during the six years when its author was mayor! But one should have no quarrel with the book or with its hero on that account. So many and

such important things were done. In Mayor
Quincy there was no over-cautious and timid
reference to public opinion with its attendant
shrinking from responsibility. He found many
reforms needed and he manfully set himself
to bring them about. Street begging was almost
entirely suppressed during his time, admirable
measures for the relief and care of the poor
were introduced, a new market-house (Quincy
Market) was erected and the city was so
effectually cleansed that a striking alteration
was observable in the mortality reports. Where
one in forty-two had died during the ten years
before 1823, during the last three years of
Mr. Quincy's administration the mortality was
but one in fifty-seven! It has indeed passed
almost into a proverb that Boston had never
had clean streets before this time, — and has
never had them since. Moreover, this energetic
mayor reorganized the fire department and the
police guardians, thus making the city a safe
and a peaceful place of residence. So orderly
was the conduct of the citizens that twenty-
four constables and eighty watchmen (of whom
never more than eighteen were out at a
time) were enough to make everybody in
Boston quite at ease concerning their lives and
property. It is Mayor Quincy, also, that we
must thank for planting the splendid trees on
the Charles street mall of the Common; and

it was during his administration (in 1824) that the Public Garden was created by Samuel E. Guild on what had been an unsightly beach of salt mud on the western side of Charles Street.

As Chairman of the School Committee, however, Mayor Quincy took a stand which has caused him to be greatly criticized by women writers. Up to 1825 there had been very scanty provision in Boston for the education of girls at the public expense, and this discrimination against women led Rev. John Pierpont, then Secretary of the School Committee, to propose the establishment in the city of a High School for Girls. He gave as his reason for doing this " general expediency and to make an object of ambition and profitable employment for three years of life now inadequately occupied." The resulting school was such a success that Mayor Quincy voted its — abandonment. Though the cost for each pupil was only eleven dollars a year, Mr. Quincy seems to have felt that, in too many cases, this appropriation would be employed for the education of wealthy girls whose parents could send them to private schools, and would if there were no public high school. " The standard of public education," he said, " should be raised to the greatest desirable and practicable height; but it should be effected by raising the standard of the common schools." Boston, it is thus clear, was

JOSIAH QUINCY, SECOND MAYOR OF BOSTON.

From the painting by Gilbert Stuart in the Boston Museum of Fine Arts.

VIEW OF BOSTON FROM EAST BOSTON IN 1848.

COLONNADE ROW, TREMONT STREET SOUTH OF
WEST STREET, OPPOSITE THE COMMON.

LEONARD VASSALL HOUSE, SUMMER STREET, THE SITE
OF HOVEY'S STORE.

by no means ready yet to provide higher
education for the poorer classes. There was
a great hue and cry because many young Irish
girls, who had entered the High School and
proved to be fine scholars, were unwilling,
after enjoying this taste of culture, to become
domestic servants. Public opinion was very
strong on this issue. For the first time, we
catch a glimpse of that anti-Irish-Catholic
feeling which culminated in the burning of the
Ursuline Convent in 1834.

During Mr. Quincy's second term he had the
honor of receiving and entertaining General
Lafayette, who was made the guest of the city
and was sumptuously entertained in the building at the corner of Park and Beacon Streets,
later known as the home of George Ticknor.
I have elsewhere[1] described in detail the events
of this visit of Washington's friend; suffice
it here, therefore, merely to say that the General
was escorted (Tuesday, August 22, 1824) to the
city limits from Roxbury by Governor Eustis
and by him presented to Mayor Quincy, with
whom he proceeded through streets resplendent
with the French and American flags and spanned
at intervals with arches bearing diverse patriotic
mottoes and inscriptions giving glad WELCOME
TO LAFAYETTE.

One incident which took place as the pro-

[1] *Among Old New England Inns*, p. 356 *et seq.*

cession moved up Tremont Street towards Boylston is too picturesque not to be told here once again. Amid the throngs of people who crowded the windows and steps of the houses on Colonnade Row the keen-eyed old soldier perceived, on a balcony, the face of Madame Scott, whom he had known well as the wife of pompous Governor Hancock. She had been his hostess away back in 1781 in the elegant Hancock mansion on Beacon Street, and though Time had wrought many changes in her piquant face and figure, he instantly recognized her and, with the inborn courtesy of a Frenchman, directed his conveyance to stop in front of the place where she sat, and rising, with his hand placed over his heart, made a graceful obeisance which was gracefully returned. Then the old lady burst into tears and exclaimed, " I have lived long enough."

Another charming feature of the festival was the singing of the Marseillaise by a throng of schoolchildren on the Common, of whom Wendell Phillips, then a fourteen year old lad, was one.

The original letter in which Lafayette announced his intended visit to Boston may be found in the manuscript collection of the Boston Public Library. It reads:

ALBANY, June 12, 1825.

My DEAR SIR: — Thus far I am come to redeem my sacred and most cordial pledge: We shall reach Boston

on the fifteenth: I will tell you between us that I have
been informed the legislature intend to receive the tribute
of my personal respects in which case it becomes proper
for me to be arrived two days before the Bunker Hill
Ceremony. As to what I am to do I cannot do better
than to refer myself to your friendly advices and shall
happily offer you and family my most affectionate grateful
respects.

LAFAYETTE.

I would have been very happy to celebrate with you[1]
the Fourth of July, but am obliged to set out on the
twentieth to visit the States of Maine, New Hampshire
and Vermont and will proceed down the north river to
New York, then to Philadelphia, Baltimore, Washington
and the seat of the [manuscript illegible] Virginia expedi-
tion so as to embark on the fifteenth August.

MR. QUINCY, *Mayor of Boston.*

On the day before his departure from Boston
the general dined in a marquee on the Common
with twelve hundred people, probably the
largest number ever seated at a single dinner
table in New England. On a previous day a
dinner of ceremony was given him at the
Exchange Coffee House on State and Congress
Streets, not the magnificent building erected
by Charles Bulfinch in 1808, but the less pre-
tentious structure put up on the same site
when that stately edifice had burned. Among
the toasts on this occasion was the following

[1] Mr. Quincy's house at this time was on Hamilton Place, number 1.

offered by General Lafayette: "The City of Boston, the CRADLE OF LIBERTY. May Faneuil Hall ever stand a monument to teach the world that resistance to oppression is a duty, and will, under true republican institutions, become a blessing."

The simple social traditions of a community as yet uncomplicated either by a large foreign population or by divisive questions such as the anti-slavery conflict was soon to introduce is reflected in the accounts of this entertainment of Lafayette. Boston at this period was a veritable garden city and Summer Street was a delightful avenue which well merited its name. Here earlier in the century had been the residences of Joseph Barrell, Benjamin Bussey and Governor James Sullivan, whose house at this time belonged to William R. Gray. Nathaniel Goddard, Henry Hill and David Ellis were among his neighbors.

Other famous old gardens on Summer Street and in its vicinity had been those of Edmund Quincy, which ran back to Bedford Street; and Judge Jackson's on the corner of Bedford and Chauncy Streets. Magnificent trees skirted the entire length of the street, overarching the driveway with interlacing branches so that one walked or rode as within a grove in a light softened by a leafy screen. Here, at the intersection of Bedford and Summer Streets was

HOUSE OF WILLIAM GRAY, CORNER OF SUMMER AND KINGSTON
STREETS.

Page 12.

OLD BEACON HILL.

From a contemporary drawing by J. R. Smith.

Church Green set off by an edifice (erected in 1814) of Bulfinch design whose spire towered to a height of one hundred and ninety feet from the foundation. "As late as 1815," declares Drake, "there was a pasture of two acres in Summer Street, and the tinkling of cowbells was by no means an unusual sound there. The hospitable residents could set before their guests cider of their own manufacture or butter from their own dairies." One very beautiful old place which belongs in this category was that (on the site now covered by Hovey's store) long known as the Vassall House and occupied later by the family of Frederick Geyer. At the wedding here of Nancy W. Geyer, who married Rufus G. Amory (in 1794), the Duke of Kent, son of George II. and father of the late Queen Victoria, was present as a guest.[1]

Harrison Gray Otis succeeded Mr. Quincy as mayor in 1829. An authentic picture of the social life of Boston during his administration is derived from the Boston correspondence published in the *New York Mirror*, where, under date of April, 1831, the writer, who appears to have been pining for the freer ether of New York, laments the lack of public places of amusement in Boston. To be sure, he admits, "the gallery of the Athenæum exhibition of paintings is crowded with beauty

[1] Drake.

a week or two in the summer; and our promenade place, Washington Street, for a couple of hours every fair day is very proper for loungers and ladies. There are, too, occasional concerts during the winter that attract genteel audiences, and once in a twelvemonth some distinguished singer or tragedian may fill the boxes of the theatre.

"But this absence of public amusements," concedes the correspondent, " is accounted for and in some measure compensated by the nature of our private society and the number of balls, parties and lectures which comfortably occupy the whole compass of the week." It was a very lavish hospitality, too, which was exercised in these Boston homes. That trade with the East which was to bring wealth to so many families of the new city had now been established for some years, and quaint silken hangings, porcelain, jade and carvings, treasures of teakwood and bronze from Canton and Hong Kong formed the effective background of elegant receptions and sumptuous feasts.

The first American to reach China after the Revolution was Major Samuel Shaw of Boston, whose romantic career I traced somewhat in the book preceding this.[1] His post was that of supercargo, — one whose duty it was to sell the outer cargo and buy another to be taken

[1] See *Old Boston Days and Ways*.

back, — and his name belongs at the head of the long list of men, chiefly from Boston, who, in this capacity, did honor to their native town and made fortunes for their descendants. A very famous house of this kind, which dates from January 1, 1824, is that known as Russell and Company, one early member of which was John Murray Forbes, in whose *Personal Reminiscences* may be found a fund of romantic material concerning the life and labors in China of many an enterprising young Bostonian. India Wharf, designed in 1808, by Charles Bulfinch, was the Boston headquarters of Russell and Company, and so important was the trade there conducted that in 1844, when the harbor froze over from the wharves to Boston Light and a channel was cut through the ice at an expense of thousands of dollars, to open the water from the Cunard Dock at East Boston, a connecting branch of it was extended to India Wharf for the benefit of the ships operated by the India Wharf Proprietors.

From first to last there were forty-eight members in the firm of Russell and Company, and when account is taken of the fact that these men not only lived in China a portion of the time but also on some occasions had their wives and daughters there for short visits, it will be seen that no formative influence was of greater importance to Boston than the organization of this wealthy and highly successful firm. There were many Bostonians, before the middle of the nineteenth century, who could talk of the East as intelligently as Kipling does now and could echo feelingly Mr. Forbes' verses, beginning

" Know ye the land where the bamboo and queue are — "

and ending

" Where the flowers have no smell and no flavor the
        fruit,
And 'tis stupid to talk and there's nothing to shoot;
    Where the earth is burnt mud and the sky is all blaze,
Where the dew is death-fog and the air is red haze?
    'Tis the land of the East; 'tis the region of curry
That slowly we come to and leave in a hurry.
    Know ye the land? My good friend, if you do,
By the Lord, I don't envy you; I know it too! "

Though Harrison Gray Otis was one of the India Wharf Proprietors, he was never a member of the firm of Russell and Company. He seems indeed to have ceased active efforts to accumulate wealth, some time before this firm was organized, and his name was now hedged about almost with divinity. For instance, on the day fixed for the organization of the city government of 1830 he sent word that he was ill and invited the members of the city council to assemble at his private residence, 42 Beacon Street, for the purpose of being qualified for office. Though this was quite unprecedented, no one thought of questioning the propriety of holding a municipal inauguration in such a place; an invitation from an Otis was equal to a command. It is altogether likely, too, that the city fathers greatly enjoyed themselves on this occasion, for Otis was a charming entertainer and his fine old mansion house with its three beautiful rooms *en suite* and decorated with pictures by Copley, Blackburn and Smibert were of the sort not accessible to all the men in the city government. Samuel Breck hazards the guess that at this time Otis was spending about ten thousand dollars a year upon the conduct of his household, though he adds that twenty-five years earlier " he told me that the utmost extent of his desires as to riches was to be *worth* ten thousand dollars." The universal opinion seems to have been that the first Harrison Gray Otis was unsurpassed in dress, equipage, entertainment and manners. " He always reminded me," says Augustus T. Perkins, who wrote his biographical memoir, " of a fine old French nobleman, one of those we read of as uniting wit with learning and great eloquence with profound acquirements."

Associated with Harrison Gray Otis in the social chronicles of the time is the name of Emily Marshall, the great Boston beauty, who married the mayor's son, William Foster

Otis, on May 18, 1831, and who died at the
Beacon Street home of her father-in-law August
17, 1836, aged only twenty-nine. Emily Marshall was the daughter of Josiah Marshall, who
lived on Franklin Street, during the twen-
ties and thirties, and for her social charm no
less than for her beauty she became very renowned. It is said that the hackmen who
served her were so spellbound with admiration
that they forgot to open the door of her carriage, and at a Fair gotten up by the ladies of
Boston, in 1833, to benefit the building fund
of the Perkins Institution for the Blind she
personally took in $2,000 at her table, — so
great was her vogue. The late Mrs. Samuel
Eliot of Brimmer Street was the daughter of
this famous beauty, the charm of whose features
is hinted at but not adequately expressed in
the well-known portrait by Chester Harding,
still in the possession of the family. There was
a time when it was "the thing" in Boston
society to write acrostic sonnets to Emily
Marshall. One of these, from the pen of N. P.
Willis, runs as follows:

> " Elegance floats about thee like a dress,
>   Melting the airy motion of thy form
> Into one swaying grace; and loveliness,
>   Like a rich tint that makes a picture warm,
> Is lurking in the chestnut of thy tress,
>   Enriching it, as moonlight after storm

Mingles dark shadows into gentleness.
A beauty that bewilders like a spell
Reigns in thine eyes' clear hazel; and thy brow
So pure in veined transparency doth tell
How spiritually beautiful art thou —
A temple where angelic love might dwell.
Life in thy presence were a thing to keep,
Like a gay dreamer clinging to his sleep."

Merely to be seen in the company of this beauty gave one a chance of immortality. Quincy in his *Figures of the Past* speaks of seeing " Beau Watson " walking (in 1821) on the Dover Street Bridge, then a favorite promenade place, with the fair Emily, who must then have been a girl in her teens. " Beau " Watson later came to be no less a person than the Rev. John Lee Watson, D. D., assistant minister of Trinity Church.

Under Mayor Otis Boston introduced municipal concerts on the Common, the project being engineered by the Society for the Suppression of Intemperance, who declared that " such a practice would have in their judgment a tendency to promote order and suppress an inclination to riot and intemperance." This same year (1830) cows were excluded from the Common. Ever since 1660 rights of pasturage on this public ground had been enjoyed by certain householders, but latterly the kine had not been invariably respectful to the ladies, and Mayor Otis, who was nothing if not gallant, signed their decree of banishment. It was also under Harrison Gray Otis, and upon his recommendation, that the Old State House was so altered as to provide accommodation for the mayor, aldermen, common council and other city officers.

So far all the mayors had been aristocrats addicted to an elegant mode of life and a magnificent manner of doing things. As a kind of protest against them and their ways Charles Wells was now (1832) put in as the representative of the middle classes. He served without distinction and, after two years, was succeeded by Theodore Lyman, Jr., whose term of office will always be associated (though perhaps through no fault of his) with two of the most disgraceful affairs ever perpetrated in an American city. The first of these culminated in the burning of the Ursuline Convent in Charlestown (now Somerville) on the night of August 11, 1834. The other, treated at length in the chapter devoted to the rise of the Anti-slavery Movement, came in the same month of the following year.

Adequately to tell the story of " The Burning of the Convent " would take much more space than I can here command. Besides, it has recently (August 29, 1909) been very beauti-

NATHANIEL HAWTHORNE IN 1840.

*From the painting by Charles Osgood, in the posses-
sion of Mrs. R. C. Manning, Salem, Mass.*

MRS. REBECCA CODMAN BUTTERFIELD WHEN
AT BROOK FARM.

From a daguerreotype.

Page 24

MARGARET FULLER OSSOLI.
From a daguerreotype.
Page 68.

HARRIET MARTINEAU.
Page 69.

fully told [1] by Miss Mary Boyle O'Reilly, daughter of the poet, who has made a special study of the subject. Miss O'Reilly attributes the ugly spirit which fired the building on Mount Benedict to labor troubles in the first place, and to an injudicious sermon preached by Rev. Lyman Beecher in the second. A quarter of a million Irish had landed in America between 1830–1835, and as ten thousand of these had settled in Boston they naturally displaced a large number of native workmen. These men resented the coming of the immigrants and caught eagerly at any opportunity which should offer to "put them down." They found their occasion in a kind of penny-dreadful, published as the work of a girl who had been a member of the nuns' community, the same production which supplied Lyman Beecher with his text. And the preacher's inflammatory words, in turn, served to give specious authority to the acts of these sore-headed truckmen who had constituted themselves the "defenders" of Boston against the corrupting (?) influence of a little band of nuns whose sole offence seems to have been that they were offering rare and very precious educational opportunities to the girls of eastern New England. The truckmen had given notice, on wretchedly printed posters scattered through-

[1] In the *Boston Globe*.

out the city, that they would demolish the
nunnery on a certain date, and there seems to
have been no reason — except that of criminal
negligence — for the failure of the authorities
to have a stout guard on duty that night at the
convent. No wonder five thousand good Boston citizens assembled in Faneuil Hall (after
the damage was done!) to protest against what
they might well call " an unparalleled outrage."
But though such men as Robert C. Winthrop,
William Appleton, Theophilus Parsons, David
Child, Nathan Appleton and many more signed
a paper and

Resolved, That in the opinion of the citizens of Boston
the late attack on the Ursuline convent, in Charlestown,
occupied only by defenceless females, was a base and
cowardly act, for which the perpetrators deserve the
contempt and detestation of the community.

Resolved, That the destruction of property and the
danger of life caused thereby calls loudly on all good citizens to express individually and collectively the abhor-
rence they feel in this high-handed violation of the laws.

Resolved, That we, the Protestant citizens of Boston,
do pledge ourselves, collectively and individually, to
unite with our Catholic brethren in protecting their
persons, their property and their civil and religious rights.

THEODORE LYMAN, JR., *Chairman.*

FANEUIL HALL, Aug. 12, 2 p. m., 1834.

no judgment was ever brought in against those
who committed the nefarious deed and no
indemnity was ever paid to the poor nuns

who had been made " the innocent victims of a public calamity." Obviously the new city of Boston had still much to learn about justice and effective government.

CHAPTER II

NOT a single Brook Farmer was ever known to admit that this experiment in communism was not a success. Even Dana and Hawthorne and George William Curtis bore testimony, years afterwards, that they had passed in this Arcady, nine miles from Boston's Beacon Hill, some of the happiest days of their lives and had brought away from their sojourn there an enduring impulse to high and noble things.

The only Brook Farmer with whom I have had an opportunity to talk (almost all who were members of the community have now passed away) is Mrs. Rebecca Codman Butterfield, a lady of eighty-five, who spent five years of her young womanhood at the community and who today speaks of it with the utmost enthusiasm and with a deep glow of reminiscent happiness in her still fine dark eyes. " My husband was a Brook Farmer, too," she said proudly, " one of the printers of the *Harbinger*, the organ of the movement, and we used often to say, after our children began to come, that we wished ardently that it were possible for us to give them anything like what we had got at Brook Farm. It was a place where the humblest could fulfil their deepest aspirations. The cobbler was a fine Shakespeare scholar, and Mr. Ripley loved above everything to work in the barn with the animals. Mrs. Ripley used to wash hours at a time, and I recall that when one particularly disagreeable piece of work on the place had to be done volunteers were called for, with the result that two of the finest young men of the community accomplished a ' drainman ' chore one night while the rest of us slept."

Mrs. Butterfield's brother, Dr. John Thomas Codman, has written in *Historic and Personal Memoirs of Brook Farm* the only long account of the community's ups and downs ever put out by one who had intimately shared its life. Ripley would have been the natural person to write such a story and there is reason to believe that he contemplated doing so. But the work was never done, perhaps because the whole thing meant so much more to him than it could possibly have meant to anybody else.

Carlyle described Ripley, who once called on him in England, as " A Socinian minister, who had left the pulpit to reform the world by cultivating onions." This gibe always makes me hate Carlyle; Ripley's essay in brotherhood

was so heroic without at all meaning to be!
That Ripley had a pulpit which he was glad to
abandon is true; he found himself (in 1840)
far from comfortable in his Purchase Street
Church and took counsel with the members of
the Transcendental Club, so-called, to see
whether it might be possible " to bring cultivated, thoughtful people together, and make a
society that deserved the name." There is
mention, in this connection, of a conference at
the house of Dr. John C. Warren, which ended
" with an oyster supper crowned by excellent
wines." One does not wonder, after hearing
the setting for his appeal, that the ex-minister
did not win many converts that night and that
all his hearers found themselves with other
things to do.

Even Emerson, when approached in the
matter, replied negatively, giving as his frank
reason for so doing that investments in Concord
were securer than they were likely to be at
Brook Farm. (Later, he compared Brook Farm
to " a French Revolution in small.") Yet his
refusal seems to have been due less to disin-
clination to venture his money than to his
inherent dislike of organization, and to his
exaggerated reverence for his own selfhood.
A discerning woman once said that it would not
be difficult to confess to Mr. Emerson, " but
that he would be shocked at the proposition

to take charge of even one soul." Certainly
he shrank, almost with horror, from the as-
sociative life implied in the Brook Farm proposition, though, all the while, the idealist in him
gave the movement secret encouragement and
applause.

Mr. Ripley had already in mind the spot upon
which to try his experiment, for, in the summer
of 1840, he and his wife had boarded at a
pleasant milk-farm in West Roxbury through
which a little brook ran cheerfully down to the
Charles River near by, and in which he found
many of the possibilities he sought. They had
left the place full of eagerness to return and
carry out what had become their dearest wish:
a movement " to insure a more natural union
between intellectual and manual labor than
exists; to combine the thinker and the worker
as far as possible in the same individual; to
guarantee the highest mental freedom by providing all with labor adapted to their tastes and
talents, and securing to them the fruits of their
industry; to do away with the necessity of
menial services by opening the benefits of
education and the profits of labor to all; and
thus to prepare a society of liberal, intelligent
and cultivated persons, whose relations with
each other would permit a more wholesome
and simple life than can be led amidst the
pressure of our competitive institutions."

The means to this end were set forth as the
cultivation of a garden, a farm, and the establishment thereon of a school or college in which
the most complete instruction should be given
from the first rudiments to the highest culture.
Thirty thousand dollars, it was decided, would
supply land and buildings for ten families
and allow a sufficient margin to cover the first
year's expenses. This sum Ripley proposed
to raise by forming a joint-stock company
among those who were friendly to his enterprise,
each subscriber to be guaranteed a fixed interest,
and the subscriptions to be secured by the real
estate.

The first step towards the execution of the
project was the purchase (in the winter of
1840–1) of Brook Farm by Ripley himself, he
taking the responsibility of its management and
success. Never did a man more conscientiously
discharge an obligation! Every debt was paid
off by him even when he himself was obliged
to work at a wretched wage for the money with
which to do this. The business arrangements of
the enterprise, from its hopeful beginning to
its saddened end, are carefully traced by Lindsay
Swift in one chapter of his charming volume,
*Brook Farm, its Members, Scholars and Vis-
itors*. Suffice it here, therefore, merely to say
that, in the spring of 1841, one third of the
necessary amount was actually paid in, and the

nucleus of the community took possession of
the farm-house which, with a large barn, was
already on the estate.

In Ripley's mind, and in the minds of the
more thoughtful of those who began the experiment with him, the idea of Brook Farm was
not at all, as has been generally supposed, to
secure an idyllic retreat for a favored few, but
to express belief in the brotherhood of man and
to proclaim through community life faith in the
possibility of realizing this belief. George P.
Bradford, who was of the original family, has
(in his chapter of the *Memorial History of
Boston*) expressed the thing thus: " The
movement was one form of the strong and rising
feeling of humanity and of the brotherhood of
man, then so widely pervading the community.
With it, too, came the desire and hope for better
conditions of life in which the less fortunate
classes might come to share in the privileges,
comforts, and various advantages belonging to
civilized society. The feeling which at this
time manifested itself in an excited form in the
anti-slavery agitation may indirectly have had
some effect in suggesting or stimulating this
movement. Mr. Ripley and others with him,
while sympathizing with the objects of the
Abolitionists, thought that as the evils of which
slavery is so signal and conspicuous a form lay
deep in the present constitution and arrange-

ment of society, so their remedy could only be found in a modification or radical change of ordinary life.

" The feeling, then, which lay at the bottom of the Brook Farm enterprise, and from which it mainly sprang, was dissatisfaction with the existing conditions of society, — that under these some classes enjoy the advantages of high culture and the gratification of the intellect and taste, and if obliged to work in some way for subsistence they yet have leisure and opportunity for refined recreation and for the enjoyment of comfortable or elegant modes of living, and are in some respects subject to more favorable moral influences; while, under these also, other classes are doomed to wearisome or painful drudgery and incessant toil, without opportunity for the enjoyment of intellect and taste, confined to dreary, squalid conditions of existence, and more exposed to temptations at least to the more flagrant crimes. Then, again, there was the feeling that there is something wrong in the mode of industry as now constituted, namely, competitive industry; . . . in which one man's gain is another man's loss, and the necessities of which make it the interest of each to get away from others and to appropriate to himself as large a share as possible of this world's goods, — a condition of things seemingly so contrary to the spirit of Christian brotherhood. Consequently a mode of life was desired . . . in which this evil condition of the relations of society might be corrected."

It would seem from the above-quoted statement that the ideals which inspired the movement were nothing more or less than those embodied in what we are today calling " Christian Socialism," one of whose disciples has put the thing thus succinctly: " If manual labor is a blessing, not a curse, I want my part of it; if it is a curse, not a blessing, I ought to take my turn." [1]   Of course, there were other and more superficial motives inciting to an interest in the enterprise and a desire to have a part in it. The prospect of a pleasant social life, with congenial society, somewhat free from distasteful conventions, moved some.   Others were attracted by the idea of a life of mingled physical and intellectual labor as exhilarating and healthful.   And young women, especially, to whom in that day comparatively few interesting occupations were open, hailed eagerly the opportunity thus afforded to earn a living amid congenial surroundings.

Hawthorne was one of the first to embrace community life at Brook Farm, and in what has come to be known as the epic of the place, *The Blithedale Romance*, he analyzes with characteristic acumen the psychology of his

[1] Vida D. Scudder in *A Listener In Babel*.

co-laborers for the common good, — " our little
army of saints and martyrs," as he rather
scathingly calls them. " They were mostly
individuals who had gone through such an
experience as to disgust them with ordinary
pursuits, but who were not yet so old, nor had
suffered so deeply, as to lose their faith in the
better time to come. On comparing their
minds, one with another, they often discovered
that this idea of a Community had been growing
up, in silent and unknown sympathy, for years.
Thoughtful, strongly lined faces were among
them; sombre brows, but eyes that did not
require spectacles, unless prematurely dimmed
by the student's lamplight, and hair that
seldom showed a thread of silver. Age, wedded
to the past, incrusted over with a stony layer
of habits and retaining nothing fluid in its
possibilities, would have been absurdly out of
place in an enterprise like this. Youth, too,
in its early dawn, was hardly more adapted to
our purpose; . . . We had very young people
with us it is true, — downy lads, rosy girls in
their first teens and children of all heights
above one's knee, — but these had chiefly been
sent thither for education, which it was one of
the objects and methods of our institution
to supply. Then we had boarders, from town
and elsewhere, who lived with us in a familiar
way, sympathized more or less in our theories

and sometimes shared in our labors. On the whole it was a society such as has seldom met together. . . ."

It was indeed. And nothing about it was more anomalous than the presence in it as a regular Community member of Nathaniel Hawthorne, poet and romancer. His deciding motive in joining the enterprise does not appear; but it seems more than possible that he was himself among those in whom recent experience of the world had awakened "disgust," for he had just severed his relation with the Boston Custom House, and it was with the thousand dollars that he had saved from his government earnings that he purchased shares 18 and 19 of the Association stock. He arrived in the midst of one of those late spring snow-storms, "which, as Lindsay Swift says, 'never fail to impress a New Englander with their unseasonableness, though they are as invariable as the solstices.'"

To set out on such an untoward April day for an adventure in Arcady might well give any man pause. Hawthorne superbly voices the reflections such a situation would engender: "The greatest obstacle to being heroic is the doubt whether one may not be going to prove oneself a fool; the truest heroism is to resist the doubt; and the profoundest wisdom to know when it ought to be resisted, and when to be obeyed." There is a life philosophy for you, apropos of an April snowstorm! And the paragraph — in *The Blithedale Romance* — which immediately follows this one, and describes as only an artist in words could that long-ago snowstorm and the way in which its exhilarations and its buffets reacted upon the sensitized mind of our tyro in altruism, is a masterly piece of writing. Then comes this, — and it is the crux of the matter: "Whatever else I may repent of, however, let it be reckoned neither among my sins nor follies that I once had faith and force enough to form generous hopes of the world's destiny, — yes! — and to do what in me lay for their accomplishment."

Hawthorne's immediate duty, at Brook Farm, was "to play chambermaid to a cow." At any rate that is the way he put the thing after he had tired of it. At first the scenery delighted him and he evinced considerable enthusiasm over his tasks. In a letter to his sister Louisa he wrote, "This is one of the most beautiful places I ever saw in my life, and as secluded as if it were a hundred miles from any city or village." Presently he writes, "I have milked a cow!" One of his first bucolic experiences was with the famous "transcendental heifer" which was named (very likely by Hawthorne) "Margaret Fuller" because the beast proved rather strong minded and had finally to be sent to Coventry by the more docile kind, always to be counted on as more or less conservative. Hawthorne later refers to this animal as having " a very intelligent face " and " a reflective cast of character." They all got a good deal of fun at Brook Farm, over the qualities imputed to their four-footed friends. Dr. Codman tells of a fine imported bull who, because he did not seem to be doing his share of work in their very industrious community, was harnessed up with a ring through his nose and made to draw a tip cart. His name was " Prince Albert." Then there was " Cyclops," too, a large raw-boned gray mare so christened because she had only one eye.

Ripley loved working with the animals, but Hawthorne never did, and by the middle of the August which followed the April of his arrival we find him writing, " In a little more than a fortnight I shall be free from my bondage — free to enjoy Nature — free to think and feel. . . . Oh, labor is the curse of the world and nobody can meddle with it without becoming proportionably brutified! " Yet he stuck it out for a whole year and referred always to his stay at Brook Farm as the romantic period of his life. When he came to write his epic of the place he closed the story with this beautiful passage: " Often in these years that are darkening around me, I remember our beautiful scheme of a noble and unselfish life, and how fair in that first summer appeared the prospect that it might endure for generations and be perfected, as the ages rolled by, into a system of a people and a world. Were my former associates now there — were there only three or four of those true-hearted men now laboring in the sun — I sometimes fancy that I would direct my world-weary footsteps thitherward, and entreat them to receive me for old friendship's sake."

The reproach hurled today at nearly all socialistic enterprises — that they stand for " free love " — early came to be used as a boomerang to throw at Brook Farm. Mrs. Butterfield tells me that her father and mother were looked upon as most rashly endangering the souls of their young children when they took them, the second year of the experiment, to " that regular free love institution." Now, of course, this charge was grossly untrue. But it soon began to militate very powerfully, none the less, against the success of the school which, at the start, was to have been a chief source of income. In the fall term of 1842 the school's teaching staff was composed of the following instructors: George Ripley, Intellectual and Natural Philosophy and Mathematics; George P. Bradford, Belles Lettres; John S. Dwight, Latin and Music; Charles A. Dana, Greek and German;

John S. Brown, Theoretical and Practical Agriculture; Sophia W. Ripley, History and Modern Languages; Marianne Ripley, Primary School; Abigail Morton, Infant School; Georgiana Bruce, Infant School; Hannah B. Ripley, Drawing. The infant school was for children under six years of age; the primary school for children under ten; the preparatory school for pupils over ten years of age intending to pursue the higher branches of study in the institution. A young man could fit for college in six years at Brook Farm or he could take a three years' course in theoretical and practical agriculture. In any case he was expected to spend from one to two hours daily in manual labor. Now with such teachers, such a well-planned course and a healthy country background upon which to live a free and happifying life, it would seem as if the school ought greatly to have succeeded. For a while, indeed, it did flourish like the proverbial green bay tree; Harvard College sent to its stimulating care young men who needed to study hard for a while in a community less exciting than Cambridge, — and their presence added not a little, as the presence of college boys always does, to the color and variety of the life.

Charles A. Dana was one of the Harvard youths who found his way to the farm in the the middle of his college career, but he came as

a " professor " and not as a pupil. Born at
Hinsdale, New Hampshire, in 1819, he had
passed his boyhood in Buffalo, and there fitted
himself for Harvard College, which he entered
in 1839. In the middle of his course his sight
became seriously impaired from reading " Oliver
Twist " by candle light. When at three in the
morning he finished the badly printed volume
he found that he could scarcely see. Study,
therefore, had to be abandoned for the time,
and he was very glad to accept the invitation
of the Harvard men already at Brook Farm to
go there as instructor in Greek and German.
He did his work as a teacher well, contributed
articles to the *Harbinger*, — when that organ
of the Brook Farmers came to be established, —
and was throughout his five years of connection
with the movement loyal and interested.

Another famous editor who passed valuable formative years at Brook Farm was George William
Curtis, who, with his brother Burrill, went out
there as a boarder in 1842. Miss Amelia Russell,
who has written charmingly of the home-life
at Brook Farm, calls the Curtis brothers
" Greek gods," — so handsome were they. Tra-
dition recalls that they had an especial fondness
for picnics and that he, whom we now associate
chiefly with an Easy Chair, danced, at a certain
Brook Farm junket, in a short green skirt
modelled on that worn by Fanny Ellsler!

CHARLES A. DANA.

After a daguerreotype.

Page 38.

DR. ORESTES A. BROWNSON AS HE
LOOKED WHEN AT BROOK FARM.

Page 47.

GEORGE RIPLEY.

Page 44.

FATHER HECKER IN HIS PRIME.

*From a rare photograph in the pos-
session of the Paulist Fathers,
New York.*

Page 47.

BROOK FARM BUILDINGS. _Copyright, 1910, by M. G. Cutter._

After a contemporary drawing.

BROOK FARM PHALANX.

Good for **5** Cents

A seeker after country beauty might well choose Brook Farm today as an ideal place in which to take refuge from a jarring world. It still has a slender little brook gurgling through its undulating meadows and there is a happy air of peace resting upon its woods and hill-tops. The accompanying picture is a photograph of a painting done in 1845 by Josiah Wolcott, then a resident at the community. It is owned by Mrs. Butterfield and is interesting as an authentic contemporary reproduction of the actual " set " of this inspiriting drama of brotherhood. At the extreme right is shown the Hive, the farm house which stood not far from the road when the life of the little community began and which was immediately utilized. Here was the heart of the community: Mr. Ripley's library; the first day nursery ever known in America, — a room where mothers could leave their children in care of the Nursery Group while they did their daily work; " Attica," a large upper room where the unmarried men slept; and the low-studded dining-room with its old-fashioned fireplace of brick and its pine tables set off with white linen and white table-ware and having white painted benches on either side.

At the highest point of land which the farm contained (and the second building from the right in the picture) was built, in 1842, the Eyrie, a square wooden structure of smooth

matched boards painted, after the imitative
fashion of the day, the color of gray sandstone.
The house was reached by a long flight of steps
from the farm road and the view from it was a
delight. Into this house the Ripleys moved as
soon as it was finished. The Cottage — which
alone of all the community buildings remains
today — was the next house erected after the
Eyrie. The remaining building, at the extreme
left of the picture, was called Pilgrim House,
and was built by Ichabod Morton for the use of
his family. It is interesting to us as having been
the editorial office of the *Harbinger*.

And now let us see what manner of daily
life was led in this community by those who
had there withdrawn from the world to help
in the world's reformation. Emerson always
rather poked fun at Brook Farm, though he
admitted that it was a pleasant place where
lasting friendships were formed and the " art
of letter writing was stimulated." He implies
that there was a shirking of labor on the part
of some, and perhaps that is true. Human
nature is pretty apt to be human nature even
at Brook Farm. " The country members," he
says, " were naturally surprised to observe that
one man ploughed all day and one looked out
of the window all day — and perhaps drew his
picture, and both received at night the same
wages."

The work of the household as well as of the farm was organized by groups, and Mrs. Butterfield is as sure today as she was then that necessary labor can be greatly lightened as well as sweetened by working in this manner. " Let us suppose it is Tuesday," she says. " The rising horn sounded at five o'clock in summer. I often used to get up and go around from house to house with a peculiar whistle as a signal to some members of the singing group to sing under John S. Dwight's windows from 6 to 7. We sang Mozart's and Haydn's masses, and it was glorious to hear that sacred music in the still, beautiful morning air. I never can forget it. I think it was one of the holiest and most inspiring things in my life.

" Then came breakfast in the Hive and after breakfast our work. I greatly enjoyed ironing, and on Tuesday I would work all the morning with that group. Dinner was at twelve o'clock and in the afternoon there were German and French classes to which any one who wanted to study could go. The cobbler would stop in his mending of shoes to go to the Shakespeare class, making up time afterward. As a rule the women did the housework, and the men that connected with the farm, but the men helped in the housework too when that seemed advisable. The baker was a man — Father Hecker, founder of the Paulist order, he came to be afterward, — another man was assistant in the laundry and one of the young fellows carried water for the dormitories.

"I shall never forget the impression made upon my youthful mind, the day our family arrived at the farm, by seeing one of the cultivated gentlemen from Concord hanging out the morning's washing. Yet that was not inappropriate work in rough weather for a man. Our women seldom participated in outdoor work, though I remember that, on one or more occasions when help in that direction was imperatively needed, half a dozen of our young women did very active work in the hay field. In several of the groups, notably the waiting groups, the young men and women were about equally divided. Charles A. Dana was at one time head waiter. After washing for three hours every Monday morning Mrs. Ripley would have her classes at the school in the afternoon. Ah! but she was a rare and lovely soul."

Rare! indeed. Too much emphasis can scarcely be laid, in writing about Brook Farm, upon the exquisite quality of this woman who upheld the hands and sustained the courage of the founder of the enterprise. Granddaughter of Chief Justice Dana, our first minister to Russia, she had been a teacher, — when Ripley came to love her, — in a boarding and day school for young ladies held in Fay House, Cambridge. In that house she was married to Ripley (August 22, 1827) by the father of Oliver Wendell Holmes. Their alliance was " founded not upon any romantic or sudden passion, but upon great respect for her intellectual power, moral worth, deep and true Christian piety and peculiar refinement and dignity of character," wrote the young husband to a friend. Ripley came of farmer stock — his boyhood home was in the beautiful Connecticut valley, — but he was a lover of books, a graduate of Harvard College, and he had chosen the ministry for his profession.

It seemed indeed as if the life the pair would lead must be that of a quiet Boston parson and his wife, for he was soon called over the church at the corner of Pearl and Purchase Streets, and he stayed there preaching Unitarianism as he saw it for fourteen years. But, during those years there came to him a vision of that great truth which is now bursting afresh upon the minds of earnest-minded ministers, — that, under existing social conditions it is well-nigh impossible to harmonize Christian doctrine and Christian life. He tried to preach the social gospel, but his people were not responsive. Finally, therefore (in October, 1840), he wrote them from Northampton a manly letter in which he set forth with absolute open-mindedness the reasons for the faith which was in him, and his reluctant conviction that he and they could not longer work together. This letter was accepted as definitive by his congregation, and on March 28, 1841, they listened respectfully but with resignation, to their minister's farewell sermon.

The compact description of Ripley given by his biographer, Rev. O. B. Frothingham, warms one's heart to the man. " He was no unbeliever, no sceptic, no innovator in matters of opinion or observance, but a quiet student, a scholar, a man of books, a calm, bright-minded, wholesouled thinker, believing, hopeful, sunny, but absorbed in philosophical pursuits. Well does the writer of these lines recall the vision of a slender figure wearing in summer the flowing silk robe, in winter the dark blue cloak of the profession, walking with measured step from his residence in Rowe Street towards the meeting house in Purchase Street. The face was shaven clean, the brown hair curled in close crisp ringlets, the face was pale as if in thought; the gold-rimmed spectacles concealed black eyes; the head was alternately bent and raised. No one could have guessed that the man had in him the fund of humor in which his friends delighted, or the heroism in social reform which, a few years later, amazed the community." To Emerson Ripley wrote that his idea of personal happiness would be to rent a place upon which he could live independently — " and one day drive his own cart to market and sell greens." As a matter of fact he possessed neither the taste nor the temperament of a magnetic leader of men.

Mrs. Ripley was quite different. She supplied what he lacked in this way. She was ardent, impulsive, deeply sympathetic. Her power of enthusing those who came in contact with her was extraordinary and " impossible seemed a word unknown to her." She was a tall and graceful woman with fair coloring. When it is said of her that, by reason of being chief of the wash-room group, she made the laundry " a place of almost seductive cheerfulness," one has perhaps given the strongest proof needed of her magnetism and buoyancy.

With such people as Mr. and Mrs. Ripley at its head and such men as Dana and John S. Dwight acting as effective lieutenants, Brook Farm was sure to be a mecca for visitors. The popularity of the place helped towards its undoing, indeed. Dr. Codman records that, in one year, more than four thousand people came out to the farm to stay for a longer or shorter period. At first these people were made welcome to meals without charge and members of the community were drafted to show them about. But when their number came to be

" legion " it was found necessary to exact a fee
for the food consumed, and they were left to
wander as they would. " Yet every pleasant
day from May to November," the historian
of the place declares, " men, women and children were passing from Hive to Eyrie and over
the farm back to the Hive, where they took
private carriage or public coach for their departure. Among these people were some of the
oddest of the odd; those who rode every con-
ceivable hobby; some of all religions; bond and
free, transcendental and occidental; anti-slavery
and pro-slavery; come-outers, communists,
fruitists and flutists; dreamers and schemers
of all sorts." In a word cranks galore. Such
was Bronson Alcott's friend Lane, who was
opposed to eating anything that was killed or
had died, so ate neither fish nor flesh; who was
opposed to wearing wool because it was an
animal product and implied robbing the sheep
of its protection; who was opposed to wearing
cotton and would use neither rice nor sugar
because they were products of slave labor; for
whom no way of getting to Brook Farm but
on his legs seemed possible and no encompassing
garment but a linen suit could be regarded as
sufficiently moral. Alcott himself did not come
often. He found Concord a more favorable
spot in which to follow his peculiar genius.
Moreover, he was fresh from the failure of

his own recent experiment in community life at Fruitlands, near Harvard, Massachusetts.

Orestes Augustus Brownson was one of the interesting characters who wandered back and forth between Brook Farm and the outer world. Brownson had experienced so many kinds of religion before he " walked backward into the Catholic Church " that it was once remarked of him, when a preacher invited to the communion table the members of all Christian churches, that Brownson was the only person in the congregation who could " fill the bill."

Brownson it was who brought to the farm Isaac Hecker, — already referred to as the family baker, — who became the head of the Paulists and, in his day, the best interpreter of the Roman Catholic Church to the cool-headed practical American. His sojourn at Brook Farm may very well be credited in tracing out the influences which made him what he was. " To leave this place is to me a great sacrifice," he wrote as he was going away. " I have been much refined by being here." Hecker was a " partial " boarder when he first entered Brook Farm; he paid four dollars a week and gave his services as a baker in exchange for instruction in German, philosophy, French and music. Later he became a " full " boarder, paying for the greater freedom five

dollars and a half a week. Hecker was of the
Grahamites, while at the Farm. In the dining-
room there was always one table of vegetarians
— those who used no flesh meats and generally
no tea or coffee, who were, in fact, followers
of the dietary principles of Dr. Sylvester
Graham, whose name is still connected with
bread made of unbolted flour because it was by
him considered the very perfection of human
food. When the plans for the Phalanstery — the
large house which was destroyed by fire before
it was completed — came to be made, it was
decided that those at the Graham tables should
be given board at a less price than the others,
because their food was less expensive.

The burning of the Phalanstery (March 3,
1846) marked an epoch at Brook Farm. For
a long time accommodations had been insuffi-
cient and high hopes were placed upon what
might be accomplished when this large, roomy
building should be available for lodging and
assembly purposes. By those who wished to
swing the Community into line with Fourierism the central house was deemed especially
desirable, and when it seemed impossible to get
together the seven thousand dollars which had
been lost through the fire their enthusiasm
dwindled gradually away. Writers on Brook
Farm are agreed that the cause of the Community's failure was its advocacy of this as-

sociationist doctrine as preached by Albert Brisbane, and that the *occasion* to which dampening of enthusiasm may be traced is the burning of the Phalanstery, the outward and visible sign of Fourierism.

When Charles Fourier, the son of a French linen draper, died in 1837, his theories were not well known in this country. But Albert Brisbane got hold of them in England, converted Horace Greeley to them, and, through Greeley, who took a very deep and real interest in Brook Farm, foisted them upon the Brook Farm Community. The old slander that Brook Farm was a " regular free love institution " now began to be repeated in the religious press as well as from mouth to mouth. And unfortunately there was just one little remark which Fourier had once made which could be interpreted as condoning irregularity in some cases. In his study of human nature he believed he had discovered inherently inconstant natures, exceptional men and women who cannot be constant to one idea, one hope or one love; and believing this inconstancy to be a normal trait of character with some persons, who are exceptions to the general rule, he simply acknowledged the fact and speculated on the result and the position such persons would have in the future ideal society. " But," he said very unmistakably, " the man has no claim as discoverer or to the confidence of the world, who advocates such absurdities as community of property, absence of divine worship and rash abolition of marriage." This would have been circumstantial enough for any unprejudiced writer. But then, as now, newspapers battened on articles in defence of " sacred institutions " nobody has attacked, and the impression that Brook Farm encouraged a laxity of moral outlook was not allowed to die. Of course this reacted disastrously upon the school attendance, which was to have been a chief source of income. Moreover, the industries, which had latterly been introduced, did not flourish as it had been fondly hoped they might. The nine miles from Boston proved too far to cart window-frames and the like profitably to market.

The organ of Fourierism in this country was the *Harbinger*, printed at Brook Farm from June, 1845, to June, 1847. Had the paper been used to tell the world the truth about Brook Farm instead of being devoted to the promulgation of doctrines already obnoxious to many, the day might have been saved in spite of the fire. As it was, the *Harbinger* was fatally associated with propaganda considered subversive of the social order. From a literary standpoint it was a great success, however; its poetry and musical criticism were excellent, and the first number contained an admirable translation of George

DANIEL WEBSTER'S HOUSE WHICH STOOD ON THE COR-
NER OF SUMMER AND HIGH STREETS.

DANIEL WEBSTER.

*From a daguerreotype made by Richards, of
Philadelphia, about 1850.*

Page 67.

ELIZABETH PEABODY.

From a portrait in the possession of the Elizabeth Peabody House, Boston.

MASONIC TEMPLE, CORNER OF TREMONT STREET
AND TEMPLE PLACE.

Page 66.

Sand's "Consuelo," contributed by Francis Gould Shaw, a neighbor and very kind friend of the Brook Farmers. Dr. Codman recalls that Mr. Shaw, on his horse, with his young son, a tiny little fellow, on a pony by his side, often galloped over to the Farm to call. The "little fellow" is now commemorated in Boston's beautiful Shaw Memorial, opposite the State House.

Another West Roxbury neighbor whom those at the Farm were always glad to welcome was Theodore Parker. Parker was a warm friend of Ripley, and as he was then having troubles and religious perplexities of his own it is probable that he found it a great comfort to tramp two miles across the fields and talk things over with one who had been through the mill. On Sundays some members of the Community would usually turn out to hear Parker preach.

Sunday was a delightful day at the Community. Hawthorne has reproduced for us something of its flavor in his talk about Eliot's pulpit in *The Blithedale Romance*, and Dr. Codman has given us a charming snapshot description of a certain occasion when William Henry Channing held a religious service in the nearby beautiful pine woods and his hearers, like the Pilgrims and reformers of old, raised their voices in hymns of praise and listened to a sermon of hopefulness. That must have been a thrilling moment when Channing bade the assembled company, seated on the pine-needles at his feet, " to join hands and make a circle, the symbol of universal unity, and of the at-one-ment of all men and women."

But life at Brook Farm was more than work and study and preaching. Of pure fun there was always a good deal. As Lindsay Swift has whimsically put it, " Enjoyment was almost from the first a serious pursuit of the Community. It formed a part of the curriculum and was a daily habit of life." Dancing was much in vogue, and after the dishes had been done in the evening it was quite the custom to clear away the dining-room tables and have a joyous hour or two. Then the talk at meals was apt to be good. The immediate effect of a visit from Alcott was the direction to cut pie " from the centre to the periphery," and Mrs. Howe avers that the customary formula at table was, " Is the butter within the sphere of your influence? "

The fact that, for a long time, there were more men than women in the Community made things very pleasant for the girls who had housework to do. George William Curtis occasionally trimmed lamps, Dana organized a band of griddle-cake servitors composed of four of the most elegant youths in the Community, and there is a story that one young fellow confessed his passion while helping his sweetheart at the sink. Of love-making there was quite a little. No less than fourteen happy marriages may be traced to acquaintance begun there. Dr. Codman thinks this was due, in part, to the fact that the girls in their neat costumes — very like that afterwards associated with Mrs. Bloomer — never looked anything but attractive. The men must have made a fine appearance, too, in their tunics of brown linen or Rob Roy flannel.

Yet since the financial conditions for marriage were not inviting, only one union was consummated at the Farm. This was the wedding of Dwight's sister, Marianne, to John Orvis. Rev. W. H. Channing tied the knot, and the usually eloquent Dwight made a speech of just five words, — " I like this making one." Perhaps he put his maturer thought about what he felt that night into his *Harbinger* poem, one verse of which runs:

" Come, let us join hands. Let our two flames mingle
        In one more pure;
    Since there is truth in nothing that is single,
        Be love love's cure."

Twenty-five years had been more or less vaguely set by the first Brook Farmers as the length of time which would be necessary to prove their experiment a real success. It had been going a fifth of that period with ever-increasing numbers and no decrease of enthusiasm when the Phalanstery burned. A year after that event Mr. Ripley was authorized by the creditors and stockholders to " let the farm." The intervening period covers the gradual dissolution of the Community. Quietly, almost imperceptibly, the members withdrew into the big outside world. Dr. Codman says there was " no sadness of farewell." All had the feeling that they would some day be together again in another Community whose finest building would not burn down just when things were at their best.

The farm itself passed into various hands and suffered several vicissitudes of fortune. The Community buildings fell away one by one until today but one roof-tree of that happy time is left standing. It is that known as the Margaret Fuller Cottage, perhaps because it is the only house at which that famous lady never stopped while visiting Brook Farm.

So ends the story of this romantic essay in socialism, this brave adventure in brotherhood which has well been called " the sweetest dream ever dreamed in America." Shall we not in leaving it repeat the benediction Hawthorne pronounced upon it: " More and more I feel we at Brook Farm struck upon what *ought* to be a truth. Posterity may dig it up and profit by it."

CHAPTER III

THE REAL ZENOBIA

THAT Hawthorne meant Margaret Fuller by Zenobia is quite as certain as that he meant Brook Farm by the Arcady he so wonderfully depicts in *The Blithedale Romance*. Of course this is not to say that he even attempted to describe Brook Farm or Margaret Fuller photographically in his story. He was first, last and always the great American *romancer*. Besides, Margaret was never a member of the community at West Roxbury. She was, indeed, only an occasional guest there. Yet, so persistent is belief in what the world wishes to believe and so muddled does literary history ere long become that a learned German work has actually been written under the title *Margaret Fuller und Brook Farm*. And Brook Farm pilgrims inquire to this day "for the pool in which Margaret Fuller was drowned!"

Whether absent or present Margaret Fuller's influence pervaded the place however, — just

as her influence pervaded all the transcendental
aspiration and all the literary activity of her
time.[1]   Necessarily, therefore, we must rehearse
her story in a book covering the Boston of this
period.   The accident that she was born in
Cambridge, did her largest literary work in
New York and found the culmination of her
life in Italy makes no real difference.   For the
best that Boston people were and felt and
thought in the nineteenth century they owe —
very largely — to Margaret Fuller.

Yet Poe called Margaret " that detestable
old maid," Carlyle was similarly scathing and
uncomplimentary in his comment on her, and
Nathaniel Hawthorne wrote down in his Roman
Journal a sketch of her character, afterwards
indiscreetly published by his son, which, if
taken by itself, would brand as arrant idiots
all those wise and cultivated folk who were
proud to be known as Margaret's admiring
friends.   For, said Hawthorne, " Margaret Fuller
had a strong and coarse nature which she had
done her utmost to refine with infinite pains;
but of course it could only be superficially
changed. . . . Margaret has not left in the
hearts and minds of those who knew her any
deep witness of her integrity and purity.   She

[1] " Her personality never ceased to hover about Concord, even
after her death," wrote Rose Hawthorne Lathrop.   " She is a
part of its fascination."

was a great humbug — of course with much
talent and moral reality, or else she could
never have been so great a humbug. . . .
Towards the last there appears to have been
a total collapse in poor Margaret, morally
and intellectually; and tragic as her catas-
trophe was, Providence was after all kind in
putting her and her clownish husband and her
child on board that fated ship."

Julian Hawthorne, certainly, was *not* kind
in giving to the public (in 1884) this unflattering
estimate of a woman, long dead. Happily,
though, Margaret had still surviving several
friends who were eager and able to set her
right with the world. James Freeman Clarke,
who had been one of her intimates, promptly
published in the *Independent* an account of
her relations with the Hawthornes which makes
one feel very sure that the great romancer
intended only for his *private* note-book this
estimate of one to whom he had been a friend.[1]
His gentle wife really loved Margaret and he
gave the appearance of doing so. As witness
this letter written by Miss Sophia Peabody
just before her marriage to Hawthorne:[2]

[1] Dr. Clarke's article embodied, also, the suggestion of one of
Hawthorne's intimates that the paragraph in the Roman Journal
was really a sketch for a future imaginative character and
not meant to be taken, as it too often has been, for Hawthorne's secret feeling about Margaret Fuller and her claims.

[2] Quoted by J. F. Clarke in the *Independent*.

"DEAR MOST NOBLE MARGARET: — I have now something to tell you which I know will give you great pleasure. The decision was not made till last evening; and I feel that you are entitled, through our love and profound regard for you, to be told directly. Mr. Hawthorne — in plain words the splendor of the world — and I are going to dwell in Concord at Dr. Ripley's old manse. . . . We shall be married in June, the month of roses and of perfect bloom.

"Mr. Hawthorne, last evening, in the midst of his emotions, so deep and absorbing, after deciding, said that Margaret can now, when she visits Mr. Emerson, spend part of the time with us. . . .

"Your very true and loving friend
"SOPHIA."

If Hawthorne had always disliked Margaret Fuller, as his son Julian contends, he would scarcely have paused, in the ecstasy of betrothal, to make plans that she should visit at his future home. Moreover, the following passage in his *American Note-Book* [1] shows that their relations actually turned out to be those of capital friends: "After leaving Mr. Emerson's I returned through the woods, and entering Sleepy Hollow, I perceived a lady reclining

[1] *American Note-Books*, I, 221.

near the path which bends along its verge. It was Margaret herself. She had been there the whole afternoon meditating or reading, for she had a book in her hand with some strange title which I did not understand and have forgotten. She said that nobody had broken her solitude, and was just giving utterance to a theory that no inhabitant of Concord ever visited Sleepy Hollow, when we saw a group of people entering the sacred precincts. Most of them followed a path which led them away from us; but an old man passed near us, and smiled to see Margaret reclining on the ground and me standing by her side. He made some remark upon the beauty of the afternoon, and withdrew himself into the shadow of the wood. Then we talked about autumn, and about the pleasures of being lost in the woods, and about the crows whose voices Margaret had heard; and about the experiences of early childhood whose influence remains upon the character after the recollection of them has passed away; and about the sight of mountains from a distance, and the view from their summits; and about other matter of high and low philosophy." One does not talk of these things a long summer afternoon through with a person whom one does not at least like.

Yet Margaret Fuller had a side to her nature with which Hawthorne could only coolly sympa-

thize at best. She was a superb lover! Of her
culture much has been written. Of her extraordinary conversational gifts the descriptions
have been so manifold and so awe-inspiring
as quite sufficiently to have prejudiced against
her the many who hate " haranguing women."
But only in Higginson's biography of her is
any emphasis laid upon her passionate love
of humanity. And even there this phase is
merely touched upon in passing because the
task which had been set for the writer (in the
American Men of Letters Series) was that of
studying Margaret Fuller as a literary woman.
Loving service was, however, far more the
expression of her inmost personality than was
writing or the pursuit of that culture with which
she is chiefly associated by her contemporaries.
Had this not been the case she would never
have stood by the side of Mazzini, as she did
in Italy's pitiful struggle for independence;
nor would young patriots, dying in the hospital,
have called for her that they might clasp her
hands and cry " Viva l'Italia " with their
expiring breath. At the very moment indeed
when Lowell was satirizing her in his *Fable
for Critics* as one who

> " . . . will take an old notion and make it her own
> By saying it o'er in her Sibylline tone,
> Or persuade you 'tis something tremendously deep
> By repeating it so as to put you to sleep,"

she was leading the life of heroic action for which she had long been yearning.

Margaret Fuller was born, May 23, 1810, in a house on Ellery Street, Cambridgeport, which is still standing. She was drowned, with her husband and child, off the coast of Fire Island soon after she had passed her fortieth birthday and when her real work in the world had only just begun. Yet the impress of her personality was such, and her book, *Woman in the Nineteenth Century* so remarkably prophetic, that hers may well be regarded as the most successful woman-life of her century, with the single exception of that which gave to the world the slave-freeing *Uncle Tom's Cabin*.

As a child she was subjected by her father to a forcing-house system of education which, as she herself has said, " made her a youthful prodigy by day and, by night, a victim of spectral illusions, nightmare and somnambulism." As one reads her journal one's heart aches with pity for the little girl who, having recited Virgil to her father, late in the evening, dreamed, when she came to sleep, of horses trampling over her and of trees that dripped with blood. Yet Virgil, Horace and Ovid were early numbered among her dear friends " and reading became a habit and a passion." Shakespeare, too, soon claimed her devotion, the first play she assimilated being that which tells the tragic tale of two young people in Verona.

How largely the appeal which *Romeo and Juliet* made to this child was due to the impassioned love lines we are not told; but since Margaret Fuller was a very ardent creature and was soon to experience the first love of her young life, there is little question that this aspect of the drama must have moved her profoundly. All her life long she loved many people with a deep absorbing devotion which, as she herself has said, "lavished away her strength." After a lapse of many years, she wrote of her first friend: "My thoughts were fixed on her with all the force of my nature. It was my first real interest in my kind and it engrossed me wholly. . . ." She was twelve at the time.

Two inexorable descriptions of the maiden Margaret have come down to us. One sets her before us as she appeared at the ball given by her father to President Adams: a young girl of sixteen "with a very plain face, half shut eyes and hair curled all over her head; she was laced so tightly, by reason of stoutness, that she had to hold her arms back as if they were pinioned; she was dressed in a badly cut, low necked pink silk, with white muslin over it; and she danced quadrilles very awkwardly, being withal so near-sighted that she could hardly see her partner." Again, Oliver Wendell Holmes, with whose class she may be said to have " danced through college " — to quote Howells' phrase, — tells us graphically of her " long and flexile neck, arching and undulating in strange, sinuous movements, which one who loved her would compare to a swan, and one who loved her not to those of the ophidian who tempted our common mother."

There were always many who loved Margaret Fuller and many who loved her not. No woman ever inspired such deep feelings both of attraction and of dislike. James Freeman Clarke, writing of Margaret and her friendships, says that the persons she might most wish to know often retired from her and avoided her. But she was " sagacious of her quarry " and never suffered herself to be repelled by this. She saw when anyone belonged to her and never rested until she came into possession of her property. This is so reminiscent of certain passages in Emerson's essay on *Friendship* that it seems natural to remark, just at this point, that the Sage of Concord was one of Margaret's most true and devoted friends.

" I became acquainted with her," he writes, " in 1835 . . . when she came to spend a fortnight with my wife. I still remember the first half hour of her conversation. She was then twenty-six years old. She had a face and frame that would indicate fulness and tenacity of life.   She was rather under the middle height; her complexion was fair with strong fair hair. She was then, as always, carefully and becomingly dressed and of lady-like self-possession. For the rest, her appearance had nothing prepossessing.   Her extreme plainness — a trick of incessantly opening and shutting her eyelids, — the nasal tone of her voice, — all repelled; and I said to myself, we shall never get far."

Yet they became dear and lifelong friends, writing to each other constantly and passing long afternoons in the close intimacy of kindred minds during her frequent and protracted visits to Concord.   Emerson was seven years her senior and very grave.   Yet to him, rather oddly, Margaret showed herself a wit; of all the people who have written of her he alone points out that she possessed a huge fund of anecdotes and drolleries and that what most call satire in her was really due only to a superabundance of animal spirits.   He was very proud to become her close friend, for he says, " she had drawn to her every superior young man or young woman she had met. . . .

" When I first knew her," he continues, " she wore this circle of friends as a necklace of diamonds about her neck. . . . The confidences given her were their best and she held them to them.   She was an active inspiring companion

OLD BOSTON CUSTOM HOUSE IN WHICH HAWTHORNE SERVED AS A
YOUNG MAN.

Page 57.

SOUTH SIDE OF TEMPLE PLACE ABOUT 1865.

BOSTON FROM THE STATE HOUSE, ABOUT 1858.

and correspondent, and all the art, the thought and the nobleness in New England seemed at that moment related to her and she to it. She was everywhere a welcome guest. The houses of her friends in town and country were open to her and every hospitable attention eagerly offered. Her arrival was a holiday. . . . Of personal influence she had, I think, more than any other person I ever knew."

Margaret Fuller honestly believed that not only between men and women can there be deep, passionate love. Witness the following passages from her journal and her letters: "At Mr. G's we looked over prints the whole evening. Nothing fixed my attention so much as a large engraving of Madame Recamier in her boudoir. I have often thought over the intimacy between her and Madame De Staël. It is so true that a woman may be in love with a woman and a man with a man. I like to be sure of it, . . . for I loved —— for a time with as much passion as I was then strong enough to feel. Her face was always gleaming before me. . . . I do not love her now with passion, but I still feel towards her as I can to no other woman. I thought of all this as I looked at Madame Recamier."

While sustaining all this remarkable current of affection Margaret was earning her living in the only way then open to women — by school-

teaching. Her father had died and there was a
brood of young brothers to be educated. She
was very glad, therefore, to avail herself of the
chance which came to her, through Emerson,
to teach (1836) in the school which Bronson
Alcott had opened in Boston, in a part of the big
stone building on the corner of Temple Place
in which, until last year, the R. H. Stearns
Company had their headquarters. She was a
welcome guest at the choicest parties of which
Boston could boast, and we are indebted to her
for this picture of the " society " of the day.
" Last night I took my boldest peep into the
' Gigman ' world of Boston. I had not been to
a large party before, and had only seen said world
in half-boots. So I thought, as it was an
occasion in which I felt real interest, to wit, a
fête given by Mrs. Thorndike for my beautiful
Susan, I would look at it for once in satin
slippers. Dr. Channing meant to go but was too
weary when the hour came. I spent the early
part of the evening in reading bits of Dante
with him and talking about the material sublime
till half-past nine, when I went with Mrs. C.
and graceful Mary.

" It was very pretty to look at. So many
fair maidens dressed as if they had stepped out
of their grandmothers' picture frames, and
youths with their long locks, suitable to represent pages if not nobles. Signor Figaro was

there also. . . . And Daniel the Great (Webster), not however, when I saw him, engaged in an operation peculiarly favorable to his style of beauty, to wit, eating oysters. Theodore Parker was there, and introduced to me. I had some pleasant talk with him, but before I could get to Spinoza, somebody seized on me and carried me off to quite another S, — to supper. On the whole, it all pleased my eye; my fashionable fellow-creatures were very civil to me, and I went home glad to have looked at this slide in the magic lantern also."

A form of dissipation much more in Margaret's line than fancy-dress balls were the meetings of the Transcendental Club and the famous "Conversations" which began (November 6, 1839) at the rooms on West Street where Miss Elizabeth P. Peabody maintained at this time a circulating library and foreign bookshop. This place had become a kind of Transcendental Exchange where many who had no thought of purchasing books dropped in for the sheer delight that it was to "talk of many things" with the keen-witted little lady who was the proprietor of the shop.[1] No better setting could have been devised for the proposed classes, subscriptions to which were obtained through the circulation of a letter setting

[1] The idea of the Church of the Disciples first occurred to Dr. Clarke in this room.

forth " the advantages of a weekly meeting for
conversation " in a class which should " supply a
point of union to well-educated and thinking
women, in a city, which, with great pretensions
to mental refinement, boasts at present nothing
of the kind."

Twenty-five cultivated Boston women were
present at the first meeting of Miss Fuller's
class, which soon grew to be a famous Boston
institution, meeting weekly for five winters
to consider everything from vanity to soci-
ology. The sessions opened at eleven in the
morning, ten or a dozen, besides the leader,
usually taking active part in the talk. The
leader's own account of the first days, as sent
to Emerson and by him quoted in the *Memoirs of Margaret Fuller Ossoli*, is as follows:

" 25th November, 1839. — My class is prosperous. I was so fortunate as to rouse at once
the tone of simple earnestness, which can
scarcely, when once awakened, cease to vibrate."

No reports of the " Conversations " are
extant, but this sprightly picture of the eighth
meeting, as sent by one who was there to a
friend in New Haven, is very pleasantly illuminating: " Christmas made a holiday for Miss
Fuller's class, but it met on Saturday at noon.
. . . Margaret, beautifully dressed (don't de-
spise that, for it made a fine picture), presided
with more dignity and grace than I had thought

possible. The subject was Beauty. Each had written her definition and Margaret began with reading her own. This called forth questions, comments and illustrations on all sides. The style and manner, of course, in this are different, but the question, the high point from which it was considered, and the earnestness and simplicity of the discussion as well as the gifts and graces of the speakers, gave it the charm of a Platonic dialogue. There was no pretension of pedantry in a word that was said. The tone of remark and question was simple as that of children in a school class; and, I believe, every one was satisfied."

Not quite everyone; not Harriet Martineau, for instance, whom Margaret had come to know through her friend Mrs. John Farrar, and to whom, upon the publication of the book, *Society in America*, Margaret protested that undue emphasis had there been placed upon the anti-slavery movement. This Miss Martineau appears to have resented, for when she came to write her Autobiography, she incorporated in the work the following utterly unfair criticism of the " Conversations: " " The difference between us [Margaret and herself] was that while she was living and moving in an ideal world, talking in private and discoursing in public about the most fanciful and shallow conceits which the Transcendentalists of Boston

took for philosophy, she looked down upon
persons who acted instead of talking finely,
and devoted their fortunes, their peace, their
repose and their very lives to the preservation
of the principles of the republic. While Margaret Fuller and her adult pupils sat ' gorgeously
dressed ' talking about Mars and Venus, Plato
and Goethe, and fancying themselves the elect
of the earth in intellect and refinement, the
liberties of the republic were running out as
fast as they could go, at a breach which
another sort of elect persons were devoting
themselves to repair; and my complaint against
the ' gorgeous ' pedants was that they regarded
their preservers as hewers of wood and drawers
of water, and their work as a less vital one than
the pedantic orations which were spoiling a
set of well-meaning women in a pitiable way."

Now, as a matter of fact, the women in the
West Street classes were almost identically the
same women of whom Miss Martineau here
speaks as " another sort of elect persons."
The wives of Emerson and Parker, the only
daughter of Channing, Mrs. Lydia Maria Child,
Mrs. Ellis Gray Loring, and the lady who afterwards became Mrs. Ednah D. Cheney, were
among those who sat at Margaret's feet. And
they were all ardent workers for the cause of
anti-slavery! It was the office of Margaret
Fuller to stimulate these women morally and

mentally, not so much, however, by the discussion of a concrete evil then existing in the world as by deepened appreciation of all that is beautiful in art, in literature and in life.

One aged lady still living, who belonged to the conversation class, has said that the influence of their leader's sympathy upon the thoughts and hopes of those before her was so great that, metaphorically speaking, the lame walked and the blind received their sight. And Mrs. Cheney spoke to me, very enthusiastically, shortly before her death, a few years ago, of all that Margaret Fuller had meant to her — and to many since.

" Her most distinguishing characteristic, next to her love of love," she said, " was her personal magnetism. I myself first came under her spell when she began to hold her ' Conversations.' I was eager enough for any intellectual advantage, but I had imbibed with the thoughtlessness of a school girl the common prejudices against Miss Fuller.

" So, though I believed that I should learn from her, I had no idea, when I joined her class with thirty or forty others, that I should esteem, and much more, love her. She was about twenty-five at the time I came under her influence, and I was, I think, sixteen or so.

" The class used to meet in the morning, and she would talk gloriously on whatever subject, perhaps Greek literature, she had set herself for that day. I early found myself in a new world of thought; a flood of light irradiated all that I had seen in nature, observed in life, or read in books.

" Whatever she spoke of revealed a hidden meaning, and everything seemed to be put in true relation. Her influence might be best expressed by saying that I was no longer the limitation of myself, but I felt that the whole work of the universe was open to me. It was this consciousness of the divinity in the soul, so real to Margaret herself, which gave her that air of regal superiority which was misinterpreted as conceit.

" Perhaps I can best give you an idea of what she was to me by an answer which I made to her. One day, when she was alone with me, and it is as if I could now feel her touch and hear her voice, she said, ' Is life rich to you? ' And I replied, ' It is since I have known you.' Such was the response of many a youthful heart to her, and herein was her wonderful influence. She did not make us her disciples, her blind followers. She opened the book of life and helped us to read it for ourselves. Her intellectuality was pronounced, of course. Neither this country nor any other has ever had, I believe, a woman of such transcendent conversational power.

"But she was even more heart than mind. It is her heart, indeed, her intense sympathy with young women, and her close knowledge of all that may come to them of trial and temptation, that explains her hold today upon the women of this country. There are Margaret Fuller clubs and Ossoli circles all over this country, you know.

"This is the year of Emerson's centenary, and his influence upon the intellectual life of this country is being everywhere exalted, and properly. But I would venture the opinion that Emerson, great as he undoubtedly is, is not loved by nearly so many people as love Margaret Fuller, who was in a way his contemporary, and who was certainly his friend.

"The last time I went west to lecture, people in the most unexpected places, in Dubuque and other such cities, used to come to me and say, 'Can't you tell me something about Margaret Fuller? You knew her,' they say. 'We only know of her. Tell us, then, of her personality, her real self.'

"I told these people what I always say of Margaret, that her strength lay in her personality; nothing that adequately represents her power remains in her writing. Any one who ever came near to her grew very fond

of her. Her tenderness seems to me her most
remarkable characteristic, and of that comparatively little is known."

At the same time that the Conversations
were doing their excellent work to stimulate
morally, as well as mentally, the young women
of Boston, Margaret Fuller was the prime agent
in bringing out *The Dial*, the organ of the
Transcendental Club to which allusion has
already been made.

Emerson wrote the introduction to the first
number and Margaret Fuller the article on
" Critics " and that bearing the caption, " Allston Gallery." For two years she was not only
the editor of the sheet but the alert and resource-
ful " filler-in " of all space left vacant at the
eleventh hour. Nominally she drew a salary
of two hundred dollars a year for all this;
actually, however, she got little or nothing.
Later Emerson took the editorial responsibility,
and, after four years of precarious fortune,
The Dial expired. Apart from the romantic
associations with which its young life was bound
up it is interesting today chiefly because it
first gave to the world, in its issue of July,
1843, Margaret Fuller's essay which we now
know, in book form, under the title, *Woman
In the Nineteenth Century*. This article might
almost have been written for a suffragette
organ in the year of our Lord, 1910, so extraor-

dinarily fresh is it in tone and so nobly does
it present the innate right of woman to real
fulness of life. Because the book is rather in-
accessible I want to quote here a few of its prophetic passages:

"Whether much or little has been done or
will be done, [by broadly educated women],
whether women will add to the talent of narra-
tion the power of systematizing, whether they
will carve marble as well as draw and paint
is not important. But that it should be acknowledged that they have intellects which need
developing, that they should not be considered
complete if beings of affection and habit alone,
is important. Yet even this acknowledgment,
rather conquered by woman than proffered
by man, has been sullied by the usual selfishness.
So much is said of women being better educated
that they may become better companions and
mothers for men. They should be fit for such
companionship. . . . But a being of infinite
scope must not be treated with an exclusive
view to any one relation." And then she quotes
with approval, "We must have units before
we can have union." After which she goes
on to point out that she is urging the greater
independence of women not because she dis-
believes in marriage but because she believes in
it profoundly.

"I wish woman to live first for God's sake,"

she explains. "Then she will not make an imperfect man her god and thus sink to idolatry. Then she will not take what is not fit for her from a sense of weakness and poverty. Then, if she finds what she needs in man embodied, she will know how to love and be worthy of being loved. Woman, self-centred, would never be absorbed by any relation; it would be only an experience to her as to man. It is a vulgar error that love, *a* love is to woman her whole existence. She also is born for Truth and Love in their universal energy."

How far did Margaret Fuller measure up to her own high ideals in this matter of woman's relation to man? Did *she*, who we have seen to be one of the most ardently affectionate natures of her time, steadfastly keep herself only for the highest kind of love? In her journal we find her profoundest feeling about this whole matter: "No one loves me. But I love many a good deal and see some way into their eventual beauty. I am myself growing better and shall by and by be a worthy object of love, one that will not anywhere disappoint or need forbearance. . . . I have no child, and the woman in me has so craved this experience that it has seemed the want of it must paralyze me. . . . I cannot always upbear my life all alone."

Why had she never married? Among the many men with whom she was on warm friendly relations was there no man who cared for her supremely and for whom she could care? Her niece has told me of a clever young Portland lawyer who might have been the man. But the first real evidence that we have of such love in her as she would have wished to give the man she might marry is to be found in the letters to James Nathan, whom she met very soon after her removal to New York (in December, 1844) for the purpose of connecting herself with Horace Greeley and his *Tribune*.

Young Nathan was a Jew and it was this fact, very likely, which prevented his marriage to the woman to whom he undoubtedly made passionate love and from whom this love drew forth as noble love-letters as ever were sent to a man by a woman. But the letters should not have been published and would not have been had Nathan returned them to their writer as she asked him to do after she learned of his approaching alliance with one of his own race. That Margaret suffered a great deal while this love ran its troubled course is evident in almost every line of the letters. "You tell me to rest, mein Leibster," one passage towards the end of the correspondence runs, "but how can I rest when you rouse in me so many thoughts and feelings? What good does it do for you to stay away when, absent or present, every hour you grow upon me and the root strikes to my

inmost life? There is far more repose in being
with you when your look fills my eye and your
voice my ear, than in trying to keep still, for
then these endless thoughts rush upon me.
And then comes, too, that tormenting sense
that only a few days more shall we be together,
and how can I rest?"[1] So much did Margaret
the wise care for this man that she even liked
to have him call her a fool! "I don't know
that any words from your mouth gave me more
pleasure," she writes, "than these, 'You must
be a fool, little girl.' It seems so whimsical
that they should be addressed to me, who was
called on for wisdom and dignity, long before
my leading strings were off."

And yet, though he had "approached her,
personally, nearer than any other person"
and had "touched her heart and thrilled it at
the centre," that heart as she proudly points
out, "is a large kingdom." She would not let
him or any man spoil her life. The last letter
in the series is dated July 14, 1846. By the
fall of that year the relation between the two
had been definitively broken and, with one or
two significant allusions in her diary,[2] Margaret
dismisses the whole matter. As for Nathan,
he wedded his coreligionist and had several

[1] Reprinted from *Love-Letters of Margaret Fuller*, Copyright,
1903, by D. Appleton and Company.

[2] These allusions are in French and may be examined at the
Cambridge Public Library which now owns the Diary.

children, dying peacefully (in 1889) in his own home at Hamburg, a very rich but blind old man. W. H. Channing, Margaret's biographer, once saw the letters and suggested, as he returned them to their owner, that perhaps it would be well to destroy them. But the one to whom they had been written thought otherwise and, in the summer of 1873, he wrote for them the preface which was used when the correspondence was published by his son fifteen years after his death.

It appears to have been the rebound from this unhappy love affair which precipitated Margaret Fuller into the alliance in which, at last, her hungry heart found abundant solace. She sailed from Boston in August, 1846, to enjoy with friends a long-deferred period of European travel, in the course of which she met Wordsworth, Mazzini, Carlyle, George Sand and many other literary celebrities. In Venice she parted with the friends who had thus far been her companions, and returned to settle in Rome and work for the cause of revolutionary Italy. To Emerson she wrote that she had at last found the work for which she had long been looking. She also found now the love which was to crown her life by her marriage to the young Marquis d'Ossoli.

Margaret first met Ossoli in 1847, while at vespers at St. Peter's. The following winter

she took an apartment in the Corso in Rome,
and the young marquis was often there drawn
to his new friend by her interest in the republican
cause, which he had espoused, as well as by
what seems to have been a very real passion on
his part. In the intervals of nursing his aged
father he ardently pursued his wooing, telling
Margaret repeatedly " that he must marry her
or be miserable." " She refused to look on him
as a lover," relates Mrs. William W. S. Story,
who was her confidant, " and insisted that it
was not fitting, — that it was best he should
marry a younger woman [he was thirty and
she was nearly thirty-eight]; that she would be
his friend but not his wife. In this way it
rested for some weeks, during which we saw
Ossoli pale, dejected, and unhappy. He was
always with her, but in a sort of hopeless,
desperate manner, until at length he convinced
her of his love and she married him."

The absurd story which, even today, is repeated from time to time, that Ossoli was un-
educated and that he ill-treated his wife, I
should not even refer to were there not always
so many people who prefer to think badly of
Italians as husbands. He had the education
of an Italian gentleman of his time, and if it
had been possible to reproduce here the too-
faded daguerreotype — the only known picture
of him — which Colonel Higginson owns we

CORNER OF TREMONT AND BROMFIELD STREETS ABOUT 1870.

CHURCH GREEN.

Page 90.

OLD STATE HOUSE, WHERE GARRISON WAS MOBBED.

Page 114.

should have seen that Ossoli was exactly the
man to love and be loved by Margaret Fuller.
A poetic face, his, in which one reads the possibility of high patriotism and of the finest
chivalry! But he was never able to talk to
his wife in her own tongue; their beautiful
love-letters, which were saved from the wreck
in which they and their baby perished, were
all written in Italian. As for the secrecy of
their marriage: that was because of Ossoli's
close relation to the Papal household and by
reason of the fact that an alliance with a foreigner (who was a Protestant) would probably
have cut him off from his share of his father's
fortune. Colonel Higginson quotes a letter
from Mrs. Story which quite effectively gives
the lie to those who would believe this strange
union not a success, however. "Ossoli's manner
towards Margaret was devoted and lover-like
to a degree. He cared not how trivial was the
service if he might perform it for her. I remember to have seen him, one morning, after
they had been married nearly two years, set
off on an errand to get the handle of her parasol
mended, with as much genuine knightly zeal
as if the charge had been a much weightier one.
As he took it he said, ' How sweet it is to do
little things for you!' . . . He never wished
her to give up any pleasure because he could not
share it, but if she were interested he would go

with her to any house, leave her and call again to take her home. Such tender unselfish love I have rarely seen before; it made green her days and gave her an expression of peace and serenity which before was a stranger to her."

Margaret herself wrote (February 5, 1850) to Mrs. Marcus Spring, with whom she had gone abroad: " I have expected that those who cared for me simply for my activity of intellect would not care for Ossoli; but those in whom the moral nature predominates would gladly learn to love and admire him and see what a treasure his affection must be to me." [1] Which makes one feel how true a word was that which the American consul in Turin sent to Emerson a year after Ossoli with his wife and child had drowned off Fire Island, " It is abundantly evident that Margaret's young husband discharged all the obligations of his relation to her *con amore*. His admiration amounted to veneration, and her yearning to be loved seemed at last to be satisfied."

[1] Quoted in Sanborn's *Autobiography*.

CHAPTER IV

WHEN THE SLAVE WAS A HERO

IN these present days of social unrest, when a compact minority of American citizens are sure that certain definite things in the government of our country are very wrong, — although regretfully admitting that they see no immediate prospect of their effective betterment, — it should rebuke their faint-heartedness and cheer their souls to reflect that the great work of that other minority known as Abolitionists was accomplished in about thirty years. The men who set this tremendous movement in motion actually lived to see their cause won and were obliged to look about for further evils in need of devoted service!

The speed with which this far-reaching reform was brought about may be credited chiefly to the fact that God raised up for the work two men, Wendell Phillips and William Lloyd Garrison, who did practically nothing else but agitate their cause until the day had been won. Of Phillips I speak at length in another chapter. Let us here, therefore, pass at once to the simple

annals of Garrison's great life and to a consideration of the conditions which he had to confront
as he began his work. For he it was who
created, almost single-handed, the moral force
which overthrew slavery. When we consider
the resistance which he overcame, the result
achieved must be regarded, as James Freeman
Clarke has pointed out,[1] " as an unexampled
triumph of pure truth. The slaves held in the
Southern States were valued, at the time of
the Civil War, at about three thousand millions
of dollars. Added to this pecuniary interest
was the value of cotton lands, sugar plantations
and rice fields cultivated exclusively by slaves.
And beside the powerful money motive for
maintaining slavery there were the force of
custom, the habits engendered by despotism,
pride, prejudice and hatred of outside inter-
ference. These interests and feelings gradually
united the whole South in a determined hos-
tility to emancipation; and men professing
anti-slavery principles could not live safely
in the slaveholding states.

" This united South," continues Dr. Clarke,
" had for its allies at the North both the great
political parties, the commercial and manufacturing interests, nearly the whole press, and
both extremes of society. Abolition was equally
obnoxious in the parlors of the wealthy and to

[1] In the *Memorial History of Boston.*

the crowd of roughs in the streets, — fashion and the mob being for once united by a common enmity. It was against this immense weight of opposition that the Abolitionists contended; and their strength consisted wholly in the justice of their cause and the enthusiasm which that cause inspired."

Of this enthusiasm Boston was preëminently the breeding-place. Garrison made no mistake in early migrating to the town which had long ago shown itself intolerant of oppression. Even in those early days when many Boston folk held slaves, the sentiment of the people as a whole was opposed to slavery. In 1646 the General Court ordered a negro stolen from Africa and brought to Boston to be sent back to the place from which he had been led away captive. In 1701 the Selectmen of Boston passed a vote requesting the Representatives to " put a period to negroes being slaves." In 1766 and 1767 votes were passed in town-meeting instructing its representatives " That for the total abolishing of slavery among us, That you move for a law to prohibit the importation and purchasing of slaves for the future." In 1770 occurred the case of Prince Boston, who was hired and paid wages by a Quaker in Nantucket, — Elisha Folger; and when his owner brought an action for the recovery of his slave, the jury returned a verdict against the owner, and Prince Boston was manumitted by the magistrates. As for the attitude on this big question of the Bostonians who fought to throw off the yoke of George III it is very well expressed in the words of Samuel Adams who, with the words, " Surry must be free on crossing the threshold of my house," declined to receive as property a negro girl offered to his wife as a present.

Cotton Mather, to be sure, had been burdened with no such scruples. There is an entry in his diary of 1706 in which he records that he had " received a singular blessing " in the gift of " a very likely slave," which was " a mighty smile of Heaven upon his family." And at the very time when Adams scorned the gift of a slave, Boston folk of " respectability " were trafficking in men and women — at arm's length. Nor was slavery ever explicitly abolished in Massachusetts, though " in the famous Jennison case tried at Worcester in 1781, it was declared that slavery no longer existed." (Justin Winsor, *Memorial History of Boston*, Volume IV, page 6.)

So there is no doubt that while Boston was a pretty good place for Garrison to choose as his residence, it was not one in which his labors would be thrown away. Joseph T. Buckingham of the *Boston Courier* had printed two sonnets written in prison by the young Newburyporter

before the office of the *Liberator* was opened
on Water Street; but that by no means implies
that an over-cordial welcome would be extended to a man who had set himself to the
task of freeing all the slaves in the land.
Too many Boston folk were making a great
deal of money out of slavery and its associated
activities.

Garrison's father was a sea captain, and his
mother was a deeply religious Baptist. Thus
heredity had endowed him with strength and
personal courage on the one hand, and with
deep and fervid religious faith on the other.
Three years after Lloyd's birth (on December
10, 1805) the captain-father left his wife and
children nevermore to return. It is believed
that he found the temptations to intemperance
offered by the seaport town of Newburyport
more than he could bear, and to avoid disgracing
his family, decided to live away from them.
Thus it fell out that William Lloyd Garrison
was early thrown upon his own resources for
a livelihood, — and that his strong-souled
mother became to him, while he was a tiny lad,
all that two parents might have been. While
yet too small comfortably to support the
weight of a lapstone, he was apprenticed to a
shoemaker, but that occupation proving un-
congenial, a place in a printing office was found
for him. This work he liked and so graduated,

at the age of twenty, from an apprenticeship into the position of a self-publishing editor.

The chance of falling in, two years later (1828), with Benjamin Lundy, editor of the *Genius of Universal Emancipation*, set our young journalist in the current which was to bear him on to ever-increasing fame and usefulness. Lundy was an interesting figure, a Quaker, who travelled about from town to town, mostly on foot, carrying a heavy pack containing among other things the head rules, column rules and subscription book of his paper. When he came to a town where he found a printing office he would stop long enough to get out and mail a number of *Genius*. His writings were aflame with hatred for slavery and determination to put it down, and when one of his shabby little sheets found its way to the office in Bennington, Vermont, over which Garrison was now presiding as editor, its burning words inspired that youth to take the first definite step of his thirty years' war against slave-holding. Forthwith he wrote a petition for the abolition of slavery in the District of Columbia, which he sent to all the postmasters in the State of Vermont, begging them to procure signatures thereto. And since, in that day, postmasters enjoyed the privilege of receiving and sending letters free of postage, the petition was quite bulky when it arrived in Congress.

It immediately caused the slave-holding constituency to sit up and take notice of — William Lloyd Garrison.

Lundy, naturally, was immensely pleased at the ardor and resourcefulness of his new recruit, and in order to make him an offer of partnership walked all the way from Boston to Bennington, staff in hand and pack on back. The result of this conference was their joint proprietorship for a time of the *Genius*. The paper was now issued weekly from Baltimore, to which city young Garrison removed.

Garrison believed in immediate emancipation and wrote all his articles to this end, signing them with his initials that they might easily be distinguished from those of Lundy, who believed in getting the slaves emancipated gradually. Inevitably the younger editor soon got the sheet and himself into hot water. Baltimore was one of the principal marts of the domestic slave trade and Francis Todd of Newburyport was the owner of a vessel which now came to that port to take to New Orleans a cargo of eighty-eight slaves. Here was a first-rate case of Northern complicity in the infamous traffic, and Garrison lost no time in vigorously denouncing Todd for his share in a transaction which, as he pointed out, was in no way different in principle from taking a cargo of human flesh on the coast of Africa and carrying it across the ocean to market. The law denounced the foreign slave trade as piracy, but the domestic slave trade was every whit as wicked in the sight of God, declared Garrison. A libel suit instituted by Todd followed hard upon the publication of this article, and as a trial in a slave-holding court before a slave-holding jury could have but one outcome, Garrison soon found himself in jail for lack of the wherewithal to pay the fifty dollars fine imposed upon him.

Now it was that he wrote the two sonnets which Joseph Buckingham was moved to publish in the *Boston Courier*. They had been inscribed with a pencil on the walls of the prisoner's cell and were entitled " Freedom of the Mind " and " The Guiltless Prisoner." After seven weeks of confinement Garrison's fine was paid by Arthur Tappan, a leading New York merchant, who had been a reader of the *Genius*, and who was glad thus to come to the rescue of its plucky junior editor.

To publish a paper of his own was that editor's next adventure. Boston had been decided upon as the background for the experiment not only because it promised as much hospitality as any city to such an undertaking but also because Garrison had come to know the place pretty well and to be fond of it during the year or so passed there, in a printing office, just after his majority. In the story of his life as told by his children, a wonderful four volume work which, with Johnson's *William Lloyd Garrison and His Times*, must be absorbed by all who would understand Garrison in his wholeness, — we are told that at this earlier period the color and glamour of Boston appealed as strongly to Garrison as to any healthy young man come to the metropolis from a small town. To see at church the lovely face of Miss Emily Marshall, who was renowned the country over for her beauty and charm, he even forsook, temporarily, the Baptist fold of his mother and the very great attraction offered by the preaching of William Ellery Channing and John Pierpont, reformers both. So strongly had the joys of the city impressed itself upon him that, while incarcerated in Baltimore jail, he even wrote some verses about Boston Common during the festival period called " Election Week!"

Election Day and its attendant joys appear to have appealed particularly to the Abolitionist mind, very likely because it was " everybody's day; and emphatically the colored people's." The blacks were wont to flock out in great numbers from what was known as " Nigger Hill," the lower part of Joy Street, and Frederick W. G. May, years afterwards, sent to Mrs. Ednah Dow Cheney for repro-

duction in her *Reminiscences* a very vivid
description of the ensuing festival. " The
wooden fence of the Common from Park Street
corner to and beyond West Street was lined
with booths and stalls where eatables and
drinkables were exposed for sale by white and
colored salesmen and saleswomen. Even oysters
by the saucerful at fo'pence ha'penney (six and
a quarter cents) found eager buyers; lobsters,
too, and candy by the ton, it seemed to my
young eyes; cakes in variety, doughnuts, ginger-
nuts; lemonade, spruce beer, ginger beer, etc.
One specially delightful feature was the ambula-
tory stall, an ordinary handcart . . . . furbished
up and fitted with a tilt or hood to shield its
delicacies from the sun, dust, etc.; inside were
boxes and shelves with the innumerable cakes
that the well-bred baker then could furnish,
buns with actual currants on them, jumbles,
waffles and I know not what else, seed cakes, —
I can see and smell them now, — PRESIDENT
BISCUIT, etc. These carts would literally cover
the field as the tide of mimic war ebbed and
flowed. . . . These laudable chariots carried
baked beans and similar necessities of Boston-
Beverly life, — brown bread hot, etc. — their
proprietors and motive power being genial
old darkey ladies with genuine wool and
gay-colored head handkerchiefs in the latest
Southern style. This was Nigger 'lection,

— the colored people very much in evidence."

Just here, because of the allusion to " Nigger Hill," it is interesting to give Mrs. Cheney's explanation [1] of the way in which Joy Street got its name. About 1820, when her parents took a house on that thoroughfare it bore the name of Belknap Street. Then as now it ran from Beacon Street to Cambridge Street and was divided by cross streets into three parts " which at that time pretty well represented three grades of society. In the upper part were some of the finest houses and most ' swell ' people in the city. In the middle part were families of good standing, and in this part was our house. The lower part was almost entirely occupied by colored people, who streamed by our house and gave us children that early familiarity with this race which, thank God, has prevented me from having any difficulty in recognizing the ' negro as a man and a brother.' But the upper ten did not relish the idea of giving their addresses on Belknap Street so associated with the despised race, and they petitioned the city government to change the name of their portion to Joy. Of course the middle class are but too prone to mimic the manners of the rich, and they next asked to have their portion renamed. It is a democratic country and therefore the lower

[1] *Reminiscences of Ednah Dow Cheney.*

portion of the street wished for its Joy also, and so the good old name of Belknap, once belonging to a worthy divine, was given up and has never been used again."[1] It is interesting to add that Joy Street still represents the " three grades of society."

The *Boston Courier* had published the sonnets which Garrison wrote while in prison. In the advertising columns of that sheet, therefore, the young reformer — who was now resolved to make a place for himself in Boston — printed, on October 12, 1830, this advertisement:

WANTED. — For three evenings, a Hall or Meeting-house (the latter would be preferred) in which to vindicate the rights of TWO MILLIONS of American citizens who are now groaning in servile chains in this boasted land of liberty; and also to propose just, benevolent, and constitutional measures for their relief. As the addresses will be gratuitous, and as the cause is of public benefit, I cannot consent to remunerate any society for the use of its building. If this application fails, I propose to address the citizens of Boston in the open air, on the Common.

WM. LLOYD GARRISON.

No. 30, Federal Street, Oct. 11, 1830.

Two days later the papers announced that Mr. Garrison would deliver his first lecture, on

[1] It survives, however, in Belknap Place which leads off Joy Street.

Friday evening, October 15, in Julien Hall, at the northwest corner of Milk and Congress Streets. The body which had offered him the hospitality of its headquarters was made up of avowed " infidels," men who had no personal acquaintance with Garrison and no especial sympathy with his cause; men, too, whose sect he had recently denounced in public. It was with deep shame for his Christian brethren, we may be sure, that Garrison accepted their hospitality. While he thanked them for their courtesy he declared his firm belief that slavery could be abolished only through the power of the Gospel and of Christian religion.

A good many prominent Christians were among those who came to hear that lecture in the hall of the " infidels." Dr. Lyman Beecher, then the head of the Orthodox pulpit in Boston, was there. So was Rev. Ezra S. Gannett, a well-known Unitarian divine, Samuel E. Sewall, a young lawyer whose famous ancestor, Judge Samuel Sewall, had been one of the earliest opponents of slavery in America,[1] Bronson Alcott, the Concord oracle, and Rev. Samuel J. May, afterwards very distinguished in the anti-slavery movement. Mr. May has thus described the occasion:

" Presently the young man arose, modestly, but with an air of calm determination, and

[1] See *St. Botolph's Town*, p. 282 et seq.

delivered such a lecture as he only, as I believe, at that time could have written; for he, only, had had his eyes so anointed that he could see that outrages perpetrated upon Africans were wrongs done to our common humanity; he, only, I believe, had had his ears so completely unstopped of ' prejudice against color ' that the cries of enslaved black men and black women sounded to him as if they came from brothers and sisters. . . .

" Never before," declares May, " was I so affected by the speech of any man. When he had ceased speaking I said to those around me: ' That is a providential man; he is a prophet; he will shake our nation to its centre, but he will shake slavery out of it. We ought to know him and we ought to help him. Come, let us go and give him our hands.' Mr. Sewall and Mr. Alcott went up with me and we introduced each other. I said to him: ' Mr. Garrison, I am not sure I can endorse all you have said this evening. Much of it requires careful consideration. But I am prepared to embrace you. I am sure you are called to a great work and I mean to help you.' Mr. Sewall cordially assured him of his readiness, also, to coöperate with him. Mr. Alcott invited him to his home. He went and we sat with him until twelve that night, listening to his discourse, in which he showed plainly that immediate, unconditional emancipation without expatriation, was the right of every slave and could not be withheld by his master an hour without sin. That night my soul was baptized in his spirit, and ever since I have been a disciple and fellow-laborer of William Lloyd Garrison.

" The next morning, immediately after breakfast, I went to his boarding-house and stayed until two P. M. I learned that he was poor, dependent upon his daily labor for his daily bread and intending to return to the printing business. But, before he could devote himself to his own support, he felt that he must deliver his message, must communicate to persons of prominent influence what he had learned of the sad condition of the enslaved, and the institutions and spirit of the slave-holders; trusting that all true and good men would discharge the obligation pressing upon them to espouse the cause of the poor, the oppressed, the down-trodden. He read to me letters he had addressed to Dr. Channing, Dr. Beecher, Dr. Edwards, the Hon. Jeremiah Mason, and Hon. Daniel Webster, holding up to their view the tremendous iniquity of the land and begging them, ere it should be too late, to interpose their great power in the Church and State to save our country from the terrible calamities which the sin of slavery was bringing upon us. These letters were eloquent, solemn, impressive. I wonder they did not produce a greater effect."

Oliver Johnson, who knew Garrison well, and has written very enthusiastically of his life and work, has an explanation to offer as to the " why " of this, and any of us who have had experience with reform movements in which the church is involved will appreciate the truth of what he says. Unhappily, the influences which chiefly sustained slavery were supplied by the people of the North. And these people were the same ones who were supporting in their pulpits the clergy to whom Mr. Garrison had addressed his letters! " The pulpit was thus sorely tempted," comments Mr. Johnson, " to swerve from the laws of humanity and rectitude and become the apologist if not the defender of slavery." Dr. Lyman Beecher, whose daughter was to do more than any other woman in the world to help in the overthrow of slavery, lost a golden opportunity at this juncture of immortality on his own account. Garrison greatly admired Beecher, who was then at the head of the Orthodox pulpit in Boston (though his former church-home on Hanover Street had just been burned and the new building of his society on Bowdoin Street — now known as the Church of St. John the Evangelist — was not yet completed), and in all simplicity and trust he turned to him for support. "I have too many irons in the fire already," was the Doctor's evasive answer. "Then," said Garrison, solemnly, "you had better let all your irons burn than neglect your duty to the slave." Whereupon, not having arguments to offer, Beecher withdrew into his robes of office, as many another priest has done before and since, replying grandiosely, "Your zeal, young man, is commendable, but you are misguided. If you will give up your fanatical notions and be led by us (the clergy) we will make you the Wilberforce of America."

Rev. Samuel J. May, however, was a different type of man and, on the very next Sunday after he had heard Garrison's lectures, he endorsed from the pulpit of Rev. Alexander Young, at Church Green in Summer Street, which he chanced to be supplying, the doctrines which this new prophet had come to preach. In concluding his sermon he said, "I have been prompted to speak thus by the words I have heard during the past week from a young man hitherto unknown, but who is, I believe, called of God to do a greater work for the good of our country than has been done by anyone since the Revolution. I mean William Lloyd Garrison. He is going to repeat his lectures the coming week. I advise, I exhort, I entreat — would that I could compel! — you to go and hear him." It takes a finely sensitized conscience

to recognize a prophet of righteousness as soon
as one has made his acquaintance, and it takes
a very high kind of courage to declare to hostile
hearers one's belief that they should heed the
message of such a man. All honor, therefore,
to Samuel J. May, for that he had the heart
to feel and the grit to proclaim the advent in
Boston of him who had been sent of God
expressly to strike the shackles from the lacer-
ated limbs of the slave.[1]

Happily, Garrison had a literary sense as
well as a compelling ethical ideal; he steadfastly refused to call the paper about to be
born the *Safety Lamp*, as suggested by Mr.
Sewall, insisting that there be given to it the
bold and appropriate title of the *Liberator*.
The first number of the epoch-making sheet
appeared on Saturday, January 1, 1831. Even
for that day of small things in the publishing
line it was an unimpressive sheet, a folio of four
pages fourteen inches in length by nine and
three-tenths in width, printed after hours in
the office of the *Christian Examiner* in return
for its proprietor's services in the day time.
At first the title was in black-letter, but, at
the end of four months, this form was changed,
and by 1850 an engraved head, which well

---

[1] How much " grit " this required may be seen from the fact that
a friend of May's father condoled with the old gentleman in all
seriousness next day, saying, " I cannot tell you how much I pity
you; I hear your son went crazy at Church Green yesterday."

VOL. I.]   WILLIAM LLOYD GARRISON AND ISAAC KNAPP, PUBLISHERS.   [NO. 17.

Boston, Massachusetts.]   OUR COUNTRY IS THE WORLD—OUR COUNTRYMEN ARE MANKIND.   [Saturday, April 23, 1831.

OUR COUNTRY IS THE WORLD—OUR COUNTRYMEN ARE ALL MANKIND.

Our Country is the World, our Countrymen are all Mankind.

THE SECOND, THIRD, AND FOURTH HEADINGS OF " THE LIBERATOR."
THE FIRST WAS PLAIN TYPE.

Page 100.

JOY STREET CHURCH, WHERE NEW ENGLAND ANTI-SLAVERY SOCIETY WAS ORGANIZED.

Page 107

DIX PLACE, SHOWING THE HOUSE OF WILLIAM LLOYD GARRISON.

repays careful examination, was being used. Hammatt Billings made the final design, which is of exceeding interest to us today in that the whole story of slavery is there told pictorially. In the background is seen the capitol of the United States, with a flag upon which is inscribed the word " Liberty " floating over the dome. In front is an auctioneer's stand with the sign, " Slaves, horses and other cattle in lots to suit the purchaser," —and a whipping post showing a slave under the lash. Balancing this — in the Billings design — is an allegorical presentation of life among the blacks when Emancipation has been declared. And between stands Christ and his cross with the scripture line, " I come to break the bonds of the oppressor."

The hardships under which the paper was gotten out during its early years are a classic tale today; but I like to rename them none the less. Garrison slept in his office (the generosity of the *Christian Examiner* lasted for the first three issues only) with the mailing table for a bed and a book for his pillow. His scanty meals he prepared himself,. and he set up with his own hand the articles which he printed, composing them as he went along. In their first issue Garrison and his co-publisher, Isaac Knapp, had announced their determination to print the paper as long as they might be able to subsist upon bread and water, and this was no empty boast. For a year and a half the two men actually had no food except such as could be obtained at a baker's shop opposite and a tiny fruitshop in the basement of their building. A friendly cat cheered their loneliness and Mr. Johnson recalls that Garrison, who was fond of animals, would often be found writing while the cat, mounted on the table by his side, caressed his bald forehead in a most affectionate way.

In his first number Garrison declared "I am in earnest — I will not equivocate — I will not excuse — I will not retreat a single inch — *and I will be heard.*"[1] Yet he avowed from the very start his opposition to war and violence under every circumstance. Naturally, however, the slaveholders could not see the matter quite as Garrison did, and when the *Liberator's* plain heading gave way, in the seventeenth number of the paper, to a cut showing slaves being sold at auction, they with one voice declared the sheet "incendiary" and began to clamor for its suppression. A highly respectable and very conservative journal published at Washington,

[1] The *Liberator* was needed, for one searches in vain for mention in such a paper as the *Advertiser*, for instance, of American slavery as an institution to be deplored. On the front page of this sheet, the year the *Liberator* was started, I find, however, in one day long articles reprobating slavery in England, and oppression in Russia and Poland!

the *National Intelligencer*, appealed to "the intelligent population of New England" and specifically to Harrison Gray Otis, then mayor of Boston, to prevent the further publication of the *Liberator*, asserting that in printing such a paper Garrison was performing "a crime as great as that of poisoning a well."

Otis had never heard of the *Liberator* when his attention was thus called to its deadly influence, but, in answer to the appeal he procured a copy and examined it carefully. Then he had its publication-office sought out and finding it to be "an obscure hole" did not bother himself much further about the matter. The State of Georgia, however, actually passed a law offering $5,000 for the conviction of those responsible for the paper's publication or for its circulation within the bounds of that State!

Meanwhile, the prophet went serenely on his way, getting out his little sheet regularly, and speaking, writing and talking everywhere his doctrine of *immediate emancipation*. Many who believed in freeing the slaves did not at all agree with him in his insistence that "now is the accepted hour for taking that righteous step." Gradual emancipation and education the while for all blacks was what they counselled. But Garrison argued thus simply: "Slavery is wrong. Every wrong act should be immediately abandoned. Therefore slavery ought at once to cease. Do right and leave the results to God." When pressed as to the consequences of this doctrine, he would explain that he did not mean that all slaveholders should turn their slaves out of doors, but that they should recognize that the blacks are free and be only their temporary guardian; that they should allow those who might wish to leave to go away whither they would, and should pay wages to all who should desire to remain. "Slavery is the holding of a human being as property." This definition, hit upon by Rev. Amos A. Phelps of Boston, himself soon to become a zealous Abolitionist, contained all that was necessary to justify to Garrison the stand he had found it imperative to take. For a creature with an immortal soul *could* not be " property."

Thus far, — for nearly a year, — the *Liberator* had been the organ of no organization; it had merely expressed the views of its high-minded editor. But the time was now come for the formation of a society which should have for its purpose the overthrow of slavery. The first meeting to form such a society was held on Nov. 13, 1831, in the office of Mr. Sewall, and on December 16 there followed another. The names of those present at the second meeting, besides Garrison and Sewall, were Ellis Gray

Loring and David Lee Child, Boston lawyers; Isaac Knapp, publisher of the *Liberator;* Samuel J. May, then settled in Brooklyn, Connecticut; Oliver Johnson, William J. Snelling, Alonzo Lewis, Dr. Abner Phelps, Rev. Mr. Blanchard (editor of an anti-masonic religious paper) and Gamaliel Bradford. A constitution was drafted by Ellis Gray Loring and Oliver Johnson, but it was voted to adjourn until January 6, at which time said constitution should be adopted.

The ensuing meeting — held in the school-room of the African Baptist Church [1] on Smith Court, off Joy Street — was one which is a landmark in American history. Writing nearly fifty years afterwards, Oliver Johnson, who had been the youngest person present, said of the occasion, " My recollections of the evening are very vivid. A fierce north-east storm, combining snow, rain, and hail in about equal proportions, was raging and the streets were full of slush. They were dark, too, for the city of Boston in those days was very economical of light on ' Nigger Hill.' But the twelve white men who there signed the Constitution of the first association ever organized in this country for the purpose of freeing the blacks were not easily to be discouraged by the frowns

[1] The building still stands but is now a synagogue, one of the 32 in Boston wherein worship more than 80,000 Jews; previous to 1840 the family of Peter Spitz represented the only Jews in Boston.

of nature. As they were stepping out into the storm and darkness, all echoed in their hearts the words of their inspired leader, ' We have met to-night in this obscure school-house; our numbers are few and our influence limited; but, mark my prediction, Faneuil Hall shall ere long echo with the principles we have set forth. We shall shake the nation by their mighty power.'" This speech and the occasion which called it forth should take its place in history alongside of Franklin's famous *bon mot* at a similarly crucial point in American affairs. " Gentlemen, if we do not all hang together we shall all hang separately." Great is the pity that no Rembrandt has arisen among Americans to send down through the ages the shadowy interior of that " obscure school-house " in which, while storm and sleet were raging outside, this bravest of all American ventures was launched by a little handful of devoted Boston citizens.

Within a year after the formation of the New England Anti-Slavery Society the women interested in freedom for the slave formed an organization, also. They appear not to have been invited to the meeting held in the African Church, but Garrison was quick to see that this was an injustice and he soon (in 1832) introduced a Ladies' Department into his paper and followed up that important step by declaring his belief that " the cause of bleeding humanity is always, legitimately, the cause of *woman*," and asserting his strong desire that women should work with men to right the great wrong of slavery. " A million females in this country," he added, " are recognized and held as property — liable to be sold or used for the gratification of the lust or avarice or convenience of unprincipled speculators — without the least protection of their chastity. . . . Have these no claims upon the sympathies — prayers — charities — *exertions* of our white countrywomen?

> " ' When woman's heart is bleeding,
> Shall woman's voice be hushed? ' "

Woman's voice had already begun to be heard concerning other issues and the Boston Female Anti-Slavery Society — founded October 14, 1832, by a little group of ladies — promptly began to make its influence felt in regard to this cause, also. Lydia Maria Child, Maria Weston Chapman, and her sisters, the Misses Weston, Louisa Loring, the wife of Ellis Gray Loring, Eliza Lee Follen, Susan Cabot, and the lady who was afterwards to become Mrs. Wendell Phillips were a few of those who, through the new organization, were soon doing yeoman service for the Abolitionist cause. In the summer of 1833 Lydia Maria Child published her famous *Appeal In Favor of That Class of Americans Called Africans*, a work which

cost her very much in income and in social
position. When she first met Garrison she was
the most successful woman writer and editor
in the United States. But she wrote later in
life, " he got hold of the strings of my conscience
and pulled me into reform work. It is no use
to imagine what might have been if I had never
seen him. Old dreams vanished, old associates
departed, and all things became new. A new
stimulus seized my whole being and carried me
whithersoever it would. I could not do otherwise, so help me God."

One important service rendered to the cause
by Mrs. Child was her share in the conversion
of William Ellery Channing, then in the height
of his influence and fame. John Pierpont, of
the Hollis Street church, Theodore Parker,
Charles Follen and Samuel J. May were
clergymen who had already rallied to the
standard of Garrison. Channing, however, had
not yet taken the decisive step. During a visit
to the West Indies (in 1830) occasioned by ill
health, he had been much impressed with the
wrong and evil of slavery and on his return to
Boston he began to express himself on the
subject. Then Mrs. Child took him in hand
and " at every interview," she writes, " I could
see that he grew bolder and stronger on the
subject, while I felt that I grew wiser and more
just. At first I thought him timid and even

slightly timeserving, but I soon discovered that I had formed this estimate from ignorance of his character. I learned that it was justice to all, not popularity for himself, which made him so cautious. He constantly grew upon my respect, until I came to regard him as the wisest as well as the gentlest apostle of humanity."

To Samuel J. May is due the credit for the definitive crossing-over of Channing to the side of the Garrisonians. The doctor had been expressing to Mr. May his agreement with the Abolitionists in all their essential doctrines, but his disapproval, none the less, of their harsh denunciations, violent language and frequent injustice to their opponents. To which at last Mr. May replied: "If this is so, Sir, it is your fault. You have held your peace and the stones have cried out. If we, who are obscure men, silly women, babes in knowledge, commit those errors, why do not such men as yourself speak and show us the right way?" To which came, after a long pause, the answer, "Brother May, I acknowledge the justice of your reproof. I have been silent too long."

But after that he was silent no longer. By his work on Slavery, his letter to James G. Birney on "The Abolitionists" (1836) and his appearance with the reformers at the State House in that same year he made it very clear

that he was with — and not against — the
work of God and humanity. His attitude in
this matter cost him many friends, too, and
drew down upon his head a great deal of abuse.
But he did not swerve in his devotion to the
principles he had at length espoused. And, in
that day, to stand firm required a great deal
of faith as well as much personal courage.
Bryant characterized the struggle as " a warfare which would only end with life; a friendless
warfare lingering through weary day and weary
year, in which the timid good stood aloof, the
sage frowned and the hissing bolt of scorn
would too surely reach its aim." Actual violence
was not unknown either. Miss Prudence Cran-
dall, a Quaker young woman of high character,
who had made colored girls, also, eligible to
her young ladies' school in Canterbury, Connecticut, was for so doing arrested and thrown
into jail after every attempt to starve or frighten
her out of her position had been tried in vain.
In New York mobs sacked the house of Lewis
Tappan, brother of that generous soul who had
paid Garrison's fine while in jail, and in Vermont
Samuel J. May was mobbed five times in one
month.

To be sure, the language of the Abolitionists
was not calculated to allay prejudice, once
aroused. For, as Margaret Fuller strikingly
put it, " The nation was deaf in regard to the

evils of slavery; and those who have to speak to deaf people naturally acquire the habit of saying everything on a very high key." The *Liberator* was, indeed, "incendiary." In all justice, therefore, we should admit that those Bostonians who honestly feared lest the violent speech which was being used by the reformers should endanger the peace of the land and result only in harm to all concerned, were not of necessity cowards or self-seekers. Often their dissent was merely as to method.

England meanwhile was supporting Mr. Garrison handsomely. In 1833 he was welcomed there with open arms by such men as Macaulay, Wilberforce, and O'Connell; and he became the close friend of George Thompson, the hero of the struggle for West India emancipation, — him of whom Lord Brougham said, in the House of Lords at the time of the passage of the Act of Emancipation, "I rise to take the crown of this most glorious victory from every other head and place it upon George Thompson's. He has done more than any other man to achieve it." Thompson was a very eloquent speaker, and Garrison felt strongly that, if he would come to America, the cause of Abolition here would be greatly advanced. Such, indeed, proved to be the case in many cities for, from the time Thompson landed in New York, in the fall of 1834, until he sailed again for home

something over a year later, he made converts
unnumbered. Frequently those who had come
to scoff remained to pray, so wonderful was his
eloquence, and so compelling his zeal for human
liberty.

Boston, however, lastingly disgraced herself
by her attitude towards George Thompson, —
though New York and Brooklyn were not far
behind in their enmity. Mrs. Child, in a
letter dated August 15, 1835, wrote thus to a
Boston friend, " I am at Brooklyn, at the house
of a very hospitable Englishman, a friend of
Mr. Thompson's. I have not ventured into the
city, nor does one of us dare to go to church
today, so great is the excitement here. You can
form no conception of it. 'Tis like the times of
the French Revolution, when no man dares
trust his neighbors. Private assassins from
New Orleans are lurking at the corners of the
streets to stab Arthur Tappan; and very large
sums are offered for anyone who will convey
Mr. Thompson into the slave States. . . . He is
almost a close prisoner in his chamber, his
friends deeming him in imminent peril the
moment it is ascertained where he is. . . ."
Within a week after these words were written,
fifteen hundred prominent citizens of Boston
appended their names to a call for a public
meeting in Faneuil Hall to denounce agitation
of slavery as putting in peril the existence of

the Union. Harrison Gray Otis was one of those who, at this famous gathering, spoke eloquently against Thompson and the friends who were working with him for the overthrow of slavery.

But though the Faneuil Hall meeting intensified the feeling against Garrison and Thompson, it was not on that occasion, but two months later, when the Boston Female Anti-Slavery Society was holding its annual meeting, that the historic demonstration of Boston " gentlemen of

THOMPSON,
THE ABOLITIONIST.

That infamous foreign scoundrel **THOMPSON**, will hold forth *this afternoon*, at the Liberator Office, No. 48, Washington Street. The present is a fair opportunity for the friends of the Union to *snake Thompson out!* It will be a contest between the Abolitionists and the friends of the Union. A purse of $100 has been raised by a number of patriotic citizens to reward the individual who shall first lay violent hands on Thompson, so that he may be brought to the tar kettle before dark. Friends of the Union, be vigilant!

Boston, Wednesday, **12 o'clock.** Oct 21. 1835

property and standing" occurred. The meeting was advertised to be held in the Society's hall, then numbered 46 Washington Street, midway between State Street and Cornhill, and an incendiary placard issued that same day at 12 o'clock from the office of the *Commercial Gazette* announced that " the infamous foreign

scoundrel, Thompson, will hold forth, this
afternoon, at the *Liberator* office. . . . The
present is a fair opportunity for the friends of
the Union to snake Thompson out." It added
that one hundred dollars had been raised to
be paid to the man who should " first lay violent
hands on Thompson, that he might be brought
to the tar-kettle before dark." This handbill
was distributed in all the places where people
were in the habit of congregating, in the insur-
ance offices, the reading-rooms, all along State
Street, in the hotels and drinking places and
among the mechanics at the North End. As
a result there gathered from every quarter of
the town men bent upon making trouble for
Thompson. Between three and four o'clock
there were, according to various estimates,
from two to five thousand people packing both
sides of Washington and State Streets in the
neighborhood of the Old State House.

Thompson was not at the meeting, however,
nor was he expected. But Garrison was there
to deliver a short address, and the ladies of the
Society, inferring rightly that the crowd, cheated
of its hoped-for victim, would try to rend Garrison, advised him to retire from the hall.
This he prudently did, but instead of leaving
the building, he went into the *Liberator* office,
adjoining the hall, and there busied himself
writing to a friend in a distant city an account

of the riotous demonstrations going on outside.
But the letter was never finished, for soon the
marauders, who had rushed into the hall in
search of him, were kicking out the panels of
his office door and, but for the presence of
mind of Charles C. Burleigh, would have seized
him forthwith and dragged him out. Friends
hustled Garrison into a carpenter's shop in
the rear of the building and for a time he was
safe. But the mob soon discovered his retreat
and he was made to descend by a ladder into
Wilson's Lane, now a part of Devonshire Street.
Then he was seized by his enemies and dragged
into State Street, in the rear of the Old State
House. From the rough handling of the mob —
they had thrown a rope around his body and
torn the clothes from his back while disputing
as to whether they should hang him or subject
him to milder treatment, — Garrison was at
length rescued by Mayor Lyman and his
officers, who succeeded in getting him into the
Old State House (then used as the City Hall
and Post-office) through the south door.

The howls of those who had been thus cheated
of their victim now became so violent, and their
acts grew so alarming, that, to save the old
building and Garrison's life, it was hastily
decided to commit him to jail as a disturber
of the peace, and he was quickly smuggled out
of the north door into a waiting hack. After

a desperate struggle with the infuriated multitude, the horses started at break-neck speed
through Court Street to Bowdoin Square,
through Cambridge into Blossom Street, and
thence to Leverett Street jail. And there, just
around the corner from his own home at 23
Brighton Street, the editor of the *Liberator*
spent in a cell the night of October 21, 1835.
The morning after his incarceration he made
upon the walls of his cell this inscription:
" William Lloyd Garrison was put into this
cell on Wednesday afternoon, October 21, 1835,
to save him from the violence of a respectable
and influential mob, who sought to destroy him
for preaching the abominable and dangerous
doctrine that ' all men are created equal,' and
that all oppression is odious in the sight of
God. Hail Columbia! Cheers for the Autocrat
of Russia and the Sultan of Turkey! Reader,
let this inscription remain till the last slave
in this despotic land be loosed from his fetters! "

The ladies whose meeting had been so rudely
interrupted made a brave attempt to pursue the
object for which they had come together.
Miss Mary S. Parker, the president, opened
the exercises by reading a portion of Scripture,
and then, in a sweet and serene voice, she
offered a prayer for the cause of the slave and
besought forgiveness for his oppressors. After
the mob had burst inside their hall, however,

WILLIAM ELLERY CHANNING.
Page 108.

HOLY CROSS CATHEDRAL, CHANNING'S CHURCH
IN THE BACKGROUND.

TREMONT STREET SOUTH OF SCHOOL STREET ABOUT 1850.

DOROTHEA LYNDE DIX.

From a daguerreotype taken in 1858.

Page 227.

MRS. WILLIAM LLOYD GARRISON.

*From a daguerreotype taken about
1852, in the possession of Francis
Jackson Garrison.*

Page 122.

the mayor urged the ladies to retire, saying that it might not be in his power, with his small force, to protect them long. This they did, the police making a passage for them through the jeering crowd outside. Francis Jackson immediately invited them to conclude their meeting at his home on Hollis Street. He was determined that there should be free speech in Boston at whatever peril. But when Hollis Street was reached it was found that Mrs. Jackson was ill, so the meeting finished its business at the home of Mrs. Maria Weston Chapman, at No. 11 West Street. It was Mrs. Chapman who, earlier in the afternoon, had replied, — when Mayor Lyman had been urging that it was dangerous for the ladies to remain in their hall, — "If this is the last bulwark of freedom, we may as well die here as anywhere."

For almost two weeks after this affair Garrison, by the advice of his friends, secluded himself at Brooklyn, Connecticut, from which place, his wife, then in her twenty-fifth year and an expectant mother of her first child, wrote as follows of her emotions on the epoch-making day to Mrs. Chapman's sister:

"BROOKLYN, Oct. 31, 1835.

"I thank you, my dear Miss Weston, for your kind letter, and the expressions of sympathy for me and mine which it contained. When I

left you at Court Street and ascertained Mr.
Garrison was not at the *Liberator* office, I
comforted myself with the reflection that he
had retired under the roof of some dear friend,
where he was safe. I made a long call at a
friend's house and then hastened home, with
the fond anticipation of meeting him; but
alas! you may judge of my feelings when my
domestic informed me a gentleman had just
left the house, who seemed exceedingly agitated,
and very desirous of seeing me. In a few
moments he returned, with a countenance
which indicated excessive grief. I prepared
myself for the worst, thinking all he would
reveal to me could not surpass what I, in a
few moments of suspense, had imagined the
real danger might be. He kindly and feelingly
related all that had transpired, from the time
the ruffians seized him at the carpenter's shop
and conveyed him to the mayor's office.

" I put on my things with a full determination
of seeing him, and ascertaining for a certainty
how much injury he had received; but before
I reached the office I met with several friends
who dissuaded me from attempting it; and
not thinking it expedient myself, when I was
apprised of the multitude that had assembled,
I concluded to tarry with my kind friend, Mrs.
Fuller, to await the result. About five I learned
he was safely carried to jail for safe-keeping.

How my heart swelled with gratitude to the Preserver of our being, for having enabled him to pass through the hands of a mob without receiving the slightest injury. My dear husband was wonderfully sustained in a calm and quiet state, during the whole scene of confusion that reigned around him; he was perfectly collected and felt willing to sacrifice his life rather than compromise principles. The two men you allude to in your letter were the ones who were most active in their exertions to save husband; why they were so no one knows, without they were bribed by someone to do it; however, let their motives be what they would, may blessings rest on them for this one act of kindness.

" I was rejoiced our dear friend, Thompson, was in his quiet retreat; for had he been in Boston they would have devoured him like so many wolves, and Bostonians would have been obliged to blush for one of the most atrocious and villainous acts that could have been committed in the sunlight of heaven. I hope he will use every precaution for his own safety that duty requires him to, for the sake of his family and friends.

" I cannot feel too thankful that Mr. May was absent from the city at the time, as he would in all probability have been the next most conspicuous in the cause, and might have received some severe blows if no more.

" I was glad the ladies, notwithstanding all they had endured for the truth, were permitted to proceed with their meeting without molestation; had I known it was their intention to adjourn to a private house, I would certainly have been one of their number.

" The many attentions I received from my friends are too numerous to mention; they flocked around me, unwearied in their exertions, and rendered me every needful assistance. How comforting and consoling the thought, that there were hearts who beat in unison with my own, and whose most fervent aspirations were ascending to the mercy-seat for a hasty and speedy deliverance from the dangers which looked so threatening.

" We are now at my Father's house, well and happy, where I think we shall remain through the winter, as I find it is impossible for us to keep house without endangering others' property, and frequently having our own domestic happiness broken in upon by a lawless mob. Husband thinks he likes the retirement of the country, and that he will be able to accomplish much more in the way of editorial than if he was in the city, where so many duties necessarily devolve upon him.

" My dear husband was deeply affected on perusing your consoling letter, especially that part of it which relates to himself. He desires

me to convey to you his warm and heartfelt
emotions of gratitude, and the same to the
Christian heroines of the Female Anti-Slavery
Society, for all your sympathies, kindnesses,
and prayers, so freely elicited in our behalf.
What he has been called to suffer he considers
not worthy to be mentioned except joyfully,
for it is a high honor and not a reproach to be
dragged through the streets by a lawless mob,
for his testimony against the great abomination
of this wicked land. I desire to bless God
that his faith was superior to the trial which he
was called to endure — that in the hour of
peril he was undaunted and cheerful; and tho'
I still tremble for his safety, yet, inexpressibly
dear as he is to me, I had rather see him sacrifice
his life in this blessed cause than swerve from
a single right principle. He expects to visit
Boston next week, and will avail himself of the
opportunity to see you. He desires to be
remembered, with all respect and esteem, to
your sisters and to Mr. and Mrs. Chapman,
for all of whom he entertains an exalted
opinion.

"Remember me very kindly to your sisters
and the Miss Ammidons, to whom I am greatly
indebted for the many favors I received the
day I was taking my departure.

"I am, very affectionately yours,

"HELEN E. GARRISON."

Surely a very beautiful and noble letter! It reminds me tardily that I have not told at all of Garrison's love-making or of the charming girl who was glad to share his uncertain income and troublous career. They had first met in Providence, just before Garrison set sail for England, and their attraction had from the beginning been mutual, though no words of love were exchanged until January, 1834, when they began a correspondence which soon culminated in an engagement. That spring, on his way to Philadelphia, the youth for the first time visited the maiden as an accepted suitor and was immensely pleased to observe that she had not " dressed up " for him! " Not one young lady out of ten thousand," he writes, — with remarkable acumen, considering his life-study had been Slavery and not Woman — " but in a first interview with her lover would have endeavored falsely to heighten her charms and allure by outward attractions." Helen Benson, then as ever, though, was inclined, (as was her father before her), to Quaker garb and Quaker ideals. At the wedding which followed, September 4, 1834, there was neither cake nor wine, both bride and groom feeling the importance of their example to the colored population, whose tendency to show and parade they understood and deplored. After a journey to Boston by carriage, the young couple began housekeeping at " Freedom's Cottage," on Bower Street, near Walnut Street, Roxbury, where they continued to live for some time. On the first anniversary of his marriage, Garrison thus wrote of his wife to her brother George,[1] who was also an ardent abolitionist, " I did not marry her expecting that she would assume a prominent station in the anti-slavery cause, but for domestic quietude and happiness. So completely absorbed am I in that cause that it was undoubtedly wise for me to select as a partner one who, while her benevolent feelings were in unison with mine, was less immediately and entirely connected with it. I knew that she was naturally diffident and distrustful of her own ability to do all that her heart might prompt. She is one of those who prefer to toil unseen, to give by stealth — and to sacrifice in seclusion. By her unwearied attention to my wants, her sympathetic regards, her perfect equanimity of mind, and her sweet and endearing manners, she is no trifling support to abolitionism, inasmuch as she lightens my labors and enables me to find exquisite delight in the family circle, as an offset to public adversity."

One of the most striking things in connection with the anti-slavery struggle was the coterie

[1] There are five large volumes of MS. letters *by* Garrison and twenty-one volumes of letters *to* him in the archives of the Boston Public Library, the gift to that institution of Garrison's children.

of beautiful and gifted women who gave themselves whole-heartedly to the cause. In Boston
alone there were enough of these to make an
imposing array, and when, to reinforce their
ranks, there came from Philadelphia such
women as Angelina and Sarah Grimké and
from England such as Harriet Martineau and
Fanny Kemble [1] the movement was sure to
make headway apace. Many of the women
workers in the anti-slavery cause grew to know
intimately other women who had been slaves
and so were moved by personal interest as well
as by principle to strike down the accursed
thing. Mrs. Cheney tells of her warm sympathy
for Harriet Jacobs, who was born a slave in
North Carolina and who suffered in her own
person all the terrible evils to which beautiful
young girls who were house servants were
habitually exposed. Through incredible suffering she escaped from slavery, being for almost
seven years hidden away in a small loft where
she could neither stand erect nor move with
any freedom. In *Linda, the Autobiography of
a Slave Woman*, a very rare book, she has
herself told the history of her life. For many
years this woman was in the service of N. P.
Willis's family and subsequently she kept a

---

[1] " I am sick and weary of this cruel and ignorant folly," wrote
Fanny Kemble of slavery, which she had studied while living in
1838–9 on a Georgia rice plantation.

boarding-house at Cambridge for Harvard students. Harriet Tubman, whose story has been told by Sarah H. Bradford, and Ellen Craft, a light mulatto woman, who escaped disguised as a young Southern planter, bringing her husband with her in the character of her body servant, likewise moved by their personal narrations the hearts and consciences of all who heard them, especially those " devout women not a few " who were already alive to the terrible wickedness of slavery.

Angelina Grimké, daughter of a Southern slave-owner, soon had an appalling example of that wickedness brought to her very door, — and she met the situation like the heroic creature that she was. Seeing in an anti-slavery paper (after the war) allusions to the academic honors being won at Lincoln University by two young colored men of her family name, she opened a correspondence with the youths, thinking they might be ex-slaves of one of her brothers. She found that they were the sons as well as former slaves of her favorite brother, who had recently died! Immediately she went south to see them at their school, acknowledged to their professors the relationship of the young men and their claim upon her, invited them to visit her at her home in Hyde Park (she had by this time married Theodore Weld, an abolitionist like herself) and there introduced them to her friends, quite naturally, as her nephews. They were good-looking, intelligent, gentlemanly young men, and in their life since (one is now a Presbyterian minister in Washington, the other a successful lawyer in Boston) they have nobly realized that " devotion to the eternal principles of justice and humanity and religion " which she solemnly enjoined on them as their duty.

No one felt the horror of the whole slave situation more than Harriet Martineau. She was the heroine of the adjourned meeting of the Boston Female Anti-Slavery Society which came on November 19 at the home of Francis Jackson, and the modest little speech in which she then declared her entire sympathy with the cause of the Abolitionists brought down upon her head a tide of denunciation only less violent than that to which George Thompson himself had been subjected. Social ostracism was henceforth her lot in Boston, and from her experience at the hands of the city's élite sprang her book *The Martyr Age of America*, which did much to bind the hearts of the Abolitionists in England to the friends of the cause on this side of the water.

Another woman who by her pen and voice rendered very valuable service to the cause at this crisis and later was Mrs. Maria Weston Chapman, wife of Henry G. Chapman, a

Boston merchant. Mrs. Chapman was a lady
of Mayflower lineage, of European culture, of
very unusual beauty and of great social charm.
When she espoused the unpopular cause of the
negro and set herself to work early and late at
whatever task would help Garrison, Boston
society was frankly disgusted. Lowell has
described Mrs. Chapman as

> " A noble woman, brave and apt,
>   Cumæan sibyl not more rapt,
>   Who might, with those fair tresses shorn,
>   The Maid of Orleans' casque have worn;
>   Herself the Joan of our Arc
>   For every shaft a shining mark."

The picture of her that I like best is, however,
that given by Miss Martineau in the following
paragraph:

" When I was putting on my shawl upstairs,
Mrs. Chapman came to me, bonnet in hand, to
say, ' You know we are threatened with a mob
again to-day; but I do not myself much appre-
hend it. It must not surprise us; but my hopes
are stronger than my fears.' I hear now, as I
write, the clear silvery tones of her who was
to be the friend of the rest of my life. I still
see the exquisite beauty which took me by
surprise that day, — the slender, graceful form;
the golden hair which might have covered her
to her feet; the brilliant complexion, noble
profile, and deep blue eyes; the aspect, meant

by nature to be soft and winning only, but that day (as ever since) so vivified by courage, and so strengthened by upright conviction, as to appear the very embodiment of heroism. ' My hopes,' said she, as she threw up her golden hair under her bonnet, ' are stronger than my fears.' "

Mrs. Chapman's husband was the cousin of Ann Terry Greene, the lady who was soon to become Mrs. Wendell Phillips. And this frail girl it was who won to the side of the Abolitionists its most valuable exponent. It was at the Chapmans' fireside, too, whither Phillips had gone to call on Miss Greene — that the most gifted spokesman of the slave met for the first time him who had long been his chief champion — another illustration of the old truth that it is love which makes the world go round.

For many years Mrs. Chapman was the prime mover in the annual anti-slavery fairs by means of which funds to carry on the work of the Society were raised. Through her wide circle of acquaintance she was able to secure for the tables many contributions from Europe — odd and beautiful things which could then be purchased at no Boston shop, and which, therefore, found a very ready sale. Garrison sent his wife, under date of December 30, 1835, the following description of one of these func-

MARIA WESTON CHAPMAN.
Page 128.

WILLIAM LLOYD GARRISON AND WENDELL
PHILLIPS

From a photograph.

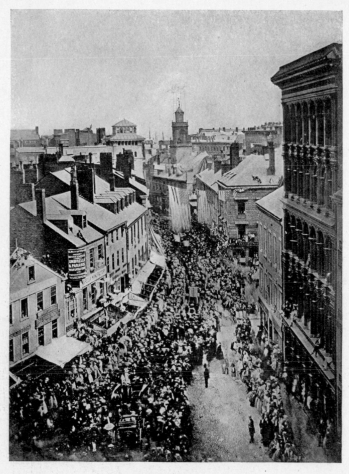

A PROCESSION IN COURT STREET.

Page 145.

tions: "To-day has been the day for the Ladies' Fair — but not so bright and fair out of doors as within doors. The Fair was held at the house of Mr. Chapman's father in Chauncey Place, in two large rooms. Perhaps there were not quite so many things prepared as last year but the assortment was nevertheless various. There were several tables, as usual, which were under the superintendence of the Misses Weston, The Misses Ammidon, Miss Paul, Miss Chapman, Mrs. Sargent (who by the way spoke in the kindest manner of you), and one or two other persons whom I did not know. I bought a few things, and had one or two presents for Mrs. Garrison. . . . Our friend Sewall's 'intended,' Miss Winslow, is now in the city and was at the Fair today with two sparkling eyes and a pleasant countenance. How soon the marriage knot is to be tied, I cannot find out. Don't you think they are unwise not to hasten matters? . . . This evening I took tea at Mr. Loring's. . . . His amiable wife was at the Fair selling and buying and giving away with her characteristic assiduity and liberality. Both of them were very kind in their inquiries after my wife. This forenoon bro. May and myself, by express invitation, visited Miss Martineau at Mr. Gannett's house. The interview was very agreeable and satisfactory to me. She is a fine woman." Miss

Martineau, on the other hand, pronounced Garrison " the most bewitching person " she had met in the United States!

To Miss Martineau's trenchant pen we are indebted for a picturesque description (in the *Martyr Age of America*) of an important State House hearing that occurred about this time (on March 4, 1836) on the question whether citizens of non-slaveholding States might or might not write and speak against slavery. " While the committee " she writes, " were, with ostentatious negligence, keeping the Abolitionists waiting, they, to whom this business was a prelude to life or death, were earnestly consulting in groups. At the further end of the chamber Garrison and another; somewhat nearer, Dr. Follen looking German all over, and a deeper earnestness than usual overspreading his serene and meditative coun-tenance. In consultation with him was Ellis Gray Loring, only too frail in form, but with a face radiant with inward light. There were May and Goodell and Sewall and several more, and many an anxious wife, sister or friend looking down from the gallery.

" During the suspense the door opened and Dr. Channing entered, — one of the last people who could, on that wintry afternoon, have been expected. He stood a few moments, muffled in his cloak and shawl-handkerchief, and then walked the whole length of the room and was immediately seen shaking hands with Garrison. A murmur ran through the gallery and a smile went round the chamber. Mrs. Chapman whispered to her next neighbor, ' Righteousness and peace have kissed each other!' Garrison, the dauntless Garrison, turned pale as ashes and sank down on a seat. Dr. Channing had censured the Abolitionists in his pamphlet on Slavery; Garrison had, in the *Liberator*, rejected the censure; and here they were shaking hands in the Senate chamber. Dr. Channing sat behind the speakers, handing them notes, and most obviously affording them his countenance, so as to be from that day considered by the world as an accession to their principles, though not to their organized body."

From this time on, events in anti-slavery circles moved swiftly. In February, 1837, a woman for the first time spoke on the subject at a State House hearing, the lady thus distinguished being the gifted Angelina Grimké, who laid down the important and far-reaching axiom that " Whatever is morally right for a man to do is morally right for a woman to do." She added that she recognized no rights but human rights and that, in her opinion, the time had gone by for woman to be " a second hand agent in regenerating the world! " Inas-

much as many of the most valued workers for
the anti-slavery cause had long been women it
was considered by the Abolitionists very fitting
that this woman, who knew slavery from
intimate childhood association, and whose powers as a speaker were soon famed throughout
the country, should appear at a Boston hearing.
But the other side did not enjoy the innovation.
Lydia Maria Child has thus described the
scene:

" The house was full to overflowing. For a
moment her sense of the responsibility resting
on her seemed almost to overwhelm her. She
trembled and grew pale. But this passed
quickly and she went on to speak gloriously,
showing, in utter forgetfulness of herself, her
own earnest faith in every word she uttered,
' Whatever comes from the heart goes to the
heart.' I believe she made a very powerful
impression on the audience. Boston, like other
cities is very far behind the country towns on
this subject; so much so that it is getting to
be Boston *vs.* Massachusetts, as the lawyers
say. The Boston members of the legislature
tried hard to prevent her having a hearing on
the second day. Among other things, they said
such a crowd was attracted by curiosity, that
the galleries were in danger of breaking down,
though in fact they are constructed with
remarkable strength. A member from Salem,

perceiving their drift, wittily proposed 'that a committee be appointed to examine the foundations of the State House of Massachusetts to see whether it will bear another lecture from Miss Grimké.' "

One interesting result of the increasing activity of women in Massachusetts was the famous Pastoral Letter of the " General Association of Massachusetts to the Churches Under Its Care," an appeal which, after deploring the slavery agitation generally, invited attention particularly " to the dangers which at present (1837) seem to threaten the female character with widespread and permanent injury." The author of this " bull," issued while the Massachusetts Orthodox churches were in session at Brookfield, was Rev. Dr. Nehemiah Adams, of Boston, who earned for himself, by his truckling to the slave power, the sobriquet of " Southside Adams." This gentleman shows himself in his " Letter " immensely solicitous for the beautiful bloom of womanhood. " If the vine whose strength and beauty is to lean upon the trellis-work and half conceal its clusters thinks to assume the independence and the overshadowing nature of the elm, it will not only cease to bear fruit," he declares, " but will fall in shame and dishonor to the dust. We cannot, therefore, but regret the mistaken conduct of those who encourage females to bear an obtrusive and ostentatious part in measures of reform and countenance any of that sex who so far forget themselves as to itinerate in the character of public lecturers and teachers." Maria Weston Chapman wittily replied to this pompous fulmination in a jingle which she called, "The Times that Try Men's Souls," and signed "The Lords of Creation." While from J. G. Whittier came the stirring verses beginning:

"So, this is all, — the utmost reach,
    Of priestly power the mind to fetter!
When laymen think — when women preach —
    A war of words — a Pastoral Letter.

.   .   .   .

"A Pastoral Letter, grave and dull —
    Alas! in hoof and horns and features,
How different is your Brookfield bull,
    From him who bellows from St. Peter's!

.   .   .   .

"But ye, who scorn the thrilling tale
    Of Carolina's high-souled daughters,
Which echoes here the mournful wail
    Of sorrow from Edisto's waters,
Close while ye may the public ear, —
    With malice vex, with slander wound them, —
The pure and good shall throng to hear,
    And tried and manly hearts surround them."

These last lines were prophetic. For the measures taken to suppress the women and to stifle the voice of the Abolitionists only served to enlarge their meetings and to win to their side converts of greater power than any they had yet known.

Chief of these was Wendell Phillips, who from 1837 on was the spokesman *par excellence* of the anti-slavery forces. Mr. Phillips' conversion to the cause came, as has been already said, through Miss Ann Terry Greene, whom he married on October 12, 1837. Ere their honeymoon was over, both were inexpressibly shocked by the news that Rev. Elijah P. Lovejoy, a Presbyterian clergyman of New England birth, who in the church organ of which he was editor had condemned the barbarous burning of a negro by a band of lynchers, had been himself shot down by a mob while in the act of defending his press from the violence of marauders. The South openly exulted over this appalling act. The North condemned the mob but lamented the " imprudence " of the victim. A petition signed by Dr. Channing and others, asking that Faneuil Hall might be assigned them for a meeting in which to protest against this violation of the principles of liberty, was rejected by the Boston authorities. Whereupon Dr. Channing issued an appeal to the citizens of Boston, calling upon them to reverse this action of the municipal government. Simultaneously, a meeting at the Supreme Court room, presided over by George W. Bond,

prepared resolutions demanding that the mayor
and aldermen change their course and give the
use of the hall. They did so and the meeting
was held, Jonathan Phillips, a wealthy kinsman
of Wendell Phillips, presiding.

It was a morning meeting, for greater safety's
sake, and the old hall was full to suffocation.
Dr. Channing made an impressive address, in
which he showed how the right of free speech
had been violated by the murder of Lovejoy.
Benjamin F. Hallett and George S. Hilliard
followed in much the same vein. The next
speaker was James Tricothic Austin, a parishioner of Dr. Channing's but one who did that
saintly man little credit in the views he was
now to set forth. For, declaring that Lovejoy
died " as the fool dieth " and that the men who
had killed him were as great patriots as those
who threw the tea into Boston harbor, he had
soon drawn to applauding approval the vast
number of those unthinking and inimical folk
who had come to the meeting because they
hoped to prevent the passage of the Resolutions
and so clog the progress of the Abolition cause
whose power they were beginning to fear.

Wendell Phillips had, until this moment, been
standing on the floor with the other listeners,
but he now leaped upon the platform and proceeded sternly to rebuke the speech of the
demagogue, Austin. " When I heard," said he,

" the gentleman lay down principles which placed the murderers of Alton side by side with Otis and Hancock, with Quincy and Adams, I thought those pictured lips," pointing to their portraits, " would have broken into voice to rebuke the recreant American, the slanderer of the dead." And then followed a marvellous speech of which Oliver Johnson, who heard it, has said, " Never before did the walls of the old ' Cradle of Liberty ' echo to a finer strain of eloquence. It was a speech to which not even the completest report could do justice . . . and the reporter [present] caught only a pale reflection of what fell from the orator's lips."

Yet it is a good speech to read even in its imperfect form. Mr. Austin had said that Lovejoy had acted with imprudence, and Phillips caught this up. " Imprudent to defend the liberty of the press! Why? Because the defence was unsuccessful? Does success gild crime into patriotism and want of it change heroic self-devotion to imprudence? Was Hampden imprudent when he drew the sword and threw away the scabbard? Yet he, judged by that single hour, was unsuccessful. After a short exile the race he hated sat again upon the throne. Imagine yourself present when the first news of Bunker Hill battle reached a New England town. The tale would have run thus: ' The patriots are routed; the red-

coats victorious; Warren lies dead upon the
field.' With what scorn would that *Tory* have
been received, who should have charged Warren
with imprudence! who should have said that,
bred as a physician, he was ' out of place ' in
the battle and ' died as the fool dieth! ' How
would the intimation have been received that
Warren and his associates should have waited
a better time? But, if success be indeed the
only criterion of prudence, *Respice finem* —
wait till the end.

" *Presumptuous* to assert the freedom of the
press on American ground! Is the assertion
of such freedom before the age? So much
before the age as to leave one no right to make
it because it displeases the community? Who
invents this libel on his country? It is this
very thing which entitles Lovejoy to greater
praise; the disputed right which provoked
the Revolution — taxation without representation — is far beneath that for which he died.
(Here there was a strong and general expression
of disapprobation.) One word, gentlemen.
As much as thought is better than money, so
much is the cause in which Lovejoy died
nobler than a mere question of taxes. James
Otis thundered in this hall when the king did
but touch his pocket. Imagine, if you can, his
indignant eloquence had England offered to
put a gag upon his lips. (Great applause.)"

And then Mr. Phillips, who was only twenty-six and comparatively unknown, closed with these words, " I am glad, sir, to see this crowded house. It is good for us to be here. When liberty is in danger, Faneuil Hall has the right, it is her duty, to strike the key-note for these United States. I am glad, for one reason, that remarks such as those to which I have alluded have been uttered here. The passage of these resolutions, in spite of this opposition, led by the Attorney General of the Commonwealth, will show more clearly, more decisively, the deep indignation with which Boston regards this outrage."

After this memorable beginning, Faneuil Hall became, each year, more and more identified with the cause of the Abolitionists. On its platform, Garrison, Sumner, Theodore Parker, Edmund Quincy, Douglass, Higginson, Howe and John A. Andrew — to name only a few on the honorable roll — reasserted whenever their testimony would help the principles of anti-slavery reform and defended as the need of the moment demanded the cause of freedom for all men.

Another Boston structure, still standing, which has deeply stirring associations for those who care about this struggle of the slave for freedom, is the Old Court House. Through the east door of this building was effected in Feb-

ruary, 1851, the rescue of Shadrach, a colored
waiter at the Cornhill Coffee House, who had
been arrested as a fugitive from slavery under
the law which Daniel Webster condemned himself by supporting. In 1851, pending the trial
of Thomas M. Sims, the Court House was
girdled with heavy chains to prevent another
rescue, and, in order to reach their tribunals
of justice, the judges of the Supreme Court of
Massachusetts were obliged to stoop under
this symbol of the slave-holders' supremacy
even in a non slave-holding State. Many
a son of Boston, however, was now fired with
mighty indignation that such things should be,
and, on the next occasion when the Fugitive
Slave Law was to be enforced in their city,
determined speeches against it were made in
Faneuil Hall and a careful plan for rescuing
Anthony Burns, the victim, was formed. Unhappily the plan did not succeed. Though a
band of Abolitionists, prominent among whom
were Thomas Wentworth Higginson and Lewis
Hayden, burst open the middle door on the
west side of the Court House by means of a
heavy beam of wood, the firing of a shot from
some unknown quarter precipitated a panic,
and the rescuers' organization was demoralized,
with the result that poor Burns was left to his
keepers and his fate. An eye witness [1] who was

[1] " Cliftondale " in the *Boston Transcript*.

on his way to school describes thus the rendition which followed:

"In passing through Court Square I was surprised at seeing a crowd of men and boys in that generally rather quiet thoroughfare. The Cadets, Colonel Amory, were in line on the City Hall side, and the open, upper windows of the Court House were filled with United States marines or soldiers. . . . From the head of State Street I saw State troops in the intersecting streets, guarding that thoroughfare. On passing down Water Street I found the City Guard.

"I returned to the square in time to witness a procession from Worcester in which a stalwart colored man carried a banner lettered with an anti-slavery motto. As it neared me a man named Allen, a stationer on State Street whose brother was a lieutenant in the Boston City Guard, rushed to the darkey, drew the pole down until he had hold of the cross-bar and the two then struggled for the possession of the banner. Others on both sides took part, and after a small riot that and other banners were torn to shreds and the pieces scattered among the crowd as souvenirs of the occasion, and the members of the procession merged with the crowd like a ' dissolving view.'

"Another procession soon emerged from the Court House door, with Burns as the central

figure, preceded by police and United States
marshals, and surrounded by United States
troops. I was in the immediate rear and against
the rope drawn across State Street when the
procession had entered it and I watched till it
reached the wharf, as it had been threatened
that bottles of vitriol would be thrown from
upper windows upon it; but I did not witness
any such proceeding. If ever ' State Rights '
were violated, though, they were on that occasion."

Miss Martha Russell, a newspaper correspondent of the period, whose heart was in the
right place and who was endowed with a
sprightly style, wrote thus categorically of what
happened just before Burns was led away:

"BOSTON, May 26, 1854.

"DEAR FRIENDS:—I have a great many things
to say to you and scarcely know where to
begin. I am in a great ' whew,' as Aunt
Lydia used to say. There is a fugitive slave
now confined in Boston Court House, and
has been there ever since Wednesday night.
His master came on, brought a man with
him and ' nabbed ' him at once. He was
going off with him but Mr. Dana interfered,
and tomorrow he will have his trial. The
whole city is in excitement; to-night there is
a great meeting in Faneuil Hall of all parties,

a regular indignation meeting, and I am going. They have not put chains about the Court House yet, as they did when they took Sims, but many people think there will be bloodshed before they get through. I shall go up to the Commonwealth office tomorrow, and as those windows command a view of State Street and Court Street, I shall see all the proceedings that can be seen outside the Court House. If Boston people allow another fugitive slave to be taken from here, and just now when that rascally Nebraska bill has passed, they deserve to be hung as high as were the Salem witches.

"I have been noticing books this forenoon. Mr. Giddings, Mr. Hale and, I think, Mr. Whittier, will be in town this week. I hope to see them. The anniversaries of the different moral and benevolent societies are held here next week. I wish you could hear some of the speeches. I go to hear Theodore Parker preach.

"Men say that he is not orthodox and all that; he says some things I do not believe, yet he never gives his hearers a stone when they ask for bread. He is a noble, fearless, but somewhat impulsive man. I care less for his theological notions and dogmas than I do for the great human heart within him.

.   .   .   .

" Sunday morning. I hoped by this time to tell you that the fugitive slave was free, but he is now in the Court House, guarded by three companies of troops — the marines from the navy yard, the regular United States troops from Governor's Island and a company of volunteers. The city is one great ferment. On Friday evening I went to Faneuil Hall. As I expected, the hall was a dense jam; there are no seats on the lower floors and the whole surface was packed with men standing. The galleries, the window-sills, the ante-rooms, were crowded with men and women, and outside was a great crowd that could not get in at all, so they made speeches out there. The meeting was organized by appointing George Russell of Roxbury chairman. There were several speakers, among them Wendell Phillips and Theodore Parker. Dr. Howe read the resolutions. I liked Mr. Phillips best of all. There seemed but one voice among speakers and people and that was that the slave, Anthony Burns, should not go back to Virginia. Such shouts and groans and hisses and cries of, 'To the Court House!' 'Let us free him tonight!' It was all Wendell Phillips could do, with his wondrous eloquence, to pacify them and show them the madness of an attempt to rescue him until after he had had his mockery of a trial. Before he had done speaking a man crowded himself into the doorway crying that there was a crowd collected around the Court House in Court Square, and they were about to attack the Court House. There was one general rush for the door. When we got out, which was not until among the last, the crowd were hurrying up to the Court House. We came up to the Commonwealth office. There was a crowd up there but we gave them a wide berth and came home, meeting on the way a company of military. Another passed the house soon after we reached it. The crowd attacked the Court House, broke one door, broke windows, etc., and were met by persons who were guarding the prisoner, the tools of the United States marshal, who was there himself, all armed with revolvers and swords. There were some pistols fired and one man killed. The man killed was said to have been inside the house and one of the men hired to guard the prisoner. The alarm bells were rung [and] as soon as possible, the mayor was there with the police. The mayor then ordered out two or three companies of military troops, while the United States marshal sent for more marines and for more regulars. None of the city troops volunteered to help the marshal, but a company of foreigners. The services of these were accepted and they were quartered in the Court House, to the great exasperation of the citizens.

The city troops guard the building and try to keep the peace.

"Yesterday morning at the hour appointed for the trial the crowd about the Court House was very great; but every avenue was guarded and at the upper windows soldiers were looking down. Commissioner Loring would let no one in on the prisoner's behalf if he could help it and so much did Mr. Dana [1] who had taken up the prisoner's defence, make of this point, that they finally granted a postponement until Monday in order that he might prepare for the defence. So all day yesterday the Court House was guarded, and it is said that the marshal has sent to Newport for more troops. I did not go up street in the morning as I had planned, for I did not think it would be wise, but when my friends came home they said I might have gone. I went just at sunset up to the Common and then down past the Court House. The troops were drawn up before the door that was battered down the night before and there was a crowd that was constantly increasing. There was a rumor that Wendell Phillips' house was to be attacked and J. went with some others to buy Colt's revolvers. These gentlemen were going to stay in Mr. Phillips' house to guard it.

[1] Richard H. Dana, Jr.

" C. has been up to the square this morning. There were not many people about and all was quiet. He heard that the merchants of Boston had offered the master his price for the slave, $1,200, for which he offered to sell him Friday, and that now he refuses to take that and wants them to pay all his expenses besides. If I had my way I would take that slaveholder down to the old Liberty Tree on the corner where they used to take Tories, with a halter round his neck and ride him on a rail out of town. That would be all the coin he would get from me for his slave. I am ashamed of their trying to buy him. The Whigs and Democrats are as much excited about the matter as the anti-slavery people, indeed, it is said they complain of the luke-warmness of the Free Soilers. They want the Free Soilers to go ahead while they stand behind the corner and cry ' Go ahead! ' The Free Soilers have done it in the times gone by and they are ready to do it now, though they would like someone to coöperate. Mr. B. very much deplores the outbreak Friday night; he thought the tone of some of the speeches made at Faneuil Hall Friday night very injudicious, and indeed the outbreak has done much to lessen the chance of the poor fellow's rescue. Tomorrow we shall see what will be done. I am to go to the office in the morning

to see the crowd and will write you all about
it.   Very truly yours,
                    " MARTHA RUSSELL." [1]

The trifling advantages gained by slavery
from such renditions as that of Burns were
vastly outweighed by the indignation against
the slave-power and all its abettors which
was fed by these transactions. In all ages and
nations it has been held odious to return fugitives into the hands of their oppressors, and no
matter how eloquently a Daniel Webster might
argue in a Seventh of March speech that it
was the constitutional duty of Massachusetts
strictly to enforce the extradition law, the
awakened conscience of Boston cried out against
such acts. To urge the enforcement of the
Fugitive Slave Law was now the surest way
to engender violent resistance to it. Moreover,
there was very good ground for belief that
the law was unconstitutional in its provisions.
The United States Constitution had provided
that " no person shall be deprived of his liberty
without due process of law " and that " in all
suits at common law where the value in con-
troversy shall exceed twenty dollars, the right
of trial by jury shall be preserved." Yet Sims
and Burns were deprived of their liberty without

---

[1] In a letter to friends in North Brandford, Connecticut, quoted
in the Notes and Queries department of the *Boston Transcript*.

seeing either judge or jury! This disregard of
the rights of the slave when in a free State it
was which started in many minds the new
and disturbing thought that, sooner or later,
force would have to be met by force. How that
thought constantly grew in power is the story
of the next ten years in Boston.

CHAPTER V

WENDELL PHILLIPS: AGITATOR

ALTHOUGH "agitating" was not a tra-
dition in the Phillips family, loving and
serving Boston was. Very early the lad
who was to do so much for the cause of the
slave began to show enthusiasm for the glorious
name and goodly fame of the city which had
chosen his father for its first mayor. Born
(Nov. 29, 1811) in the stately house of colonial
pattern which still stands at the corner of
Beacon and Walnut Streets, Wendell Phillips
grew up with the historic Common for a play-
ground, and with J. Lothrop Motley and Thomas
Gold Appleton, lads destined, like himself, to
hold an honored place upon the rolls of Boston's
famous men, for play-fellows. "Wendell Phillips, Motley and I," Appleton has recorded,
"used to frolic in the gallery of the Motley
House [at the corner of Walnut and Chestnut
Streets] and I recall that their favorite pastime
used to be to strut about in any fancy costume
they could find in the corners of the old attic
and shout scraps of poetry and snatches of

dialogue at each other. It was a fine sight to watch them, for both were noble-looking fellows; and even then Wendell's voice was a very pleasant one to listen to, and his gestures as graceful as could be."

When young Phillips was eleven he began to attend the Boston Public Latin School which (till 1844) stood on School Street upon a portion of the ground now occupied by the Parker House. An impressionable lad always, he was wont to think much as he went back and forth to school of the famous dead who had made Boston what it was. " Boston boys had reason to be thankful for their birthright," he declared in referring to these memories. " The noble deeds and sacred places of the old town are the poetry of history and the keenest ripeners of character." Such, at any rate, they proved to be in his case. And the mere contemplation of Faneuil Hall and the Old South Church strengthened in him his early determination to be a great orator even as James Otis and Dr. Warren had been. " What led me first to observe him," a fellow-student has said, " was his elocution; and I soon came to look forward to declamation day with interest, mainly on his account. The pieces chosen were chiefly such as would excite patriotic feelings and an enthusiasm for freedom." Wendell Phillips, however, did not need to have such " pieces " chosen for him. Already he had studied and committed most of the famous speeches of history, and he lost no opportunity to go where he could hear such speeches pronounced by the great men of his own time and town. Like the younger Pitt he made the study of oratory the diversion of his boyhood. Hearing Harrison Gray Otis or Edward Everett talk of policies and politics in Boston was to him as fascinating an occupation as visiting the circus is to the country lad who has been performing acrobatic stunts with the old farm horse.

When Wendell was fourteen a very great thing happened to Boston; Washington's friend, Lafayette, came to be the guest of the city. In a charming address made, years afterwards, to an audience of schoolchildren in Music Hall, Phillips thus recalled this stirring occasion, and no one of us who has ever been a hero-worshipper can listen coldly to his words: " I was a little boy in a class in the Latin School at the time and we were turned out on yonder Common in a grand procession at nine o'clock in the morning. And for what? Not to hear fine music — no; but for something better than music, that thrilled more than eloquence — a sight which should live in the memory forever, the best sight which Boston ever saw — the welcome of Lafayette on his return to this country, after an absence of a score of years.

I can boast, boys and girls, more than you. I
can boast that these eyes have beheld the hero
of three revolutions, this hand has touched
the right hand that held up Hancock and
Washington. Not all this glorious celebration
can equal that glad reception of the nation's
benefactor by all that Boston could offer him —
a sight of her children. It was a long procession;
and, unlike other processions, we started punc-
tually at the hour published. They would not
let us wander about and did not wish us to
sit down. I there received my first lesson in
hero-worship. I was so tired after four hours'
waiting I could scarcely stand; but when I
saw him — that glorious old Frenchman! — I
could have stood until today."

At sixteen the boy entered **Harvard** and
formed that friendship with Edmund Quincy,
the president's son, which was to mean so
much to both as well as to the Abolition cause.
In college, however, Phillips was still what he
had been made by the circumstances of his life,
a proud leader of the aristocracy, a handsome,
well-born, well bred lad who, though distinguished above all his mates for purity of
character and earnestness of purpose, seemed
predestined to conservatism and to a prosperous
career as the defender of the rights of those who
possessed, — and who wished to retain. Such
a youth, of blue Boston blood, went naturally,

then as now, after being graduated from college into the Harvard Law School, and Phillips proved no exception to the rule. At college Charles Sumner had been one of Phillips' friends and in the Law School the two continued their intimacy counting themselves very fortunate to be students together under Judge Story, the legal luminary of that day. When Phillips had completed his course the judge foretold for him an unprecedented career, little thinking in how extraordinary a sense the prophecy was to be a true one.

A trip to Philadelphia followed Phillips' release from studies and, on his way home after its enjoyment, he made the acquaintance, in New York, of Aaron Burr. The slayer of Hamilton was exceedingly polite to the young law graduate, showing him the sights of the metropolis and otherwise making him feel at home. Thus it was that, when Burr came to Boston for a visit, soon after Phillips' return, the younger man called on him at the Tremont House and returned the courtesies. Among other places he took Burr to the Athenæum, then on Pearl Street, to see the treasures of the place. "As they walked down the hall between the alcoves," records F. B. Sanborn (in his *Recollections of Wendell Phillips*) "Phillips caught sight of a bust of Hamilton, one of the ornaments of the library, which he had forgotten was there. He tried on some pretext to draw Burr in another direction; but he, too, had seen the bust and marched straight up to it. He stood facing it for a moment, then turned and said: 'A remarkable man — a very remarkable man.'" After which he wheeled about and walked composedly away.

The old sign "Wendell Phillips: Office" which hung outside the Court Street building in which the young man began his law practice, still hangs against the bricks of a Boston wall. Now, however, its owner is the keeper of an "old curiosity shop" on Park Street, just opposite the State House, and the fact that he will not sell the sign for any sum whatever, — because of its value to him as an advertisement, — proves that Wendell Phillips' name is still one to conjure with in Boston. Seventy-five years ago, also, the sign "drew business." During his first two seasons of practice the young lawyer paid all his own expenses; and he was beginning to get cases with fame as well as fees attached to them when what some would call chance and others Providence arrested the current of his life and turned it in quite another direction. Sumner, as has been said, was Phillips' warm friend. He had an office near by at 4 Court Street and they were often together. One day, as they sat chatting in Phillips' office, a mutual friend burst in, informed

them of his engagement to a Miss Grew of
Greenfield and added that, with his fiancée
and a cousin of hers, a Miss Ann Terry Greene,
he was to make a stage journey to Greenfield
on the morrow.

" But you know," he added, " that in my condition ' two's company,' etc., and I wish you
to go, both of you, and take care of the other
lady. She will require the two of you, for she is
the cleverest, loveliest girl you ever met. But
I warn you that she is a rabid Abolitionist.
Look out or she will talk you both into that ism
before you suspect what she is at."

Goodnaturedly, the two young men promised
to be on hand next morning and to entertain
the fair Abolitionist while the fiancés enjoyed
each other. But when the next day dawned in
a furious rainstorm, Sumner faithlessly kept
his comfortable bed and Wendell Phillips had,
all to himself, during the long journey, the
attention and the conversation of Miss Ann
Terry Greene. As it happened, his mind was
hospitably inclined towards the Abolition arguments with which she plied him, for he had been
a witness to the indignities heaped upon Garrison by the " broadcloth mob " and so was
theoretically on the anti-slavery side. But
the burning words of this gentle girl, who had
herself been in the little company of women
whose meeting the mob had interrupted, awoke

an unwonted response in his soul and, finding
that she lived in Boston, he asked and received
permission to call on her. Carlos Martyn, to
whose vivid *Life* of Wendell Phillips I am
indebted for this anecdote of a romance at its
dawn, says that Phillips confessed, after he had
married the lady, " Yes, my wife made an out
and out Abolitionist of me, and she always
preceded me in the adoption of the various
causes I have advocated." But Mrs. Phillips
was never in the public gaze after their marriage, — long invalidism claimed her, poor lady!
For the rest of her days she was able to serve
only through her husband.

Phillips' maiden speech for the anti-slavery
cause was made, June 14, 1837, in Lynn. Four
months later he and Miss Greene were married,
and ere their honeymoon was over he came out
at Faneuil Hall, as has been related in the
preceding chapter, for Garrison, for freedom
and for the slave.

The cause of Woman, also, was one which
Phillips early espoused. Allusion has already
been made to the fine quality of the women
in the anti-slavery movement and to their
tenacity of purpose in pushing this reform.
It is as if they had resolved to illustrate afresh
the truth of Luther's saying, " I have often-
times noted when women espouse a cause they
are far more fervent in faith, they hold to it

more stiff and fast than men do; as we see in
the lovely Magdalen who was more hearty and
bold than Peter himself." But though the
anti-slavery societies welcomed women they
gave them no voice and no vote, when it came
to be a question of electing officers and shaping
policies. Some of the women resented this, —
just as they are resenting today the necessity
of obeying laws they have had no chance of
making. Phillips among the first saw the justice
of the women's claim. In a letter written in
1838 (to Arthur Tappan) he states unmistakably his view of this matter, " Since woman
is interested equally with man in righting the
wrongs of slavery; since among the blacks she
suffers vitally as wife and mother, as daughter
and sister, just as he does as husband and
father, as son and brother; why is she not
entitled to utter her indignation anywhere,
everywhere, and most of all in anti-slavery
committee-rooms and upon anti-slavery plat-
forms? "

A capital opportunity to take a notable stand
on this important matter now came Phillips'
way. He was accredited the representative
abroad of the anti-slavery movement and
after a year spent in travelling up and down
Europe in the hope of benefiting Mrs. Phillips'
health the two found themselves (June, 1840) in
London for the meeting of the World's Anti-

Slavery Convention. The call to this convention had been addressed to " friends of the slave of every nation and of every clime." Accordingly, when the various American societies appointed delegates they sent women as well as men, following their recent resolution on this matter. Garrison and Phillips were among the men appointed, Mrs. Phillips and Mrs. Chapman among the women. But when Wendell Phillips proceeded to present the credentials of the delegates he found that women were not expected to sit with the body. This was his opportunity and he decided to appeal the matter to the convention itself. On the morning the convention was to open his wife instructed him as he left their boarding-place:

" Wendell, don't shilly-shally."

He obeyed her. In a speech which has become historic as the first ever made by a man in advocacy of the rights of women he declared that, with the delegates from Massachusetts, this was a matter of conscience. " We think it right for women to sit by our side in America," he asserted, " and we think it right for them to do the same here. We could not go back to America to ask for any aid from the women of Massachusetts if we had deserted them when they chose to send out their own sisters as their representatives here." None the less, it was decreed that women should be welcomed to the *galleries only*, and then merely as spectators, not as participants in the proceedings of the Convention. Garrison had been detained at sea by storms and did not reach London until the Convention was nearing its end, but as soon as he learned that the credentials of the women delegates had been dishonored he declared that, he, too, would sit in the gallery. Afterwards he said, "If there is any one act of my life of which I am particularly proud it is in refusing to join such a body [the London Conference] on terms which were manifestly reproachful to my constituents and unjust to the cause of liberty." Necessarily, however, that gallery where the head of the American Abolitionists sat surrounded by the excluded women-delegates became one of the most interesting places in the hall!

To the stand which Phillips and Garrison had taken upon this mooted matter Daniel O'Connell the great Irish liberator rallied also, it is interesting to note, though at first his feeling had been against accrediting the women. His support naturally strengthened the great admiration which Phillips had for him, an admiration which was to do much, in America, for the young orator, as well as for the famous Irishman.

The summer of 1841 found the Phillipses back in Boston making preparations to begin housekeeping. Mrs. Phillips had inherited from her father a modest brick house at 26 Essex Street and here they took up their abode. The Garrisons, the Chapmans and the Lorings were all within five minutes' walk, and soon Theodore Parker, also, was to be a near neighbor. Phillips greatly enjoyed his home. To Miss Elizabeth Pease, a friend whom he and Mrs. Phillips had made in England, he wrote:

" November 25, 1841.

" I am writing in our own parlor — wish you were in it — on Thanksgiving Day. Did you ever hear of that name? 'Tis an old custom in New England, begun to thank God for a providential arrival of food from the mother-country in sixteen hundred and odd year, and perpetuated now, wherever a New Englander dwells, some time in autumn, by the Governor's appointment. All is hushed of business about me; the devout pass the morning at church; those who have wandered to other cities hurry back to worship to-day where their fathers knelt, and gather sons and grandsons, to the littlest prattler, under the old roof-tree to — shall I break the picture? — cram as much turkey and plum-pudding as possible; a sort of compromise by Puritan love of good eating for denying itself that ' wicked papistrie ' Christmas." [1]

[1] *Memorial of Ann Phillips.*

A pleasant little glimpse of the young couple's life together at " No. 26 " as they often called it to their friends is afforded by this letter of Mrs. Phillips to Miss Pease: " There is your Wendell seated in the arm-chair, lazy and easy as ever, perhaps a little fatter than when you saw him, still protesting how he was ruined by marrying. Your humble servant looks like the Genius of Famine, as she always did, one of Pharaoh's lean kine. She laughs considerably, continues in health in the same naughty way, has been pretty well for her this winter. Now what do you think her life is? Why, she strolls out a few steps occasionally, calling it a walk; the rest of the time from bed to sofa, from sofa to rocking-chair; reads, generally, the *Standard* and *Liberator*, and that is pretty much all the literature her aching head will allow her to peruse; rarely writes a letter, sees no company, makes no calls, looks forward to spring and birds, when she will be a little freer; is cross very often, pleasant at other times, loves her dear L— and thinks a great deal of her; and now you have Ann Phillips.

" Now I'll take up another strain. This winter has been marked to us by our keeping house the first time. I call it housekeeping; but, alas! we have not the pleasure of entertaining angels, awares or unawares. We have a small house, but large enough for us, only a

THE HOME OF WENDELL PHILLIPS, 26 ESSEX STREET.
Mr. Phillips is shown just entering the door.

WENDELL PHILLIPS' STUDY.
From a photograph in the possession of Francis Jackson Garrison.

RALPH WALDO EMERSON.

After the Hawes Portrait.

Page 169.

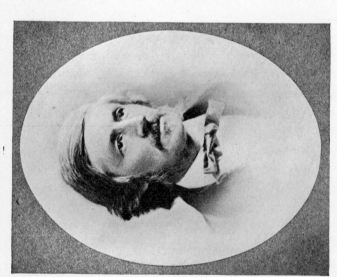

FRANK SANBORN.

From an early photograph.

Page 154.

few rooms furnished — just enough to try to make me more comfortable than at board. But then I am not well enough even to have friends to tea, so that all that I strive to do is to keep the house neat and to keep myself about. I have attended no meetings since I helped to fill ' the negro pew.' What anti-slavery news I get, I get second-hand. I should not get along at all, so great is my darkness, were it not for Wendell to tell me that the world is still going on. . . . We are very happy, and only have to regret my health being so poor and our own sinfulness. Dear Wendell speaks whenever he can leave me, and for his sake I sometimes wish I were myself again; but I dare say it is all right as it is." [1]

The *Standard*, to which allusion has here been made, was the organ of that faction of the Abolitionists which had withdrawn from the Garrisonian camp. Phillips remained the at-torney-general of the Boston forces whose organ was *The Liberator*, and in that capacity he was very glad soon to be the spokesman at Faneuil Hall of the seventy thousand Irishmen who, with Daniel O'Connell and Father Mathew at their head, had sent over to their fellow countrymen here an urgent appeal to identify themselves with the Abolitionists. Up to this time the Irish in America had, almost without

[1] *Memorial of Ann Phillips.*

exception, been on the side of slavery. The
reason for this appears to have been that they
feared the competition which would be offered
in the labor market by the negro if free. Phillips,
however, by the power of his matchless eloquence, as he held that imposing petition in his
hand, won to the side of freedom for the black
man this huge Irish audience all of whom knew,
themselves, only too well, the meaning of
oppression. " Ireland," he said, " is the land
of agitation and agitators. We may well learn
a lesson from her in the battle for human rights.
. . . I trust in that love of liberty which every
Irishman brings to the country of his adoption,
to make him true to her cause at the ballot-box,
and throw no vote without asking if the hand
to which he is about to trust political power
will use it for the slave. When an American
was introduced to O'Connell in the lobby of
the House of Commons, he asked, without
putting out his hand, ' Are you from the South? '
' Yes, sir.' ' A slaveholder, I presume? ' ' Yes,
sir.' ' Then,' said the great liberator, ' I have
no hand for you! ' and walked away. Shall his
countrymen trust that hand with political
power which O'Connell deemed it pollution to
touch? "

Soon after this Phillips took a step for which
he was greatly criticized: he personally seceded
from the Union because, as he held, its Con-

stitution was a pro-slavery one! The occasion
for this step was the famous ruling of Judge
Shaw in the case of a mulatto named Latimer,
who, in October, 1842, came to Boston from
Norfolk, Virginia, and was thrown into jail
on a charge of theft. It soon became clear that
all that the man had stolen was — himself, and
friends rallied to his side and demanded a trial
by jury. Judge Shaw, however, denied this
privilege on the ground that Latimer was a
fugitive slave. "The Constitution of the
United States," he declared, "authorizes the
owner of such an one to arrest him in any State
to which he may have fled." At a Sunday
night meeting in Faneuil Hall, called together by
the Abolitionists to denounce this decision, Phillips, referring to Judge Shaw's ruling exclaimed,
"We presume to believe the Bible out-weighs
the statute-book. When I look on those
crowded thousands and see them trample on their
consciences and on the rights of their fellow-
men at the bidding of a piece of parchment, I
say, my curse be on the Constitution of these
United States!" The case of Latimer had made
him see clearly that his real quarrel, in all this
advocacy of the black, was with the old pro-
slavery Constitution, a document which demanded that a Civil War must be fought before
it could be effectually amended. From this
time on Phillips neither practised in the courts

— because, as an attorney he would have had to take an oath to support the Constitution — or used his right of ballot, since to vote would have been to participate actively in governmental affairs.

As soon as Phillips' eyes had been opened to the fact that the Constitution was a pro-slavery document he " came out." Nor was he long to be alone in the position he had taken. There was soon a band of come-outers, with Garrison and Quincy to officer them. The question thus raised became the topic of debate at every anti-slavery meeting, and in 1843 the Massachusetts Society adopted " come-outer " resolutions, their example in this matter being followed, the next year, by the societies in New England and throughout the free States generally. " No Union with Slave-holders " was now their motto. To be sure, there remained other earnest Abolitionists who did not see the matter thus, and they it was who formed the Liberty Party in the hope of attaining reform through the ballot — just as the Socialist Party now hopes to do. Thus it came about that the " moral suasionists and the political actionists " lined up in opposition each to the other.

Phillips certainly made out a wonderful case for his side in his argument *The Constitution a Pro-Slavery Compact*, which he wrote and published in 1845. And his brochure, published

in the same year, " Can Abolitionists Vote
or Take Office under the United States Constitution? " is full of wit and telling stories.
There is no better way of making plain his
position as a " come-outer " than to quote a
few paragraphs from this pamphlet. " My
object," he says, " in becoming a disunionist
is to free the slave, and meantime to live a
consistent life. I want men to understand me.
And I submit that the body of the Roman
people understood better and felt more earnestly the struggle between the people and the
princes, when the little band of democrats
left the city and encamped on Mons Sacer,
outside, than while they remained mixed up
and voting with their masters. . . . Because
we refuse to aid a wrongdoer in his sin we by
no means proclaim that we think our whole
character better than his. It is neither phari-
saical to have opinions nor presumptuous to
guide our lives by them. He would be a strange
preacher who should set out to reform his
circle by joining in all their sins. This reminds
me of the tipsy Duke of Norfolk, who seeing
a drunken friend in the gutter hiccoughed:
' My dear fellow, I can't help you out, but
I'll do better — I'll lie down by your side! ' "

Of course, Phillips was branded as a crank
and a zealot by reason of the position he had
taken, and he was told that he was meanwhile

losing a golden opportunity to help amend the
Constitution by voting right, but to this he
replied that he could not, on that account, swear
to support it " as it is. What it may become
we know not. We speak of it as it is and
repudiate it as it is. We will not brand it
as Pro-Slavery after it has ceased to be so.
This objection to our position reminds me of
Miss Martineau's story of the little boy who
hurt himself and sat crying on the sidewalk.
' Don't cry,' said a friend, ' it won't hurt you
to-morrow.' ' Well then,' whimpered the child,
' I won't cry to-morrow! ' "

A man who would refuse to vote because
the Constitution under which he must needs
exercise the suffrage defended an institution
he abhorred would, not unnaturally, proceed
to cut himself off, also, from an organized
church whose officers were, most of them,
advocates of slavery. Phillips had had a
very religious mother and he was himself
deeply religious. To a personal friend who
asked him, not long before his death, whether
he had ever consecrated himself to God he
replied, " Yes, when I was a boy fourteen years
of age, in the old church at the North End, I
heard Lyman Beecher preach on the theme,
' You belong to God,' and I went home, after
that service, threw myself on the floor of my
room, with locked doors, and prayed, ' Oh God,

I belong to Thee; take what is Thine own. I ask this, that whenever a thing be wrong it may have no power of temptation over me; whenever a thing be right it may take no courage to do it.' From that day to this," added Phillips, " it has been so. Whenever I have known a thing to be wrong it has held no temptation. Whenever I have known a thing to be right it has taken no courage to do it."[1] A man who could honestly say this when arrived at old age would not lightly have broken away from the institution through which so much of moral power had come to him. Phillips continued to hold fast to his ancestral faith, but he, none the less, denounced the Church as it existed precisely in the spirit in which many good men today are denouncing it. Yet at many a meeting of the Radical Club he testified in no uncertain fashion to his own strictly orthodox beliefs. He was not a member of this club, which was wont to meet at the Chestnut Street home of Rev. John T. Sargent and his wife, but he was a frequent guest there, and he always took the conservative ground when religious radicalism was being advanced. On one occasion, when Emerson had read an essay on religion in which he claimed that Christianity was only one faith more, a modifica-

[1] Evidence of Rev. O. P. Gifford, D. D. Reported in the *Golden Rule* August 15, 1889.

tion of Judaism or Buddhism, Phillips, in a
masterly rejoinder, maintained that Christianity had in it something essentially different
from the religious experience of other races.
On another occasion, at the same place, he
commented thus on the paper which Rev. W.
H. Channing had just read on " the Christian
Name: " " Jesus is the divine type who has
given His peculiar form to the modern world.
. . . Europe shows a type of human character
not paralleled anywhere else. The intellect
of Greece centred around power and beauty;
that of Rome around legal justice. The civilization of modern Europe was inspired by a
great moral purpose. Imperfect as it was and
limited in many ways, the religious element
there had steadily carried those nations forward. The battle for human rights was finally
fought on a Christian plane. . . . *The power
that urged the world forward came from Christianity.*" And one day, when John Weiss spoke
on " Heart in Religion," contending that Jesus
was effeminate, Phillips said, " You speculate
as to whether Jesus was a masculine character.
Look at the men who have learned of Him
most closely, — at Paul and Luther and Wesley.
Were they effeminate? Yet the disciple is
but a faint reflection of his Master. The
character from which came the force which has
been doing battle ever since with wrong and

falsehood and error was nothing less than
masculine; but sentiment is the toughest thing
in the world, — nothing else is iron." A man
so honoring Christ could not be anti-Christian
though he was " anti-Church." " He distinguished," says his biographer, Carlos Martyn,
(writing in 1890) " between Christianity and
Churchianity; the distinction may be needed
again sometime." How interestingly history
repeats itself in the case of reformers! I am
constantly hearing this distinction made today
by men who think the Church of Christ is not
living up to the Truth Christ came to proclaim.

Because Wendell Phillips was no longer a
practicing lawyer, with a lawyer's natural
means of self-expression and self-assertion; because, too, he had cut away from church
organization and the help that might have
afforded him, he now proceeded to construct
for himself a platform, — he became, in a word,
that new thing in American life, a professional
agitator. It was his firm belief that in every
age there are wrongs which must be righted,
and he maintained that neither the press, nor
political parties, nor the pulpit could do so
much towards getting them righted as a free
citizen who should have the will and the skill
to present to the attention of the people at
large the particular question under debate.
He was by no means deceived as to the diffi-

culties which would be encountered in winning
adherents to an unpopular cause. For he saw —
none more clearly — that, " in a country like
ours, of absolute democratic equality . . . there
is no refuge from the tyranny of public opinion.
The result is that, if you take the old Greek
lantern and go about to seek among a hundred,
you will find not one single American who
really has not, or who does not fancy at least
that he has, something to gain or lose in his
ambition, his social life or his business from the
good opinion and the votes of those around him.
And the consequence is that, instead of being
a mass of individuals, each one fearlessly
blurting out his own convictions, as a nation,
compared with other nations, we are a mass of
cowards." [1]

Phillips, however, was just enough not to
blame the pulpit or the press unduly for being
bound by the average sentiment. " As the
minister's settlement and salary," he said,
" depend upon the unity and good will of the
people he preaches to, he cannot fairly be
expected, save in exceptional and special cases,
to antagonize his flock. If all clergymen were
like Paul or Luther or Wesley they might give,
not take orders. But as the average clergyman
is an average man he will be bound by average

[1] Oration delivered at the O'Connell Celebration in Boston,
August 6, 1870.

conditions." [1] Similarly, he held it to be unreasonable to expect of the press a loftier tone than that taken by the constituency who support it. " The moment therefore," he concluded, " that a large issue, twenty years ahead of its age, presents itself to the consideration of an empire or of a republic, just in proportion to the freedom of its institutions is the necessity of a platform outside of the press, of politics and of the Church, whereon stand men with no candidate to elect, with no plan to carry, with no reputation to stake, with no object but the truth, no purpose but to tear the question open and let the light through it."

Especially in a republic is agitation necessary, he insisted, in his lecture on Public Opinion. " Only by unintermitted agitation can a people be kept sufficiently awake to principle not to let liberty be smothered in material prosperity." Surely we of today know the truth of that great saying, first set forth at the Melodeon, in Boston, January 28, 1852. " Republics," he then went on, " exist only on the tenure of being constantly agitated. . . . Never, to our latest posterity, can we afford to do without prophets like Garrison, to stir up the monotony of wealth and reawake the people to the great ideas that are constantly fading out of their

[1] Extract from a lecture on Agitation.

minds — to trouble the waters that there may
be health in their flow." One other axiom held
by Wendell Phillips, agitator, was that he and
others like him should, on the platform, tell " the
truth, the whole truth and nothing but the
truth." Under this rule he used a plainness
of speech which often considerably shocked a
generation inured to euphemism. Words " with
which we have no concern," to paraphrase
Barrie's Tommy, abounded in his lectures.
But, like Whitman, he was coarse, not for
coarseness' sake but because he wished to goad
his hearers to attention. As when he declared
the South to be " one great brothel," or again,
when, speaking of the defection of Webster,
he said, " It is not often that Providence per-
mits the eyes of twenty millions of thinking
people to behold the fall of another Lucifer,
from the very battlements of Heaven, down into
that ' lower deep of the lowest deep ' of hell."

Of course, under the present system, a man
who should speak his mind thus freely would
need to have a modest inheritance upon which
to live. Phillips, happily, was so circumstanced
that, even before he began to earn large fees
from his lectures, he was independent in matters
of money. And he had a very happy home life
in spite of the invalidism of his beloved wife.
Dr. Samuel A. Green, ex-Mayor of Boston,
who was a near neighbor of Phillips when the

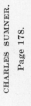

CHARLES SUMNER.

Page 178.

DR. SAMUEL A. GREEN.

From the painting by Frederic Vinton in the
possession of the Groton Library.

Page 174.

WASHINGTON STREET, SOUTH OF MILK STREET IN 1858.

Page 212.

orator lived on Essex Street, tells me that, though he was often at the Phillips home, he never saw Mrs. Phillips. Yet he constantly felt her presence, for her husband quoted her wit and wisdom to all his friends and so passed on to them something of the inspiration he himself drew from her brave and buoyant spirit. Debarred from attendance at concerts, of which she was very fond, Mrs. Phillips derived much pleasure in listening to the strains of the hand-organs which played often under her window, and it is said that her last word to Mr. Phillips, when he was going out, would always be, " Wendell, don't forget the organ money." The meals in their little home were always served in the invalid's room, he on this side and she on that of a tiny table, and at such times the married lovers were wont to converse in the language of Molière. As the husband put it to a friend, " We eat in French."

Early in 1857 a new neighbor came to take up his abode near the Phillips home, Theodore Parker, whose house in Essex Place was henceforth directly in the rear of " 26 Essex Street." Though Phillips and Parker differed greatly in their theology they were united in love of books and in zeal for human freedom. Their intimacy became a source of great joy and stimulus to both. Both needed it, too, for Abolitionists were bitterly hated by those who

would not or could not understand them, and
Phillips and Parker often carried their lives
in their hands as they walked down Essex
Street to their homes after a stormy meeting.
Frederick Douglass, in a letter to Mary Livermore, tells of one occasion in particular when
it was proposed to shed the blood of Phillips
to appease the slave god of the South, and when
Phillips and Maria Weston Chapman literally
hazarded their lives by walking through the
dense excited mass of people from Cambridge
Street through Belknap [Joy] Street " to the
little Baptist Church once presided over by
Father Snowdon." It took great courage in
those times even to express sympathy with
Parker or Phillips! What has been characterized
as " one of the bravest acts of Henry Ward
Beecher's life " was when, in 1850, after the
Abolitionists had been mobbed in New York,
that gifted preacher (then not an Abolitionist
himself) opened Plymouth Church to Phillips
and appeared with him on the platform to
signify his appreciation of free speech. Phillips
was always perfectly serene on these dangerous
occasions. " I was amazed," Beecher wrote
afterward, " at the unagitated Agitator, — so
calm, so fearless, so incisive, — every word a
bullet. I never heard a more effective speech
than Mr. Phillips' that night. He seemed inspired and played with his audience (turbulent,

of course) as Gulliver might with the Lilliputians. He had the dignity of Pitt, the vigor of Fox, the wit of Sheridan, the satire of Junius, — and a grace and music all his own."

To Phillips, as to all other right-minded New Englanders, Webster's advocacy of the Fugitive Slave Law was a severe trial of faith in human nature, — as well as a keen disappointment. Webster had previously done yeoman service on the side of freedom. Moreover, it would seem to have been true, as Henry Cabot Lodge says, that " no man in all history ever came into the world so equipped physically to serve a noble cause by speech." The impression Webster commonly produced was like that made upon the English navvy who pointed at Webster in the streets of Liverpool and said, " There goes a king." Sydney Smith exclaimed when he saw him, " Good heavens, he is a small cathedral by himself." And Carlyle, who did not too much love America, wrote to Emerson, " Not many days ago I saw at breakfast the notablest of all your notabilities, Daniel Webster. . . . As a logic fencer or parliamentary Hercules, one would incline to back him at first sight against all the extant world. The tanned complexion; that amorphous crag-like face; the dull black eyes under the precipice of brows, like dull anthracite furnaces needing only to be *blown;* the mastiff mouth accurately closed;

I have not traced so much *silent Berserker rage*
that I remember of in any man. " Yet when all
eyes were fixed upon Webster and he had the
chance of his life for power and prophecy he
faced South instead of North — and betrayed
the constituents who trusted him. Whether
the dominant desire of his seventh of March
speech was to arrest the whole anti-slavery
movement and in that way put an end to the
dangers which threatened the Union, or whether
his only thought, as his harshest critics aver,
was so to curry favor with the South that he
would gain the Presidency he coveted, the
result was the same: for him moral and political
suicide; for those who had believed in him
bitter disappointment and disillusion.

`Happily there was raised up, just then, to
furl the flag of freedom which Webster had
allowed to be trampled in the dust, Charles
Sumner, who had been Phillips' friend in college
and who had latterly been growing greatly in
power and in the confidence of the public.
Sumner was Bostonian to the core. The family
home, where he was born, was on the corner
of Revere and Irving Streets and in the upper
part of the house his aunt kept a private school
at which he received his first instruction.
At the university Sumner had had a brilliant
career and after he began the practice of law
in Boston he was able to build up a lucrative

practice much more quickly than is usually the
case with young lawyers.   But as yet he had
felt no overwhelming interest in public affairs.
Instead, it was literature and literary men which
fascinated him, and when (in 1837) he went on
a European tour it was Carlyle, Wordsworth,
Lady Blessington and Mrs. Jameson in whose
society he delighted, not in that of George
Thompson or his co-workers.   Even when he
returned to Boston (in the spring of 1840) and
was welcomed back into a circle which included
Judge Story, Washington Allston, Jeremiah
Mason, Dr. Channing, Rufus Choate, Prescott,
Bancroft, Longfellow, Dr. Howe and Felton
(some of whom were ardent Abolitionists) his
interest in the anti-slavery cause was only a
mild one.   Always, however, he was distinguished by a fine sense of duty and by an inclination to unselfish service.   To Horace Mann he
gave substantial aid in his efforts to improve
educational methods in Massachusetts, and Dr.
Howe he helped in such ways as he could in his
work for the blind.   Howe, who was one of his
warmest friends, wrote him, about this time,
" I know not where you may be or what you
may be about; but I know what you are *not*
about; you are not seeking your own pleasure
or striving to advance your own interests; you
are, I warrant me, on some errand of kindness
— some work for a friend or for the public."

So the soil was ready. Should Sumner once become aroused to the overwhelming importance of the anti-slavery cause none could be more depended on than he to give it enthusiastic support. His début as a public speaker came in 1845 when he was invited to deliver the Fourth of July oration in Boston. The subject he chose was — Peace. It was a significant choice, not so much because Peace was an unusual topic for a Fourth of July oration (though it was that), as because of the way in which the speaker proceeded to marshal his arguments against the horrors of war, its sinful wastefulness, its absurdity and its utter failure, in most cases, to accomplish the object for which it had been waged. It was a speech fifty years ahead of its time, and it demonstrated conclusively that Charles Sumner possessed high courage as well as marked eloquence and rare scholarship. Though he was still less than thirty-five, Sumner was, from that moment, a recognized leader of men!

His next noteworthy speech was a Phi Beta Kappa oration in the summer of 1846, and in this he " took advantage of the occasion to express himself freely, especially on the two great questions of slavery and war." About the former topic he had been thinking deeply since the Fourth of July of a year ago, and of the result Emerson wrote in his journal: "Sumner's oration was marked with a certain magnificence which I do not well know how to parallel;" and Everett said, "It was an amazingly splendid affair. I never heard it surpassed; I don't know that I ever heard it equalled." The following month Sumner broke into politics, being sent as a delegate to the Whig State convention and voicing very effectively there the sentiments of the anti-slavery faction in that party. When Webster, however, became, in his famous speech of March 7, 1850, the apologist of slavery, the swan-song of the Whig party was sung, in Massachusetts. And when Charles Sumner was elected to replace Webster in the Senate (the great Daniel having been called into President Fillmore's Cabinet) it was as the choice of the Free Soil party, the child and successor of the old Liberty party, that he entered upon his duties. This "party of freedom," as Sumner termed it, was founded on the principle that new States admitted to the Union should be free States. Gloriously did Charles Sumner uphold this principle in Washington!

In Massachusetts, meanwhile, Wendell Philips, agitator, embraced a new cause. In London, it will be recalled, Phillips, at a crucial moment in the anti-slavery movement, championed the cause of Woman. Naturally, therefore, he was glad, with Mrs. Phillips, to sign the call for the Women's Rights Convention which met at Worcester, Massachusetts, October 23 and 24, 1850. The year is important because in Old England, as in New England, the women's cause — to which Mary A. Livermore and Lucy Stone here gave their lives — dates from this Worcester gathering; the *Westminster Review*, apropos of the convention, gave space to an exhaustive article on the subject written by Mrs. John Stuart Mill. The attendance at Worcester was large, women naturally being in the majority; but Phillips, Garrison and Douglass were there, also, to represent the anti-slavery interest, and Sargent and Channing found their way to the meetings in behalf of the liberal pulpit. The illiberal pulpit commented upon the gathering in characteristically unpleasant fashion. A certain Universalist clergyman — whose name Carlos Martyn says it would be cruel to give but which I should give just the same if I knew it — thus announced a meeting at which Lucy Stone was to speak: " Tonight, at the Town Hall, a hen will attempt to crow." One very interesting thing about this convention was that Wendell Phillips there made a prophecy, for which he was rebuked by Lucretia Mott, but of which time has, none the less, proved the truth: i. e., that " the cause would meet more immediate and palpable and insulting opposition from women than from men." Only now, after sixty years, are women in any appreciable numbers espousing the principles for which that convention first stood, principles set forth for all time by Phillips a year later in that matchless speech of which George William Curtis has said: " . . . All the pleas for applying the American principle of representation to the wives and mothers of American citizens echo the eloquence of Wendell Phillips at Worcester." This address is easily accessible in the collected speeches of Phillips. But I would advise all men who prefer to " protect " women and keep them in " their place, the home," (forgetting that more than six million women in the United States are already earning their living outside the home) I would advise such men and women, I say, not to read the speech. It will make them feel so silly!

When Phillips met Theodore Parker, after returning from the Women's Rights Convention, the clergyman said to him:

" Wendell, why do you make a fool of yourself? "

" Theodore," was the reply, " this is the greatest question of the ages; you ought to understand it."

Inside of a year Parker had not only espoused the cause but had preached four sermons on it.

It was in the year 1851, which we have now reached in our story of Phillips' life, that Kossuth came to America, seeking the intervention of the United States in the cause of Hungary against Austria. Kossuth is remembered by a few " old-timers " as a " short thick-set man with brown hair, a full brown beard and large blue eyes." He was a graceful and impressive speaker, aflame with patriotic devotion to his oppressed country. But, unhappily for his cause in Boston, he ignored the fact that in this country also, a large question concerning human freedom was being debated. He accepted the hospitality of slave-holders while in the South and he carefully refrained from raising his voice on what, to the Abolitionists, was the most important issue then connected with the word, freedom. Wendell Phillips, accordingly, improved the opportunity offered by the annual anti-slavery Bazaar in Boston to make (on December 27, 1851) a perfectly tremendous speech on Kossuth's anomalous position. He showed that the patriot had been informed of the condition of the American struggle before he left the old world, so that he could not plead ignorance as his excuse, and he contrasted — greatly to Kossuth's disadvantage — his attitude in regard to the institution of slavery with that of Lafayette and O'Connell. Not that Phillips felt it necessary that Kossuth, who had come to raise money for Hungary, should take a pronounced anti-slavery stand; but he did feel that this friend of freedom might at least have withheld sweeping praise of American institutions, praise so fulsome and so enthusiastic as to convince the slave-holders that their visitor distinctly approved of them and of their ways. The only report of the speech is in the *Liberator* (vol. XXII, p. 3), but it is well worth searching out there, for Phillips never rose to greater heights than when he pointed out to Bostonians the paradox of Kossuth's position in America and lashed with sarcasm this eminent patriot who was endorsing the " great American lie, that to save or benefit one class a man may righteously sacrifice the rights of another." Webster, who since his speech in behalf of the Fugitive Slave Law had systematically adhered to the position then taken, fittingly did the honors for Boston at the dinner given here to Kossuth.

A year later Webster was no more and Boston honored *him* in the last rites that may be paid to any man. Though the use of Faneuil Hall for a reception had been refused the great Daniel by the Boston board of aldermen only a year before, his faults were now forgotten in genuine grief at the passing on ~~July~~ 9, 1852, *October* of a mighty intellect. The burial was at Marshfield, Webster's summer home, and though the nearest railway station then was at Kingston, eight miles distant, and transportation was not easy, twenty thousand people went out for the services. Crowded memorial services were subsequently held in Faneuil Hall and in the Hollis Street Church, and beautiful and appropriate mourning was displayed for days throughout the city. From Faneuil Hall was hung a banner inscribed, " Like Daniel of Old: His Trust Was In God. Upon Whom Shall His Mantle Fall? " And from Bunker Hill where he had made two of the greatest speeches in the English language floated the legend, " Bunker Hill Mourns the Departed Patriot."

One other important thing happened in Boston that year of our Lord 1852. J. P. Jewett, a young and hitherto unknown publisher, brought out in book form Harriet Beecher Stowe's *Uncle Tom's Cabin*. Mrs. Stowe had known Boston well as a girl, for her father had been a prominent pastor here. But during her maturity the city seems to have made its impression upon her chiefly through the *Liberator*. Not only had she diligently read this and other anti-slavery papers; she had seen slavery at work in Kentucky. For nearly twenty years before the publication of "Uncle Tom " she had been brooding over the wrongs of the slaves. When comparative leisure came to her the story, as she has said, " wrote itself."

(At the time it found its way to paper she was living in what was then known as the Titcomb house in Brunswick, Maine, where her husband, Professor Stowe, had lately been called as the incumbent of the chair of natural and revealed religion at Bowdoin College.)

No woman with Mrs. Stowe's heritage and character could have had intimate knowledge of the horrors of slavery without being deeply moved by them. Yet, until she came back to New England, by way of Boston, she had not felt impelled to the duty she afterwards undertook. On her journey to Maine she happened to stop at the Boston home of her brother, Dr. Edward Beecher. Daniel Webster's Seventh of March speech was still ringing in the ears of the people and all good men were aflame with the infamy of the Fugitive Slave Act which he had been defending. The heart-rending scenes which occurred in connection with slave-renditions under this Act were rehearsed and commented on in all Abolition homes and terrible stories told of men frozen while trying to escape in the dead of winter through rivers and pathless forests to Canada. After Mrs. Stowe reached Brunswick her Boston sister-in-law wrote her, " Hattie, if I could use a pen as you can I would write something to make this whole nation feel what an accursed thing slavery is." While Mrs. Stowe was pondering this saying she came upon an authenticated account, in an anti-slavery magazine, of the escape of a woman with her child on the ice across the Ohio River from Kentucky. This suggested a plot which soon crystallized in *Uncle Tom's Cabin*. The *National Era*, published in Washington, was glad to bring the story out in numbers and for this Mrs. Stowe received three hundred dollars. But it remained for J. P. Jewett, of Boston, to see the great possibilities of the story when it should be brought out in book form. None the less he hesitated over the step, for the work was longer than he would have wished. When, however, the competent literary critic to whom he had submitted it for an opinion reported, "The story has life in it; it will sell," he hesitated no more. Finding that Professor Stowe could not share equally with him the expense and the profits of bringing out the work Mr. Jewett offered the usual ten per cent. royalty, which was accepted.

The success of the book was immediate. Three thousand copies were sold the first day and within a few days ten thousand copies had gone. Then a second edition went to press, and thereafter eight presses, running night and day, were barely able to keep pace with the demand. Within a year three hundred thousand copies were sold and newspapers and pulpits were alternately defending and attacking the book.

Mrs. Stowe was now comparatively rich as well as famous. When her husband, four months after the book's publication, was asked by Mr. Jewett how much he expected to receive as royalty, he replied whimsically that he hadn't the slightest idea but hoped it would be enough to buy Mrs. Stowe a new silk dress. The publisher handed him a check for ten thousand dollars. Yet because the author had neglected to secure the dramatic rights of her work she derived no profits from the great success the story had as a play. It was first presented on the stage in August, 1852, — and today it is being played by scores of travelling companies in the United States. From its enormous success, both as a book and as a play, the story earned vast sums in Europe also. But from

these Mrs. Stowe made no money; and by the
laws of her own country even her ten per
cent. on the American sales of the book ceased
before her death.

But Harriet Beecher Stowe had written
Uncle Tom's Cabin to advance a cause and
not to accumulate wealth. How wonderfully
it did this every American school boy knows.
Charles Dudley Warner (in the *Atlantic Monthly*
of September, 1896) attributes to the vigorous
and noble appeal which Mrs. Stowe addressed
to the women of England, — while the Civil
War was going on, — a great measure of the
sympathy that England felt for the North
during that " irrepressible conflict." And this
appeal was directly due to a remarkable document sent to the women of America by the
women of England just after " Uncle Tom "
was brought out in the mother country. There
had then (in 1853) been presented to Mrs.
Stowe as a result of a meeting at Stafford House
a huge petition against slavery together with
an address composed by Lord Shaftesbury.
This petition had previously been put into the
hands of canvassers in England and on the
continent as far as Jerusalem, with the result
that signatures of 562,848 women were obtained " with their occupations and residences
from the nobility on the steps of the throne
down to the maids in the kitchen." All who

GOVERNOR JOHN A. ANDREW.

From the painting by William Morris Hunt, in the possession of the Massachusetts Historical Society.

Page 232.

COLONEL ROBERT GOULD SHAW.

From a photograph taken in 1862 and in the possession of Mrs. George William Curtis.

Page 232.

LUCY STONE.
Page 182.

HARRIET BEECHER STOWE.

From the drawing by George Rich-
mond, London, 1853, in the pos-

MARY A. LIVERMORE.
Page 182.

signed the petition acknowledged England's complicity in the sin of slavery but prayed for aid in removing from the country " our common crimes and common dishonor."

Personally, Mrs. Stowe was the most interesting member of a highly interesting family. She was attractive to look at, too, though the portraits of her which are usually given would not in the least lead one so to believe. Mrs. Fields, who has written her life, tells us that once, after she had accompanied Mrs. Stowe to a well-known house in Boston, the hostess came to her exclaiming, " Why did you not tell me that Mrs. Stowe was beautiful? " Mrs. Stowe herself relates that during her triumphant tour of England, after the publication of *Uncle Tom's Cabin*, the general topic of remark on meeting her seemed to be that she was " not so badlooking " as they were afraid she was.

Lincoln characterized Harriet Beecher Stowe as " the little woman who made this great war." Before the publication of her book, slavery, though *the* question *of* questions for a devoted body of reformers, was an academic question to people generally. After the book came out it became a matter of wide popular interest. This interest the anti-slavery societies carefully fanned. Meeting after meeting was arranged with stirring addresses and special anti-slavery hymns or songs in which all could join. Moreover, Bostonians, who had heretofore been comparatively conservative, began to concern themselves that territories about to be admitted to the Union should be of the " Free State " variety. By the autumn of 1854 Amos A. Lawrence and his associates began to send men out to Kansas in order to make that a free State, and these parties would go swinging across the intervening territory singing the words of Whittier:

> " We cross the prairie as of old
>   The Pilgrims crossed the sea,
>   To make the West, as they the East,
>   The homestead of the free."

Now it happened that, ten years earlier, a certain John Brown, who had meanwhile grown more and more interested in the suppression of slavery, had been the buying agent in Ohio of the wool firm in which Amos Lawrence of Boston was a member. We are beginning, are we not, to smell powder? It seems, at any rate, to be a fact that Amos Lawrence and his co-workers in the Massachusetts Emigrant Aid Company were soon giving not only moral support to the men who were going out to help make Kansas a free State; they were also, as Frank Sanborn makes very clear (in his *Life and Letters of John Brown*), helping them, as early as 1855, by supplying them with Sharpe's rifles!

John Brown's first visit to Boston, for the purpose of advancing his plans for Kansas (to which place he had gone, two years earlier, from his home in North Elba, New York), occurred just after Christmas, 1856. He came at the invitation of George Luther Stearns, a wealthy Boston manufacturer whose home was in Medford and who had married the niece of Lydia Maria Child. The next Sunday, the first in January, 1857, Brown went to the Boston Music Hall to hear Theodore Parker preach. He seems indeed to have met a number of the Abolitionists of the city during his stay here and to have stimulated very effectively the determination which existed to make Kansas a free State. The crisis called for action. For in spite of yeoman service rendered by Sumner in the Senate the Missouri Compromise had been repealed and the Kansas-Nebraska Bill passed. This Bill provided that the question of slavery in a State should be determined by those who settled there. The need of the moment was that Kansas should be settled by colonists who would be anti-slavery men, men who should send forth an "everlasting No" to every scheme to advance the Southern interest.

Boston became the centre of operation for the ensuing organization. Dr. Samuel Gridley Howe, who had fought for Greek independence and participated also in the revolutionary strug-

gles of Poland and France, took an especially
deep interest in making Kansas a Free State,
and at his office on Bromfield Street were to be
met those men and women who were similarly
concerned. For while the men were raising
funds to furnish the Kansas colonists with
Sharpe's rifles and ammunition the women were
getting together clothing and money for food
to be forwarded by a committee of which Mrs.
Samuel Cabot, Jr., was the efficient and admirable head.

Sumner imperilled his life, as the event
proved, for a free Kansas. At first the pro-
slavery element had been successful out there —
thanks to neighboring Missourians who de-
liberately rode across the line to vote fraudu-
lently, to shoot and to rob. The Legislature
which these men put in promptly took steps
to make Kansas a slave Territory and passed
a severe code of laws for the protection of
slavery. Northern men proceeded to ignore
this government as illegitimate, by meeting in
convention at Topeka, forming a State Constitution and in turn seeking admittance to
the Union. Thus there were two authorities
in Kansas, one pro-slavery, the other anti-
slavery, and for about two years the history of
the settlement was one of disgraceful violence.
From November first, 1855, until that December
when John Brown came to Boston and heard

Theodore Parker preach it was estimated that about two hundred persons had been killed in the Territory, and property worth not less than two million dollars destroyed.

For Bostonians and for the future, however, the most far-reaching issue raised by the Kansas question came in the savage attack made on Charles Sumner, in May, 1856, following what Whittier termed the " grand and terrible philippic " delivered by that senator against the terrible wrong to freedom which had been committed in the Territory by the slave-power. " The Crime Against Kansas " Sumner called his speech, and he attacked with special severity Senator Butler of South Carolina. Preston S. Brooks, a representative from that State and a kinsman of Butler, determined to take revenge, and on May 22, while Sumner sat at his desk engaged in writing letters, crept up upon him and struck him again and again over the head with a heavy walking stick. So seriously was Sumner injured by this dastardly attack that he did not recover for a number of years; but the most important result of it all was the indignation which was everywhere fomented in the North against the South by a sympathy for Brooks which was shown by returning him again to Washington. Nothing that had occurred before the outbreak of the war did more to estrange the two sections than this. Sumner magnanimously charged the whole thing up where it belonged — to the slaveholders of the South. Years afterward, when walking with George William Curtis in the Congressional Cemetery, his attention was called to the cenotaph of Brooks, which he had not seen. " How do you feel about Brooks? " Curtis asked him. " Only as to a brick that should fall upon my head from a chimney," came the reply. " He was the unconscious agent of a malign power."

That power was soon to array itself definitively against the North. And it was through Kansas, fittingly enough, that the long-delayed struggle was precipitated. For John Brown, as has been said, was the soul of the organization through which it was ere long recognized that slaves could not be held in Kansas. And from Brown's success in this connection it was that he mustered resolution for that daring raid upon Harper's Ferry which cost him his life and persuaded even Wendell Phillips, — who had spent years of patient effort in the endeavor to avoid a physical conflict between the North and the South, — that the question could be settled for all time in one way only and that way — *war*.

CHAPTER VI

THEODORE PARKER AND HIS MUSIC HALL PULPIT

WE have already seen that during John Brown's momentous first visit to Boston he went to Music Hall to hear Theodore Parker preach. Who else was hearing Parker? And how did it happen that this greatest of Boston Radicals was to be enjoyed on Sundays, only in a hall which had been built for concert purposes?

The answer to these two questions should contain matter of deep interest to us who are now following causes and currents in nineteenth century Boston. For Theodore Parker is one of Boston's most distinguished sons, though he was born not in Boston but near by in Lexington, and though Boston early repudiated him. His grandfather, John Parker, was that captain of minute men who commanded his band of followers, "Don't fire unless fired upon; but if they mean to have a war, *let it begin here!*" The grandson was to take a similarly indomitable tone concerning resistance to the slave power and to theological tyranny.

On the mother's side there was good stock, too. "For she was," wrote her famous son in that autobiography which, unhappily, is merely a fragment, "eminently a religious woman. . . . She saw Him in the rainbow, and in the drops of rain which helped to compose it as they fell into the muddy ground, to come up grass and trees and corn and flowers. She took a deep and still delight in silent prayer. . . . The more spiritual part of the Bible formed her favorite reading; the dark theology of the times seems not to have stained her soul at all."

So it was a goodly heritage which Parker had in the predispositions of his character. It was, however, his sole heritage. His father could not afford to support him at Harvard College (which the lad had entered without anybody's advice), and so, though Theodore took all the required studies and passed all the examinations, he got no degree, — because he had never resided in Cambridge nor paid tuition fees. His college days were passed working on the farm and teaching school in North Lexington, Quincy and Waltham! Thus he reached the age of twenty-one. Then (March 23, 1831) the Lexington home life came definitively to an end by his acceptance of a position as teacher of a private school in Boston.

Writing Dr. Howe in 1860 he describes vividly his early experience in the city he was to help make famous.[1] " A raw boy with clothes made by country tailors, coarse shoes, great hands, red lips, and blue eyes, I went to serve in a private school, where for fifteen dollars a month and my board I taught Latin, Greek, subsequently French(!) and mathematics and all sorts of philosophy. . . . I taught in the school six hours a day and from May to September seven; but I had always from ten to twelve hours a day for my own private studies out of school. . . . Judge if I did not work: it makes my flesh creep to think how I used to work, and how much I learned that year and the four next. . . . Oh, that I had known the art of life, or found some man to tell me how to *live*, to *study*, to *take exercise*. . . . But I found none, and so here I am." John White Chadwick, who has written an admirable life of Theodore Parker, calls attention to the self-conscious note in this. The lad from Lexington seems, indeed, to have been an introspective person and one who, though gay, was not very happy. Very likely this was due to the hardships he had endured and to his loneliness

[1] Culture then came cheap in Boston. In the papers for that year may be found the advertisements for the Boston Lyceum course of lectures, held Thursday evenings at 7 in the Masonic Temple. The price for 22 lectures was $2 (minors under eighteen $1). Rev. Lyman Beecher was the first speaker in the series.

during those early formative years in Boston.
All through his life he studied too 'hard and too
late. During that first Boston year he read all of
Homer and much of Xenophon, Demosthenes,
and Æschylus, studied German and French
until he could write as well as read those languages, and made decided progress, at the same
time, in mathematics and philosophy! No
wonder he shuddered at remembering all this
when, in what should have been his prime, he
was dying as a result of it.

The next year young Parker branched out and
opened a school of his own in Watertown.
Here he made friends; came into contact with
John Weiss and so with the Transcendental
school of thought; was elected superintendent
of the Sunday School — and became engaged.
At the end of the second year at Watertown his
teaching ended and (in April, 1834) he entered
the Divinity School at Cambridge for the last
term of the junior year. He had saved the two
hundred dollars which would put him through
this experience and so he settled down with high
courage in his snuggery at 29 Divinity Hall, the
front corner room towards the college buildings
and on the upper floor. His extraordinary
command of " foreign tongues " served him
well at this stage, for, besides tutoring lads in
Greek and German, he was able to earn considerable money translating Lafayette's letters

for Jared Sparks, who was then at work on his *Life of Washington*. Theologically Parker was quite sound all this time, as we see from the " creed " which he outlined in response to the request of his nephew, Columbus Greene. One sentence in this runs, " I believe that Christ was the son of God, conceived and born in a miraculous manner, that he came to preach a better religion by which man may be saved." Chadwick, who should know, declares that this creed of Parker's — from which I have quoted only one sentence, — was " a neat and comfortable statement of the conservative Unitarianism of the time."

Yet, when the young " theologue " was ready to go forth from the Divinity School we find him writing: " What an immense change has taken place in my opinions and feelings upon all the main points of inquiry since I entered this place! " His theology was now, indeed, so liberal that he found it rather hard work to get a pulpit. His preaching made everywhere a good impression, but since it was rumored that he was a " Transcendentalist," a tag as bewildering to the average intelligence in his time as in ours, committees acting upon candidates were inclined to go slow. For Emerson was a " Transcendentalist " and he had just resigned his charge in Boston because he could not conscientiously administer the Lord's Sup-

per. Finally, however, the young parson was
called to the Spring Street Society at West
Roxbury, where he had preached acceptably
several times, at a salary of $600. Thus a nine
years' ministry of deep and far-reaching import
began.

Just before this Parker had been married
(April 20, 1837) to the Lydia Cabot who had
been a teacher in the Watertown Sunday-School
when he was superintendent, and the two set
up housekeeping in a little white house a mile
distant from the church. Their garden plot
adjoined the extensive grounds of George R.
Russell, a notable parishioner and friend, and
was only slightly removed from the estate of
Francis Gould Shaw, father of the heroic
Robert Gould Shaw. So they were very nobly
neighbored, these two.

During his first year in Roxbury, Parker's
sermons were simple and practical. He had
resolved to " preach nothing as religion " which
he had not " experienced inwardly and made my
own knowing it by heart." Once he devoted the
Sunday morning period to a discourse on " The
Temptations of Milkmen! " Of these early
efforts he says himself, " The simple life of the
farmers, mechanics and milkmen about me,
of its own accord turned into a sort of poetry
and reappeared in the sermons, as the green
woods not far off looked into the windows of

THEODORE PARKER'S CHURCH IN WEST ROX-
BURY.

Page 202.

THEODORE PARKER.

From a daguerreotype.

— Page 202.

T. W. HIGGINSON, AS COLONEL OF THE FIRST SOUTH
CAROLINA VOLUNTEERS.

T. W. HIGGINSON, AET. 20.
From a crayon drawing by Eastman Johnson.

the meeting-house." That his sermons should have been thus simple in style is greatly to the man's credit inasmuch as he was already the master of twenty languages and of much of the literature in which these twenty are employed. This, too, in an age when German dictionaries were so rare that Parker once walked from Watertown to Professor Ticknor's in Boston to consult one. An ordinary day with this prodigious student, — before his marriage, — has been described thus, " Rising at seven, before the midday meal he read the books of Esther, Nehemiah, Solomon's Song, first twelve chapters of Isaiah; wrote part of a sermon; finished one hundred and fifty pages of Allan's *Life of Scott* and two of Herder's *Briefe.* After dinner read in a desultory manner; walked two or three miles; found a queer plant; gathered chestnuts; geologized a little; went to ride . . . took tea " and reluctantly devoted the evening to social intercourse.

Obviously this man greatly needed a wife who should curb his terrifying devotion to books. Mrs. Parker was of quite different fibre from most of the women we have been encountering in these pages, for she was not at all intellectual. She could not share in the least her husband's passion for books and it was not until his humanitarianism developed that they found a field of common interest. But she satisfied at first and always the man's ardently affectionate nature. Early in the Roxbury years, while she was absent on a visit, we find this entry in his journal, " At home nominally; but since wife is gone my home is in New Jersey. I miss her absence — wicked woman! — most exceedingly. I cannot sleep or eat or work without her. It is not so much the affection she bestows on me as that she receives by which I am blessed. I want someone always in the arms of my heart to caress and comfort. . . . I can do nothing without Lydia — not even read."

It is pleasant to realize that Parker, who was soon to be branded as a heretic and carefully avoided as such by almost all of his fellow-clergy, had always at hand the love and the sympathy of this Lydia who satisfied his hungry heart. As he approached his thirtieth year there began to be many and unmistakable signs that he would not be acceptable to the other Unitarians of his day. In 1840 he and his Brook Farm neighbor, George Ripley, walked thirty miles to attend a Groton convention of " come outers " and he made a speech indicting sectarianism and pleading for religious unity and " the Christianity of Christ." That same year he records in his journal the fact that he has repeatedly solicited an exchange with this, that and the other clergyman, but in vain.

On May 19, 1841, however, he did have an opportunity to preach in another minister's pulpit and he gave an address which has become historic. The place was the South Boston Unitarian Church and the occasion the installation of Rev. Charles C. Shackford. The sermon was an impassioned assertion of the permanence and value of Christianity as embodied in the teachings of Jesus, that "pure ideal religion which Jesus saw on the mount of his vision, and lived out in the lowly life of a Galilean peasant." Yet in the same sermon Jesus was said to have founded no institutions, the preacher vigorously maintaining that "if it could be proved that Jesus of Nazareth had never lived, still Christianity would stand firm and fear no evil."

The chief offence of the sermon seems to have been Parker's denial that belief in the miracles is essential to the support of Christianity. Andrews Norton had recently been contending (in *The Latest Form of Infidelity*) "that no man is a Christian who does not believe in the Christian truth because of some miraculous affirmation." To this Parker replied, by implication, that to believe in Christian truth only as miraculously attested was to do it a great irreverence. Now this was "heresy" and the man promoting it must be ostracized. Mrs. Cheney in her *Reminis-*

cences tells an amusing story which indicates
the feeling which prevailed in regard to Parker
and his South Boston sermon. Miss Cornelia
Walter, long editorial director of the *Boston
Transcript* in the place of her brother Lynde
Walter, who had broken down in health, was
reading the sermon aloud to her invalid when
her mother, a sweet old lady, came into the
room. " Whose sermon is that? " she asked.
" It is by a Mr. Parker," answered her daughter.
The name, then unfamiliar, suggested nothing
to the questioner, so she inquired, " To what
sect does he belong? " Not wishing to shock her,
her daughter replied, " I think they call him a
Spiritualist." " I should think so," was the
old lady's comment, " for it is the most spiritual
thing I ever heard." Yet when she learned
what sermon it was she had been led to praise
she was very indignant.

The ministers in the South Boston Church
that morning the sermon was delivered appear
to have been very like Mrs. Walter in their
attitude towards it. All the hue and cry about
its heresy came after the event and in response
to the demand of an ultra-orthodox parson
who demanded Parker's arrest for heresy.
Whereupon a Unitarian layman wrote in the
Boston Courier, " I would rather see every
Unitarian congregation in our land dissolved
and every one of our churches occupied by

other denominations or razed to the ground
than to assist in placing a man entertaining
the sentiments of Theodore Parker in one of
our pulpits." This was so general a sentiment
that exchanges for which Parker had arranged
were cancelled and those solicited were refused
until, by the beginning of the year 1843, gatherings of Unitarian ministers were asking this
very particular question in regard to him,
"Can a believer in Christianity who rejects
the miracles or does not believe because of them
be considered a Christian?"

Happily, the West Roxbury people, who could
have turned Parker out of his parish, declined
to persecute as a heretic their greatly beloved
pastor. Instead, they made their faith in him
and their affection for him clearer than ever
and granted him the year's leave of absence he
desired in order that he have in Europe the
much-needed rest for which a kind friend had
furnished the means. It was during this trip
abroad that Parker called, in Berlin, on Bettine
von Arnim, whose friendship with Goethe had
made glorious her long-vanished girlhood.

He was not even shocked when Bettine told
him that she prayed to Jupiter and that, in her
opinion, Christ the person had done more harm
to the world than any other man. "I found,
however, that for the man Jesus of Nazareth
and for all the great doctrines of religion she had

the profoundest respect," Parker writes, and he adds simply, " I told her there was, to my thinking, but one religion, — that was being good and doing good."

Boston greatly needed a strong man who should preach this religion and a little group who so believed resolved " that Theodore Parker should be heard." Accordingly, soon after his return from Europe he began that series of Sunday morning sermons in the Melodeon (later the Bijou Theatre) which continued for seven years or until the Twenty Eighth Congregational Society of Worship, popularly known as " the Twenty Eighth," secured the larger quarters at Music Hall with which Parker's fame is indissolubly linked.

The first Sunday in Boston was cold, dark and rainy with the streets full of slush and a depressing air of gloom everywhere. But the hall was crowded, for lovers of truth had flocked in from the suburban towns and from all parts of Boston to hear what this " heretic " should have to say. Ere long there were 7000 (!) names on the parish register and to this multitude Parker aspired to be as much a pastor as he had been to the sixty families in his Roxbury church. For more than a year, too, he continued to keep up the Roxbury work.

Glad as he was to be preaching in Boston

there were many things in his new environment
that jarred upon Parker. He had the New
England minister's love for the homely decencies
of worship and his new flock's habit of reading
their newspapers while waiting for the service
to begin accorded ill with his inherited church
traditions. The place, too, was dingy and
unattractive. In the last sermon given there
we get a picture of it as it appeared to Parker:
" We must bid farewell to these old walls. They
have not been very comfortable. All the
elements have been hostile. The winter's cold
has chilled us; the summer's heat has burned
us; the air has been poisoned with contamina-
tions, a whole week long in collecting; and the
element of earth, the dirt, *that* was everywhere.
As I have stood here, I have often seen the
spangles of opera dancers, who beguiled the
previous night, lying on the floor beside me.
. . . Dancing monkeys and ' Ethiopian sere-
naders ' making vulgar merriment out of the
ignorance and wretchedness of the American
slave have occupied this spot during the week
and left their marks, their instruments and
their breath behind them on Sunday."

This passage is significant for its reflection
of Parker's tremendous sympathy with the
slave and his interest in the movement which
was struggling to set him free. In the same
year with his South Boston sermon he had

preached for the first time on the Great American Evil, but his most important early contribution to the anti-slavery cause was not a sermon at all but a " Letter to the People of The United States Touching the Matter of Slavery." This document (dated December 22, 1847) is a masterly presentation of the case against Slavery. Ten pages are given to the history of slavery, eight to the condition and treatment of slaves, ten to the effects on industry, two to effects on population, ten to effects on education, fifteen to effects on law and politics and five to " Slavery Considered as a Wrong." Though dignified and dispassionate the thing is simply overwhelming in its presentation of facts and figures. The closing paragraph of the " Letter " well illustrates Parker's forceful style.

" Across the Stage of Time the nations pass in the solemn pomp of their historical procession. What kingly forms sweep by, leading the peoples of the past, the present age! Let them pass — their mingled good and ill. A great People now comes forth, the newest born of nations, the latest Hope of Mankind, the Heir of sixty centuries, — the Bridegroom of the virgin West. First come those Pilgrims, few and far between, who knelt on the sands of a wilderness. . . . Then comes the One with venerable face, who ruled alike the Senate and

the Camp, and at whose feet the attendant
years spread garlands and laurel wreaths calling
him First in War and First in Peace and First
in his Country's Heart, as it is in his. Then
follow men bearing the first fruits of our toil,
the wealth of sea and land, the labors of the
loom, the stores of commerce and the arts.
A happy People comes, some with shut Bibles
in their hands, some with the nation's laws,
some uttering those mighty Truths which God
has writ on Man and men have copied into
golden words. Then comes to close this long
historic pomp — the panorama of the world —
the Negro Slave, bought, bonded, beat."

Parker could occasionally be very effective
as a satirist. In his " Anti-Slavery " Scrap
Book (now in the Boston Public Library)
may be found " Another Chapter in the Book
of Daniel," written for the *New York Tribune*
apropos of the capture of Shadrach. The
bitter allusions to Webster make this lampoon
very interesting. " Now it came to pass in
the latter days that Daniel was King over all
the children of Jonathan, which had waxed
many and fat in the land. And by reasons
which the prophet detaileth not Daniel's head
was turned and he went after the strange
gods. . . ." Then comes an account of
Daniel's gradual surrender to these gods of the
" Southernites " followed by several very telling

paragraphs about " the great city of the North-
ernites which lieth to the eastward on the sea
shore, as thou goest down to the old country
and it is called Boston. . . .

" And in that city there was a street called
Milk, peradventure because it is the dwelling
place of so many of the babes and sucklings
of commerce. And also another called State,
wherein be the priests' offices, and the temples
of their chief gods.

" For in that city they did worship many
strange gods, whereof the chief was called
Money, an idol whose head was of fine gold,
the belly of silver and legs of copper; but second
thereto was another notable idol called Cotton.

" Unto this latter they did sacrifice, and built
him high places and factories, by the brooks
that run among the hills, and bowed down and
worshipped him saying, Cotton, help us! Cotton, help us! . . .

" Then they held a meeting and cried out,
' Great is Cotton of the Bostonians; there is
no God but Money, no Lord but Cotton; no
King but Daniel; nothing better than Riches;
and no Justice but only the laws of Daniel.'
Then said they, we be a great people." After
which comes a description of the capture of
Shadrach, " a servant in an inn " whom they
" took away from his frying pans and his
skillets and his ovens and his gridirons and

his spits " but whom, none the less, the Lord
delivered. Whereupon

" The Worshippers of Money and of Cotton
fell down on their faces and wept sore, and they
said, Alas for us, the Lord has triumphed and
Cotton has fallen down! Lo Daniel will hate
us, and will make a proclamation and send a
message and the Southernites will be upon us
and take away our hope of a tariff. We will
be all dead men! And their hearts became as
a dog's heart when he barketh, but knoweth
not whom he may bite."

Parker's later service to the anti-slavery
cause came largely in his sermons. Every event
bearing on this great topic was " improved "
by him. Thus his enormous following heard
the annexation of Texas, the rendition of
fugitive slaves, the war with Mexico and every
related event discussed with the fiery ardor
which marked his pulpit style. At Faneuil Hall
and on the lecture platform throughout the
Free States he was frequently heard in the same
cause. Unlike Garrison and Phillips he defended the Union as the instrument by which
slavery would be abolished, thus showing his
clear vision. He differed from Garrison, also,
in his estimate of the negro character. Chadwick says: " Edward Everett had a more
favorable opinion of it. Emerson's was more
genial and more just. Parker's estimate of

the negro, intellectually and morally, was low.
He exaggerated the sensuality of the negro
as he did that of the Jew, whom he placed
only a little higher in this respect. Moreover,
the negro had for him a certain physical repulsion. But his humanity easily absorbed the
instinctive repulsion and the theoretic doubts.
He could see no human creature wronged and
not feel the pain in his own side. The limitations of the negro, as he conceived them, were
not reasons for degrading him. They were
appeals to his benevolence and were responded
to as such."

Half the leaves in the Scrap-Book already
referred to (and called by Parker " Memoranda
of the Troubles Occasioned by the Infamous
Fugitive Slave Law from March 15, 1851, to
February 19, 1856 ") are devoted to posters
warning the fugitives of danger and summoning
their friends to the rescue; and many of these
bear unmistakably the mark of Parker's hand.
In William and Ellen Craft, of which one sees
repeated mention, he was especially interested,
marrying them at a colored boarding-house in
Boston, — and using a Bible and a bowie knife
in the place of the usual symbols! These two
defences happened to be lying on a table and
Parker put them into the husband's hands,
telling him to use the one for his soul and the
other for his body's safety. When the kid-

nappers were in hot pursuit of Ellen Craft
she was sheltered in his house, and after her
marriage Parker started the pair off to England
armed with a letter commending them to
James Martineau's parochial care. Occasional
communications from the Crafts may be found
in late numbers of the *Liberator*.

The year 1852 in Parker's life is marked by
two events of note: his Webster funeral oration
and his removal to Music Hall. The former
antedates the latter by three weeks and this
is rather a pity since we may not ascribe to
the more dignified background such a sentence
as this, in which the complicity of the North
with Slavery is described: "Slavery the most
hideous snake which Southern regions breed,
with fifteen unequal feet came crawling North;
fold on fold, and ring on ring, and coil on coil
the venomed monster came: then Avarice,
the foulest worm which Northern cities gender
in their heat, went crawling South; with many
a wriggling curl it wound along its way. At
length they met and twisting up in their obscene
embrace, the twain became one monster." An
extraordinary funeral oration this and unspeakably bitter in its reproaches of certain public
acts of Webster! Yet it is generally conceded to
be, in its tenderer passages, as fair an estimate
of Webster's private character as any essay
or oration of which he is the subject.

Parker's first sermon in Music Hall was preached November 21, 1852, on " The Position and Duty of a Minister." Therein he told his people with his usual directness and simplicity that he had " great faith in preaching; faith that a religious sentiment, a religious idea will revolutionize the world to beauty, holiness, peace and love." On this occasion, as on many a subsequent one, this immense hall, then brand new, was crowded to the doors, 1500 people in the chairs on the main floor, 700 in the two narrow galleries or balconies and a few hundred more standing or overflowing upon the stage where a kind of body guard of Parker's personal friends usually sat, a little withdrawn from the central figure who dominated the whole. The crowd was promiscuous and there was no collection and no " sittings," the expenses being met by voluntary contributions from an inner circle of devoted friends. The service was very plain: Bible reading with anything omitted which offended the minister's moral sense and hymns sung by the choir from what Parker was wont to call " The Sam Book " — because it was compiled by Samuel Johnson and Samuel Longfellow. The sermon, read from manuscript, was accompanied by no graces either of manner or of delivery. But the preacher had lived and thought and felt and read deeply, and his strong simple sinewy

THE CITY HALL OF PARKER'S DAY.

BOSTON MUSIC HALL, WHERE PARKER PREACHED.

Page 216.

HOWARD ATHENÆUM ABOUT 1865.

OLD NATIONAL THEATRE, PORTLAND STREET.

Page 246.

words went straight to the intelligence of his hearers, of whom more than one went away to say, like a certain plain man whose comment has come down to us, "Is that Theodore Parker? You told me he was remarkable *but I understood every word he said.*"

There were prayers, too, at this "church," "talks with God" which heartened all who heard them, so simply beautiful were they. Louisa Alcott first heard Parker when he was preaching to "laborious young women" and the sermon helped her and inspired her. Yet her most appreciative word is for the prayer, "unlike any I had ever heard; not cold and formal as if uttered from a sense of duty, not a display of eloquence nor an impious directing of Deity in his duties towards humanity. It was a quiet talk with God, as if long intercourse and much love had made it natural and easy for the son to seek the Father . . . and the phrase, 'Our Father and our Mother God' was inexpressibly sweet and beautiful, seeming to invoke both power and love to sustain the anxious overburdened hearts of those who listened and went away to labor and to wait with fresh hope and faith."

Parker was very happy at Music Hall and he gave himself more devotedly than ever to his Sunday preaching. Sometimes his sermons were roughly blocked out four years in advance!

And the crowds continued to come gladly because, as Lowell puts it in his Fable for Critics,

" Every word that he speaks has been fierily furnaced
In the blast of a life that has struggled in earnest: . . .
You forget the man wholly, you're so thankful to meet
With a preacher who smacks of the field and the street."

Nothing that is a part of human life seemed to Parker beyond the pale as pulpit matter. Like Whitman he believed in the excellence of the human body; his sympathy with Mother Nature in her manifold aspects was likewise akin to Whitman's. And often he would preach of these things, exalting as part of the God-given scheme man's passional nature and all that marriage should mean to the young people who sat at his feet. " A real happy marriage of love and judgment between a noble man and woman is one of the things so very handsome," he once said in a sermon, " that if the sun were, as the Greeks fabled, a god, he might stop the world and hold it still now and then in order to look all day long on some example thereof and feast his eyes on such a spectacle." Yet, when all is said, the strength of Parker's preaching lay chiefly in the fact that he was the exalter of righteousness. It was in this, of course, that the poignant appeal of his anti-slavery sermons lay.

Such a man as Parker, with a strong grasp on the homely verities, with profound scholarship, — which he yet knew how to adapt to a popular audience, — and with an impelling ethical ideal would be sure of a warm welcome on the hospitable lyceum platform of the day. During the winter following his return from Europe he lectured forty times and from that time on an ordinary year with him ranged anywhere from fifty lectures to ninety-eight, his record. When the comparatively slow means of transportation is taken into account and the fact recalled that he almost always preached in his own pulpit on Sunday it will be seen that this represents enormous activity. Moreover, he was a voluminous correspondent, writing exhaustive letters with his own hand to scholars who wanted criticism, students who wanted suggestions, common folk who wanted advice and friends who wanted — him. In the biographies of celebrities of this period one encounters scores of these letters. One which I have just happened to see in a " Life " of Parkman embodies long and careful criticism of the most stimulating kind of *The Conspiracy of Pontiac* which had just been published. And this was only one of a thousand such letters written by Parker that year in the scant leisure left after his many other more pressing duties were performed!

Partly because it gives a good picture of Parker at work and partly because of its interesting observations on the Lyceum as an institution I want to quote here from a letter once sent to his friend, Miss Sarah Hunt, while *en tour:* " The business of lecturing is an original American contrivance for educating the people. The world has nothing like it. In it are combined the best things of the Church, i. e., the preaching, and of the College, i. e., the informing thought, with some of the fun of the Theatre. . . . But none know the hardships of the lecturer's life. . . . In one of the awful nights in winter I went to lecture at —— It was half charity. I gave up the Anti-Slavery Festival, rode fifty-six miles in the cars, leaving Boston at half-past four o'clock and reaching the end of the railroad at half-past six — drove seven miles in a sleigh, and reached the house of —— who had engaged [me] to come. It was time; I lectured one hour and three-quarters and returned to the house. Was offered no supper before the lecture, and none after, till the sleigh came to the door to take me back again to the railroad station seven miles off [near which] I was to pass the night and take the cars at half-past six the next morning.

" Luckily, I always carry a few little creature comforts in my wallet. I ate a seed-cake or two and a fig with lumps of sugar. We reached a tavern at eleven, could get nothing to eat at that hour, and as it was a temperance house not a glass of ale which is a good night-cap. It took three-quarters of an hour to thaw out: — went to bed in a cold room, was called up at five, had what is universal — a tough steak, sour bread, potatoes swimming in fat, — wanted me to deduct from my poor fifteen dollars the expenses of my nocturnal ride, but I ' could not make the change.' " Usually Parker's fee for lecturing (after he had reached his full intellectual stature, that is) was " F. A. M. E., i. e., Fifty And My Expenses." Thus he was able to buy himself more and more books and to cut down voluntarily his salary at Music Hall.

Very reluctantly he now (1847) gave up his white cottage in West Roxbury and made his home in Essex Place, his house there touching gardens with that of Wendell Phillips. Phillips records that often, as he looked from his own chamber window late at night, when some lecture engagement had kept him out until the " wee sma' hours," he would see in Parker's study the unquenched light which meant that the insatiable student was still hard at work. These night vigils ere long were to cost the man his life. By the time he was forty-three Parker had warnings that he was not to live to be an old man, and three years later, while lecturing in New Bedford, sight, hearing and speech suddenly gave out. Yet after taking a glass of sherry at a nearby drug-shop he was able to return and finish his lecture. He would not allow himself, indeed, the luxury of being ill, and the result was that, in January, 1859, he was told that the consumption which he knew to be a family tendency, had obtained such a hold upon him that there was only one chance in ten of his recovery. In pursuit of this chance he spent a year in Italy and there, in Florence, he died May 10, 1860. Among his last words were, " There are two Theodore Parkers now: one is dying here in Italy; the other I have planted in America." Neither are forgotten. For pilgrimages are constantly being made to his obscure Italian grave and, every year, his moral beauty becomes more and more revered in the America for which he did so much.

CHAPTER VII

BOSTON'S SHARE IN THE IRREPRESSIBLE CONFLICT

IT was William H. Seward who, in a speech delivered October 25, 1858, spoke of the long fight which he saw coming as "an *irrepressible conflict* between opposing and enduring forces." He meant the force that believed in slaveholding and the force that did not, but there were those — and they included Wendell Phillips — who gave his phrase a larger interpretation. Phillips saw that the war was really a contention as to whether Aristocracy or Democracy should rule in America and, being the man he was, he exulted over the impending struggle. Franklin Sargent, who as the son of Rev. John Sargent and Mrs. Sargent of the Radical Club, had rare opportunities in his youth to know the great men and women of Boston in its romantic era, has recently characterized Wendell Phillips to me as "a handsome aristocrat turned plebeian from principle." And T. W. Higginson, who also knew Phillips well, has told me that the great orator was never more aristocratic in

aspect than when walking through the streets
of his own Boston with an ugly mob howling
at his heels; yet this was the man who five
days after the attack on Fort Sumter was
giving war a warm welcome in Boston Music
Hall, saying, " I rejoice for the first time in my
anti-slavery life; I stand under the stars and
stripes [1] and welcome the tread of Massachusetts men."

The spirit in which Phillips said these words
and had all his life been calling out to the
young people with whom he came in contact,
" Throw yourself upon the altar of some noble
cause! To rise in the morning only to eat and
drink and gather gold — that is a life not worth
living," is the spirit of '61 in Boston. The
noble youth of the time welcomed with out-
stretched arms the possibility of doing something
to show their love of the Union. The sense of
romantic possibilities near at hand made them
feel, to quote Higginson again, " as if one had
learned to swim in air and were striking out
for some new planet."

Even Emerson was caught up in the whirl
of enthusiasm. While John Brown lay in
prison awaiting execution a meeting was held

[1] Cf. the lines in John Boyle O'Reilly's poem on Phillips (written
after his death February 2, 1884):

" A sower of infinite seed was he, a woodman that hewed to the light,
Who dared to be traitor to Union when the Union was traitor to
Right! "

in Boston to raise funds for the relief of his impoverished family, and Emerson, no less than Phillips, was on hand. John A. Andrew presided, and it was on this occasion that Rev. J. M. Manning of the Old South Church declared, " I am here to represent the church of Sam Adams and Wendell Phillips; and I want all the world to know that I am not afraid to ride in the coach when Wendell Phillips sits on the box." Many a man became similarly outspoken about his personal conviction now that the moment for such demonstration had arrived. Woodbury says that throughout the war Emerson was deeply moved in his patriotic feelings and rejoiced in it not only as a cause of civilization but for its reinvigoration of the spirit of the people. " The effect of it upon his own thought was remarkable," he adds. " The anti-social and anarchistic sentiments which were to be plentifully found in his writings before this time cease; and in their place there is a powerful grasp of the social unities embodied in the state as a main source of the blessings of civilization."

On the stone erected on Soldiers' Field, Cambridge, — an athletic ground given to Harvard University by Henry L. Higginson to the memory of James Savage, Jr., Charles Russell Lowell, Edward Barry Dalton, Stephen George Perkins, James Jackson Lowell and Robert

Gould Shaw, all of whom died for their country,
— is this quatrain of Emerson's:

" Though love repine, and reason chafe,
There came a voice without reply, —
'Tis man's perdition to be safe,
When for the truth he ought to die."

This high call to sacrifice was never more
courageously answered than in the case of the
Boston men who enlisted for the Civil War.
The very morning of the attack upon Sumter
forces began to rally and individuals came
forward with offers of all kinds of help. The
Hon. William Gray immediately sent $10,000
to the State House, and the banks of Boston
offered to lend the State $3,000,000 in advance
of legislative action. Physicians and lawyers
volunteered to take charge gratuitously of the
families of men who went to war, and the organ
of the Democrats, whose sympathies had long
been with the South rather than with the North,
advised the postponement of all other issues
until " this self-preserving issue is settled."
The total amount of money expended by the
city, exclusive of State aid, is set down at a
little over $2,500,000.

Yet money was the smallest part of what
Boston gave to this war. Twenty-six thousand
one hundred and seventy-five men out of a
population of about 178,000, meant a much
larger share of the city's wealth than its financial

contribution represented. Moreover, the work done for the Northern army by those two noble Boston women Dorothea Dix and Mrs. Harrison Gray Otis cannot in any way be estimated. Of Mrs. Otis I shall be speaking at some length in a later chapter, so let us here take brief account of Dorothea Lynde Dix's unique work.

As a young woman Dorothea Dix had maintained at the home of her grandmother in what is now Dix Place, Boston, one of those famous girls' schools which in the early part of the nineteenth century, did so much for the character of sensitive young women. Too much, indeed, for this school had a kind of Protestant version of the Roman Catholic system of the confessional, — a shell post-office into which daily, if possible, letters were to be dropped recording the results of the searching introspection required by the young schoolmistress and by her followed up. No wonder Miss Dix was a wreck at thirty-three as a result of such strenuousness. Yet it was during the ensuing visit to England, for the recovery of her health, that the horrible treatment then accorded the insane first came to this earnest woman's attention. Up to so late a date as 1770 Bethlehem Hospital in London, popularly known as " Old Bedlam," was regarded as the prime show in the city, superior even in the attractions it offered the pleasure seeker to a bull-baiting or a dog fight.

Country cousins of the average citizen were taken for a hearty laugh to Bedlam to see the madmen cursing, raving and fighting. The annual fees derived from this public entertainment amounted to several hundred pounds. A mad house was a menagerie — nothing more. Against the cruelties of the place Sydney Smith in the *Edinburgh Review*, 1815–1816, wrote: " Even in the new building the windows of the patients' bedrooms were not glazed nor were the latter warmed."

Barbarous England? Yes, but let us look nearer home and see what Miss Dix saw a whole quarter of a century later. One pleasant Sunday morning as she was coming out of Dr. Lowell's church after a fine sermon she overheard two gentlemen speaking in such terms of indignation and horror of the treatment to which the prisoners and lunatics in the East Cambridge, Massachusetts, jail were subjected that she forthwith determined to go there and look into the matter herself. She had now returned from abroad comparatively well, and, through the will of her grandmother, had come into a sufficient competency to enable her to live comfortably and in a leisurely fashion. At this time it was her intention to enjoy a quiet ladylike life, devoting herself to literature and study and to the social intercourse which was always so delightful to her.

The visit to Cambridge was the turning point of her life. She found among the prisoners a few insane persons with whom she talked. She noticed that there was no stove in their room, and no means of proper warmth. She saw at once that only by resorting to legal measures could this be righted, so, without delay, she caused the matter to be brought up before the court then in session. Her request was granted; the cold rooms were warmed.

Thus was begun her great work, the work at which she labored steadily for the next twenty years, or until these abuses had been reformed in nearly all the States of the Union.

When the War broke out, however, Dorothea Dix saw that the preservation of the Union must take precedence over everything else and within a week after the attack on Sumter she had offered herself and been accepted for free hospital service. Her commission from the Secretary of War declared her " Superintendent of Women Nurses, to select and assign women nurses to general or permanent military hospitals, they not to be employed in such hospitals without her sanction and approval except in cases of urgent need." Naturally, her twenty years' experience in conquering obstacles of every kind made her invaluable to the Surgeon-General. For she everywhere demanded efficiency and sentimentalism she

simply would not have. Higginson, in his
Cheerful Yesterdays, raises whimsical objection
to Miss Dix's ruling that no woman under
thirty need apply to serve in government hospitals and that all nurses should be plain-
looking persons content to be garbed in brown
or black " with no bows, no curls, or jewels,
and no hoopskirts." Yet such prohibitions
appear to have been needed. Hardly had the
first shot been fired when scores of women,
many of whom were obviously unfit for anything useful, presented themselves at headquarters saying, " We've come to nurse " and
seeing no reason why they should not be assigned work.

Even before she had organized the nurses,
however, Miss Dix rendered a signal service
to the Union cause. She it was who revealed
to the proper authorities a bit of Southern
strategy which contemplated the seizing of
Washington as the headquarters of the Con-
federacy and the prevention of Lincoln's inauguration. Miss Dix would never allow herself
to be praised for this act nor would she accept
the public demonstration for her services as
superintendent of war nurses which Mr. Stanton
wished to give her at the close of the war.
Yet, now that she can no longer object, it
seems a great pity that her unique services to
humanity should not be adequately recognized.

Let Congress put through with a rush that bill to appropriate $10,000 for a memorial to her with which they have been dallying for years!

Massachusetts was exceedingly fortunate in having as governor, when the war broke out, a man of the calibre of John A. Andrew. Committed heart and soul to the anti-slavery cause Andrew was yet keen for the preservation of the Union, — and he strongly believed in the potentiality of the negro as a soldier. Through him it was that the Fifty-fourth Massachusetts Infantry, colored, of which Robert Gould Shaw was colonel, came into being. Not easily did he secure the consent of the War Department to raise such a regiment and when he had got it he was a little at a loss where to turn for a commander. Then he lighted on Robert Gould Shaw, who at the time was an officer in the Second Massachusetts Infantry. At first the young man refused the command, doubting his own capacity. But after he had been assured by his superior officer of his entire fitness for the task he telegraphed Governor Andrew his acceptance of the offer and wrote to his mother, " I feel convinced I shall never regret having taken this step, as far as I myself am concerned, for while I was undecided I felt ashamed of myself, as if I were cowardly."

The task of training this colored regiment was

taken up by Colonel Shaw in February, 1863, and in three months his men were ready for service. On May second he was married to Miss Anna Haggerty and on May twenty-eighth the Fifty-fourth broke camp and came to Boston to take the steamer for South Carolina. Shaw was only twenty-six at this time, a handsome, well-made man with a fine complexion, blue eyes and golden hair. He must have been a striking figure as he marched with his black men and his white officers, — among them Norwood [1] and Edward Hallowell, to salute Governor Andrew, standing on the State House steps directly opposite the present site of the beautiful St. Gaudens monument, which was erected to Shaw's memory by his friends in 1897. " I know not," said Governor Andrew as he handed the colors to the Fifty-fourth, " when, in all human history, to any thousand men in arms has there been given a work, so proud, so precious, so full of hope and glory, as the work committed to you."

Shaw was immensely proud of his men and exceedingly anxious to " get them," as he wrote, " alongside of white troops and into a good fight if there is to be one." When the chance came to lead the attack on Fort Wagner, — July 18, 1863, — he seized it eagerly. But

[1] To whom I am indebted for interesting and valuable material about Col. Shaw.

GREEN ROOM OF THE BOSTON MUSEUM.
Page 258.

Copyright, 1903, by N. L. Stebbins.

FOYER OF THE BOSTON MUSEUM.

MRS. VINCENT.
Page 262.

WILLIAM WARREN.

From the painting by Frederic Vinton, in the pos-

almost immediately he fell dead on the parapet, in the midst of a terribly fierce fire in which no less than two hundred and fifty-five of his black soldiers were killed or wounded with him!

Colonel Hallowell has written very beautifully of the qualities of this man under whom he was proud to serve. "His clean-cut face, quick, decided step and singular charm of manner, full of grace and virtue, bespoke the hero. The immortal charge of his black regiment reads like a page of the Iliad or a story from Plutarch. I have always thought that in the great war with the slave power the figure that stands out in boldest relief is that of Colonel Shaw. There were many others as brave and devoted as he, — the humblest private who sleeps in yonder cemetery or fills an unknown grave in the South is as much entitled to our gratitude, — but to no others was given an equal opportunity. By the earnestness of his convictions, the unselfishness of his character, his championship of an enslaved race, and the manner of his death, all the conditions are given to make Shaw the best historical exponent of the underlying cause, the real meaning of the war. He was the fair type of all that was brave, generous, beautiful and of all that was best worth fighting for in the war of the slaveholders' Rebellion."

Yet when he died in the prime of his beautiful young manhood his body was stripped of all but underclothing, exposed for a time on the fort and finally buried in a trench with the negroes! Robert Gould Shaw of Boston was the only officer buried with the colored troops. Not that being side by side, in death as in life, with the men he had loved and trusted could have given Shaw anything but joy! It is for this reason that I like especially the wonderful St. Gaudens monument in which he and his negro followers make up an impressive and artistic unit. Each year on Memorial day the Robert Bell post of Grand Army men, all of whom are colored, hang wreaths of immortelles on the Shaw Memorial and it seems to me a particularly happy thing that they must thus honor at one and the same time their black brethren and the white hero who was their leader.

"I want to fling my leaf on dear Shaw's grave," wrote Lowell to Fields when preparing the poem "Memoriae Positum" in which the brave youth is so stirringly sung. Then he added, "I want the poem to be a little monumental." It is that. Especially the verse:

> "Brave, good and true,
> I see him stand before me now,
> And read again on that young brow,
> Where every hope was new,

How sweet were life! Yet, by the mouth firm-set,
And look made up for Duty's utmost debt,
   I could divine he knew
That death within the sulphurous hostile lines,
In the mere wreck of nobly-pitched designs,
   Plucks hearts-ease, and not rue."

The Fifty-fifth infantry and the Fifth Cavalry were other Massachusetts regiments made up of black men, while all the soldiers in the black regiment of which Thomas Wentworth Higginson of Cambridge was chosen colonel had been slaves. It was in this connection that the following " nonsense verse " began to be circulated in Boston:

" There was a young curate of Worcester
   Who could have a command if he'd choose ter;
      But he said each recruit
      Must be blacker than soot
   Or else he'd go preach where he used ter."

Higginson denies that this verse is a literal statement of the facts; but it is significant that the only title to which he clings, after a full and remarkably varied life, is that of colonel of the First South Carolina Volunteers.

Through the suffering and the sacrifice entailed upon all classes by the Civil War the old differences between parties and clans in Boston were gradually forgotten. Much of the credit for this was due to John Albion Andrew, a man of imperturbable sweetness of temper, who, though just to all his opponents, was yet capable of immensely effective service in the cause he believed to be right.

Andrew was one of those who believed that " John Brown himself was right." He stated very clearly, in 1859, that he sympathized with the *man* and sympathized with the idea because he sympathized with and believed in the Eternal Right. He made this declaration at a time that it took great courage to do so and he never retracted. Yet, the next year, he was chosen to be governor by a popular vote larger than had been received by any of his predecessors. Massachusetts' heart appears to have been in the right place after all! During the long and difficult interval when every governor was a war-minister John A. Andrew was of the greatest service to Lincoln. In many ways, indeed, his mind and that of the President worked alike. And, like Lincoln, he was always accessible, always gentle, kind and just. There is a story that, on one of the days when the pressure of details and decisions was simply tremendous he gave patient audience, at the State House, to a man who was setting forth the virtues of a patent knapsack and that he ended by having the bag packed and buckled on over his own shoulders that he might decide intelligently whether it would really be a good substitute for the regulation knapsack of the army.

For five years John A. Andrew worked early and late as Massachusetts' chief executive, tasting, in that time, more cares and sorrows, hopes and joys and labors than most men would in four score years of ordinary life. He did not long survive the great strain of this period; it has been well said "no soldier struck by a rebel bullet on the battle-field died more truly a victim to the national cause than John A. Andrew." [1] So *his* life, also, must be counted among those offered up in Boston on the altar of "the irrepressible conflict."

[1] By Albert G. Brown, Jr., in his *Sketch of the Official Life of John A. Andrew.*

CHAPTER VIII

WRITING in April, 1831, the Boston correspondent of the *New York Mirror* — whose lamentations over the Puritan city's paucity of histrionic attractions have been referred to in an earlier chapter — observes plaintively, " There is now but one theatre open." That theatre was the Tremont, on the site of the present Tremont Temple, and it had now been making its bid for public patronage for nearly two years, disparaging in every possible way, the while, the Federal Street theatre, its rival. In 1830 the latter was forced to capitulate. It then passed into the hands of the owners of the Tremont, who kept it closed, except for a brief season, until 1835.

The performances at the Tremont began at seven o'clock and the best seats cost only one dollar. Yet several of the greatest artists of the nineteenth century made their appearance here, chief among them being Edwin Forrest, who here played " Hamlet " for the first time in

Boston on November 15, 1828.   Forrest was
then only twenty-two (he had been born in
Philadelphia March 9, 1806) and he looked as
well as acted the young Prince of Denmark.
Moreover, he had not yet developed that
brusqueness of manner under which he elected,
in later years, to cloak what seems to have
been a thoroughly kind heart and a real love
of humanity. It was at the Tremont Theatre
in 1828, also, that John Gibbs Gilbert, a resident
of Boston's North End, made his début. J. B.
Booth was at this time manager and one night,
when he was in the bill, there was enacted a
sad scene which serves amply to establish the
contention of those who claim that his son,
who shot Lincoln, inherited insanity.   Upon
his first entrance on the stage, for the after-piece
in which a comic part had been assigned him,
it was observed that he was faltering in his
delivery and that jumbled scraps from other
plays were finding their way into the dialogue.
Yet he managed somehow to get through two
acts. In the early part of the third act, he
suddenly dropped all pretense of carrying his
part and fell into a colloquial chat with the
King of Naples in the play. For a moment
there was silence. Then, making a desperate
effort to regain his self-control, the actor turned
to the audience and said, " Ladies and gentlemen, I really don't know this part. I studied

it only once before and against my inclination. I will read the part and the play shall go on. By your leave the play shall go on and Mr. Wilson shall read the part for me." Hisses greeted this suggestion. Meanwhile Booth, with a silly grin, which soon broke into a mirthless laugh, was being led into the wings, by a friend in the company, muttering as he went, "I can't read, — I am a charity boy; — I can't read. Take me to the Lunatic Hospital." In later years Booth appeared several times on the Boston stage, having, to all appearances, recovered entirely from this attack of insanity.

In January, 1831, the celebrated Master Burke, announced as the "Irish Roscius," played an engagement of more than a month at the Tremont to houses that were most unusual for that time. "Balls and parties, sleigh rides and social gatherings were for the time dispensed with," says the record, "and the theatre was the centre of the fashionable and literary world of Boston. Burke opened as "Young Norval" but he played also Dr. Pangloss, Shylock, Richard III, Hamlet and Romeo, besides several things whose names mean nothing to us of today.

One very curious thing about the early theatrical history of Boston is the seriousness with which the public took the private peccadilloes of artists. Theatrical riots were of common occurrence. The most important one, since that connected with the appearance of Edmund Kean at the Federal Street Theatre,[1] came at the Tremont in 1831 when Mr. J. R. Anderson, an English singer, was hissed off the stage because he was believed to have spoken " disrespectfully of the American people." In those days this was an unpardonable sin and poor Anderson and his managers had a hard time of it notwithstanding the fact that they deluged the papers with letters and affidavits asserting that he " never did it."

The spring of 1833, at the Tremont, was marked by two very interesting events, a benefit given (April 3) to John Howard Payne by the citizens of Boston, after his absence for nearly twenty years from the scene of his early triumphs, and the first appearance in Boston, on Tuesday, April 16, of Miss Fanny Kemble. The Payne benefit was carried out by a committee of citizens appointed at a meeting held in the Tremont House and the pieces chosen for presentation consisted entirely of selections from various plays, written by him whom we now know only as the author of " Home, Sweet Home." Whether by reason of Miss Kemble's approaching season, or because the plays Payne offered were all familiar ones, and the night selected was on the eve of

[1] See *Old Boston Days and Ways*, p. 456.

Fast Day, — when it was the custom for Boston families to unite in social gatherings, — whatever the reason may have been the fact remains that the receipts for the benefit were small. Yet the occasion was an impressive one. Park Benjamin wrote for it a poem celebrating the events of Payne's varied career which makes much better reading than most " efforts " of the kind, and the affair appropriately came to a close with the rendering of " Home, Sweet Home " by the orchestra followed by a speech from Payne himself.

The season of Miss Kemble and her father was a pronounced triumph, the wealth and beauty of the city crowding the playhouse night after night to do honor to this lovely woman and charming actress. Though the Hamlet of Charles Kemble was much approved, it was when the two appeared together in " School For Scandal " or " Romeo and Juliet " that the enthusiasm of the audience reached its highest pitch. When they played their fall engagement at the Tremont, under the management of Thomas Barry, the admirable stage-manager who had just come over from the Park Theatre in New York to direct the destinies of Boston's leading theatre, the receipts were very large for that time: $11,671 in eighteen nights. Thomas Barry was then called the best stage-manager in America and he continued to deserve the title, winning and holding universal respect not only among the members of his profession but also with the general public. His first move after coming to the Tremont was to put the theatre in complete repair at an expense of $5,000 which came out of his own pocket. Gas was then introduced into the house much to the satisfaction of the ladies, " many of whom," we read, " could trace a ruined dress to a visit to the theatre, owing to the dripping of the oil from the lamps."

Charles H. Eaton, a Boston boy who became " the most capable, scholarly and polished American actor of his time," his untimely and tragic death (by a fall down a spiral staircase) bringing to a sad end what would undoubtedly have been a very brilliant career, played at the Tremont this same year. Then (in 1833) came Mr. and Mrs. Joseph Wood, whose appearance here in opera created almost as great an excitement as the coming of Jenny Lind. To us the Woods are interesting chiefly because it was with them that Charlotte Cushman, America's greatest tragic actress and the only Boston woman to attain international fame on the stage, made her début. In those days Charlotte thought herself destined to be a great singer. It is interesting to note in passing that at this period she sang Lucy Bertram at the Tremont Theatre in a musical version of

the play which was afterwards to afford her
her master-rôle.

The great event in the history of the Tremont
Theatre was its connection with Fanny Ellsler,
the first theatrical celebrity of French birth
ever to win the plaudits of conservative Bostonians. She made her initial appearance in
Boston on the evening of September 7, 1840,
and, almost immediately, became the talk of the
town. Even Emerson, who with Margaret
Fuller had gone to witness this unusual attraction, seems to have been dazzled by the grace
and charm of the lovely Fanny, for, as she was
executing one of her inimitable pirouettes,
balancing her supple body on the toe of her
left foot while she extended her right one " to
a dangerous not to say questionable height
into space," he replied to Margaret's ecstatic
whisper, " Ralph, this is poetry! " with a
fervent, " Margaret, it is *religion !* " The press
notices of the time almost persuade one to
accept these transcendental testimonies. " All
that we had imagined," says one critic, " of
poetry, of music, of sculpture, of refinement,
elegance and beauty, were realized. The
colors of the rainbow, the delicacy of the
flowers, the purity of the crystal waters, have
nothing more radiant, exquisite or transparent
than the gossamer floatings of this glorious
creature." If the following categorical descrip-

LORENZO PAPANTI.

From a painting in the possession of the Bostonian Society

Page 314.

FANNY ELLSLER.

From a drawing by W. K. Hewitt.

Page 244.

LOBBY OF THE OLD GLOBE THEATRE.
Page 273.

FOYER OF THE BOSTON THEATRE.
Page 270.

tion [1] of Miss Ellsler's charms be just, she must certainly have been " glorious: "

" La Fanny is tall, beautifully formed, with limbs that resemble those of the hunting Diana, combining strength with the most delicate and graceful style; her small and classically shaped head is placed on her shoulders in a singularly elegant manner; the pure fairness of her skin requires no artificial whiteness, while her eyes beam with a species of playful malice, well suited to the half-ironical expression at times visible in the corners of her finely curved lips; her rich glossy hair of bright chestnut hue is usually braided over a forehead formed to wear with equal grace and dignity the diadem of a queen or the floral wreath of a nymph."

No wonder our ordinarily staid citizens walked before the Tremont House for hours in hopes that the divinity would show herself at the window! Articles of use and ornament, from bread and bootjacks to cuffs and brass buttons were named in her honor; and so great was her vogue that her help was gladly accepted by " society " in raising money for the granite shaft on Bunker Hill, then nearing completion. The wags of the day declared that Fanny had kicked the cap on the Monument. During her thirteen nights in Boston she earned $15,000 by her dancing!

[1] In *Beauties of the Opera and Ballet*.

A keen rival of the Tremont Theatre at this time was the National, brought into being by the same disgruntled actor, William Pelby, who had caused the Tremont to be started. For four years he called his venture, at the corner of Portland and Travers Streets, the Warren, but, in 1836, he reconstructed its interior and announced that its name would henceforth be the National. Here it was that Jean Davenport made in 1838 the success which induced her father to lease the Lion Theatre, on the site of the present Bijou, for her. Miss Davenport was at this time stated to be only " eleven years of age " and was justly regarded as an infant phenomenon, equal to Master Betty in the best days of that prodigy and surpassing the wonderful Burke to whom allusion has already been made. Why anyone should wish to see a mere child playing Richard and Shylock I cannot see, but that the desire to be thus entertained was keen there seems no doubt. Her ten performances in as many parts netted nearly sixteen hundred dollars for her fond father! The National burned in 1852 but was promptly rebuilt and for many years continued to draw large audiences. Its pieces were always well mounted and its prices reasonable.

The Howard Athenæum, once characterized [1] as an edifice " which has had an experience of

[1] By Henry Austin Clapp.

more variety than any other piece of masonry
in the city of Boston," dates from 1845 and is
still given over to amusement purposes. This
place was built to be a temple of the Millerites, whose prophet, the venerable Father
Miller, predicted with such persuasiveness,

> " The end of the world will surely be
> In Eighteen Hundred and Forty-three."

that large numbers of his followers sold all their
possessions preparatory to immediate departure
for a land more blessed. When the day set
apart for the closing up of all earthly affairs had
however passed with no sign of being the Last
Day Father Miller reviewed his calculations
and discovered that he had been wrong in his
arithmetic to the extent of a few thousand
years. Whereupon the Millerites reluctantly
consented to lease their former gathering-place
to a group of men desirous of establishing
another theatre in Boston. At the time of its
opening (October 13, 1845) this new theatre
had a regular stock company, which included
James H. Hackett, afterwards the manager of
the Howard. One feature of Hackett's acting
was his originality. It is related that, on a
certain occasion when he had been vociferously
applauded for his work in Nimrod Wildfire, a
piece that concludes with a dance in which the
star kicks over a table spread with tea things,

the gallery gods continued their applause out of all limits. Whereupon Hackett advanced to the footlights and said, " I should be most happy to repeat the dance, but I am out of breath, and what is worse, the manager is out of cups and saucers! "

It was at the Howard Athenæum on its opening night under Hackett's management (October 5, 1846) in a new building which replaced the wooden structure of the Millerites, that William Warren, whom we of today inevitably connect with the Boston Museum, made his first appearance in this city as Sir Lucius O'Trigger in " The Rivals." The crowning theatrical achievement of that season in this house was, however, the dancing of the Viennoise Children; in opera the year is marked by the fact that here, for the first time in Boston, genuine Italian opera was presented, the vehicle being Verdi's " Ernani " and the stars Tedesco and Perilli. Before the theatre ceased, in 1868, to be the home of " the legitimate " it saw many opera seasons worthy of note, not the least of these being one in the spring of 1853 of which Madame Sontag was the star. It also had many distinguished managers, among them E. L. Davenport, John Gibbs Gilbert, Lester Wallack the elder, Sothern the elder, Isaac B. Rich and John Stetson. Joseph Jefferson was a member of the company at this house during the season of 1853–54. Clever advertisements have always been a feature here and, even today, when the talent to be exploited is by no means of a high order, the emanations from the press room of the " Old Howard " are gems of their kind. In 1845 it was announced by a soulful press agent:

" As Rome points proudly to her Coliseum,
So Boston treats her Howard Athenæum."

Someone has observed that this deference on Boston's part may have arisen from the fact that the Howard was the first Boston theatre to have cushioned seats.

The first Boston theatre to have a " nigger heaven " was the Tremont. An early program stated that the central gallery, to which the admission was fifty cents, was " reserved for people of color." It would be interesting to know how largely these people took advantage of the special provision made for them. Lyman Beecher hated with a godly hatred this Tremont Theatre and he once boasted that he " would yet preach " in the building then desecrated by playhouse use. He lived to fulfil the boast; for following a religious revival of unusual fervor, it was decided to sell the theatre to Rev. Mr. Colver's Baptist Society. The bitter resentment cherished by many of the clergy towards the theatres in Boston can hardly be appreciated in these days when it is so generally

felt that the stage at its best is bent on the
same ideals as inspire the church. Yet Lyman
Beecher declared, when one of the theatres
in the city was burned down, that " another
gateway of Hell has been destroyed by the
direct intervention of divine Providence! "
After the Tremont Theatre had been modelled
over into Tremont Temple it was opened (in
the fall of 1843) with the hymn " Lord, Let
These Ransomed Walls Rejoice."

The last June of the Tremont's life as a
theatre was none the less a gala month. The
city was thronged with people who had come
to town to be present at the ceremonies incident
to the completion of Bunker Hill Monument —
for which Webster delivered the oration — and
so many people were desirous of attending the
theatre that, for the first time in history, Boston
had a playhouse open on Saturday evening. A
week later, the last performance in the old
house was held. Ere the company broke up
on this occasion two or three speeches were
made by actors which, to my mind, compare —
to Lyman Beecher's disadvantage — with some
of that divine's discourses on the subject of
the drama. Gilbert, for instance, defended feelingly his profession. There were defects,
he admitted, in the drama, but they could be
removed by judicious management so that the
most scrupulously fastidious should feel that

the theatre was a good institution and be induced
to patronize it.

The cue in all this, that " by judicious management the most scrupulously fastidious might
be made to feel the theatre a good institution
and so to patronize it " was promptly taken
up by a very clever man, Moses Kimball. Mr.
Kimball had the shrewdness to see that the
Boston public could be made to take very
kindly to a new theatre if the thing were broken
to them gradually. On June 14, 1841, he had
opened his Boston Museum and Gallery of Fine
Arts in a building on the site where the Horti-
cultural Hall stood later and the Paddock
Building stands now, and to furnish his Museum
had purchased generously from the collection
which had been in the possession of the New
England Museum. One of his choice acquisi-
tions was the famous so-called historical painting by Rembrandt Peale, representing the
Roman Daughter giving sustenance to her
father in prison, a startling canvas which
until the demolition of the Old Boston Museum greeted all who were making their exit
down the long flight of steps that led out to
the street.

In order to understand what a unique opportunity Mr. Kimball had to develop a successful
theatre from this unobjectionable beginning it
should be recalled that theatricals in Boston

were just then at very low ebb. The Boston
Theatre on Federal Street was closed, the
National Theatre was making an appeal which
was chiefly local, the Howard had not yet been
started and the Tremont Theatre was expiring.
Mr. Kimball's problem, then, was to move
so cautiously as to make no enemies, trusting
to Providence that, in good time, he should
make many friends. He opened his institution
with a "grand concert" and for two years
nothing more exciting than dioramas and pano-
ramas was offered, — in addition to music
and the curiosities.

But, no sooner had the Tremont closed its
doors than Mr. Kimball made arrangements
to give regular dramatic performances in his
Museum and several members of the Tremont
Company were engaged to float the venture.
Miss Adelaide Phillips, then a child of ten,
was among the number, and for several years
during her early connection with the Museum
she was wont to drive her hoop back and forth
to rehearsals from her parents' home on Tremont
Street.

The price of admission during all the Bromfield
Street period of the Museum's history was 25
cents, "children under twelve years of age
half price." Great emphasis was laid upon the
educational value of the curiosities and such
shows as were produced were represented to

be of the strictly " moral " variety. On the bills
for 1844 a prize of $100 was offered by the
management "for the best moral domestic
drama adapted to the stock company of the
Museum." To win this prize there was sent
in a play called " The Drunkard " the authorship of which has never been accurately known,
but which John Bouvé Clapp — who has made
a special study of the Museum's history to
which I am indebted for many of these facts —
attributes to Rev. John Pierpont, then pastor
of the Hollis Street Church. Pierpont was an
ardent worker in the movement for temperance
reform, and he was wont to thunder from his
pulpit, Sunday after Sunday, against those
who had built up fortunes by liquor manufacture. This despite the fact that three of
the pillars of his church were distillers and
stored their rum in the basement of the church —
thus giving point to the epigram:

> " Above the spirit Divine,
> Below the spirits of Wine."

Perhaps it was in the belief that he could
preach temperance to a larger audience through
the theatre than through the church that Mr.
Pierpont turned his attention to the writing of a
play. One of the parts in this highly moral
" Drunkard " was taken, it is interesting to
know, by Miss Caroline Fox, who afterwards

became famous, the world over, as the original
Topsy.

So kindly had the Boston public taken to
theatre-going at a " Museum " that Mr. Kimball now began to arrange for ampler quarters.
Hammatt Billings and J. E. Billings were com-
missioned to make plans for an adequate
auditorium and on November 6, 1846, what we
of today know as " the Old Boston Museum "
was opened. The first performance began
with the playing of " America " by the orchestra
and in the course of the evening Adelaide
Phillips danced.

When the new Museum opened its doors
the curios were displayed in the pillared promenade where the pictures hung later. Not
until the season of 1850–51 was the " wax
statuary hall 100 feet in length " fitted up as
their home and " The Murder of Miss McCrea,"
the " Scene in the Cabin of a Vessel Captured
by Pirates," the " Three Stages of Intemperance " and " The Last Supper " there " exhibited without extra charge to all who desired
to view them." The " Feejee Mermaid,"
alluded to by Barnum in his Autobiography was
also duly here. Mr. Kimball was by no means
stingy with his treasures, however, and when
the Cochituate water was let on in Boston (1848)
two of the Museum's huge stuffed elephants
were lent to be in the procession.

In that charming book, *Yesterdays With Actors*,[1] there is a Hawthornesque passage descriptive of the quaint old gentleman who was long the care-taker and preserver of the wax figures. When Mrs. Winslow, the new recruit to the company, first met him (about 1860) he conducted her to the upper gallery she says, " with a confiding yet startled air which was almost furtive and suggested fear and suspicion. I could not but believe that, engrossed with his dumb companions, when he sought human fellowship, the eyes that moved, the lips that spoke half terrified him! However, being a silent person, I was taken the rounds, and every perfection pointed out to me. Was I not smitten with the belief that Chang and Eng were before me? These Siamese, were they not real? He spoke with solemn earnestness of Miss McCrea's need of a clean gown. She should have it yet. But the school — the school. Look at it! Every face, he told me, had been wiped, every collar washed, every shoe brushed. The schoolmaster, was I not deceived by him? The scholar with the dunce's cap? Wax? No! it was life! . . . The ghastly tragedy of the drunkard's history, the verisimilitude of the sealing wax blood of poor Miss McCrea, stark staring Santa Anna, were always things terrible to me, but as I think now of the

[1] Written by Mrs. Erving Winslow, née Kate Reignolds.

pale moonlight falling on those awful spectres
[this book was written before the Museum was
demolished] I have an eerie feeling that the
little old man, though he died some time since,
still creeps about the gallery, fulfilling his
faithful task."

The great event of the season 1847–1848 at
the Museum was the first appearance at this
house of William Warren, who (with the exception of one year) was exclusively associated with
this playhouse for the next thirty-five seasons.
His initial appearance was in Pocock's old
comedy, "Sweethearts and Wives," and he
acted for the last time, May 12, 1883, playing
Old Eccles in "Caste." His career may thus
be said to cover the history of the Museum
throughout the entire period of its palmy
days. Mr. Warren was the son of an English
player and of an American lady of acting
family. He got his training through the old
stock company system and of him it might
peculiarly be said that in his time he "played
many parts." While at the Museum, alone,
his rôles numbered over 575 and the performances to his credit were upwards of 13,000.
On the fiftieth anniversary of his first appearance
in Boston he was given a testimonial and Vinton's portrait, herewith reproduced, which was
painted at the order of a number of Bostonians,
was exhibited in the lobby. The picture now

hangs in Boston's Museum of Fine Arts, a worthy memorial of one who was a gifted actor and an old school gentleman of the finest type.

For many years Mr. Warren was a most interesting Boston figure as he took his daily walks to the Museum from his boarding place kept by Miss Fisher, for he never married. Henry Austin Clapp has declared that his manners were the finest he ever saw in a man and that he remembers hearing it said at a time, near the close of the Great War, by some men who were native here, and to the best Boston manner born, that "Edward Everett, A. B., A. M., LL.D., ex-Governor of Massachusetts, ex-United States Senator from Massachusetts, ex-President of Harvard College, ex-Minister to England, litterateur, orator, statesman, was, in respect of distinction of manners, in a class with but one other of his fellow citizens: that one other appearing in the local directory as Warren, William, comedian, boards 2 Bulfinch Place." [1]

For sixteen years the stage-manager and leading man at the Museum was W. H. Smith. He was succeeded in the stage management by Mr. E. F. Keach, a dashing actor as well as a capable director. Mrs. Winslow gives us an interesting glimpse into the green room and behind the scenes when Keach was at the helm:

[1] *Reminiscences of a Dramatic Critic.*

" We entered by a narrow door from one of the galleries which gave at a touch, but fell back as quickly with the force of a ponderous spring. A door-keeper, seated at the end of a narrow aisle some three feet wide between enormous piles of dusty canvas, permitted none to pass except the actual employees of the theatre. About the same space between the inner edge of the scenery standing in its grooves and the masses stacked along the walls, allowed a scant passage down the side of the stage. At one corner, where the private box is now was a property room, behind that the manager's office.

" On the opposite side, a small space of perhaps six feet wide at one end tapering down to four at the other was the green room, its furniture a bench about the wall, a cast case, a dictionary and a mirror, over which was inscribed ' Trifles make Perfection.' . . . A hasty glance at the ' call ' in the green room for the coming plays, a word of courteous greeting for our fellow actors, the last conning of the part; such were the interludes between the appearances on the stage; and a more workaday, matter of fact place it would be hard to find."

Yet because the players were clever men and women many a good thing flashed out in that dingy room. William Warren, Mrs. Winslow relates, she saw one night surrounded by a

bevy of girls "who in their æsthetic clinging
gowns and admring attitudes could not but
remind me of the maidens in Patience grouped
around Bunthorn. In speaking to him afterwards I told him he was the lion of the night.
'Ah,' said Warren, 'I never heard of but one
man who was not hurt by lionizing, and he was
a Jew by the name of Daniel.'" It was of
Warren that the great Rachel said simply,
"He is one of us."

One of Warren's early successes at the
Museum was as Mustapha in "The Forty
Thieves," which, with "Aladdin," "Cinder-
ella," "Valentine and Orson," "The Enchanted
Beauty," "Blue Beard" and "The Children of
Cyprus" formed the series of "grand dramatic
spectacles" which served to make friends for
Mr. Kimball's enterprise because parents "took
the children," — just as we all do now when
the circus is in town. "The Children of Cyprus" is especially remembered for its bird
song rendered by Adelaide Phillips. It was the
young artist's work in this part which first
caused Jenny Lind to be interested in her, and
to help her, subsequently, to a musical education.

The naïve readiness of the Bostonians to
take the new theatre, disguised as a "Museum,"
at Mr. Kimball's shrewdly calculated valua-
tion is nowhere more amusingly shown than

in the various handbooks of the time. In the 1856 edition of *Boston Sights and Strangers' Guide* we find unbounded enthusiasm over "the spacious and superb building, its front adorned by elegant balconies and rows of ground glass globes like enormous pearls which at night are luminous with gas. Three tiers of elegantly arched windows admit light into the building," adds the writer, "and we reach the interior by a bold flight of stairs."

A bold flight of description this! Yet even more impressive matter follows, for we are told of the statuary and superb works of art, of the curios which are "products of many a clime" . . . and of an observatory surmounting all "whence splendid panoramic views of the city and harbor and its islands may be obtained." After which comes the editorial assurance that "the Museum theatre is one of the most beautifully decorated, best constructed and well managed theatres in the United States. The visitor there has no rowdyism to fear and nothing ever occurs either in the audience portion or on the stage to offend the most fastidious. As good order is maintained in Mr. Kimball's theatre as in any drawing room in the land."

The reserved seat plan was adopted at the Museum in 1848, slips entitling to the same being partly printed and partly filled out by hand. The following year Edwin Booth, called

WASHINGTON ALLSTON.

Page 284.

WILLIAM MORRIS HUNT.

From the painting by himself in the possession of the Boston Museum of Fine Arts.

Page 285.

in the bills Edwin T. Booth, was seen here for the first time on any stage, his rôle being the small one of Tressel in " Richard III " to his father's Gloster. This was September 10, 1849, young Booth being then sixteen years old.

Two very interesting things happened at the Museum in the season of 1852–53: " Uncle Tom's Cabin " was staged and Mrs. Vincent joined the company. The dramatization of Mrs. Stowe's story was made by H. J. Conway, Frank Whitman played Uncle Tom, W. H. Smith did Drover John, J. Davies was Simon Legree, E. F. Keach did the George Harris, J. A. Smith was the St. Clare, Mrs. Wulf Fries did the Eliza, Mrs. Thoman was Aunt Ophelia, Helen Western was the Eva and Miss Gazzynski acted Topsy. An interpolated character — Penetrate Partyside — who created " comic relief " in the play was done by William Warren, and Mrs. Vincent, then a slim and swift young woman, acted Cassy. On one memorable evening Mrs. Stowe and her sister, together with their father, Rev. Lyman Beecher, — who hated the theatre generally, — attended the performance.

Mrs. Vincent's maiden name was Mary Ann Farley and she was born in Portsmouth, England, September 18, 1818. Her father was a naval officer but he died when she was only two and her mother's decease soon afterward

left the child to be brought up and cared for
by an aunt, a grandmother and an old servant.
This servant married a man who lived in Gos-
port and began to take boarders, among them
several actors, including Charles Wilson, manager of the Theatre at Cowes, and his wife.
Little Miss Farley used to go to have tea with
them at the theatre; thus her stage desires were
early kindled. She made her début at Cowes
in April, 1835, in " The Review, or the Wags of
Windsor," by George Colman, Jr., playing with
much vim and vigor the part of a chambermaid. The following August, when only sixteen,
she married James R. Vincent, a comedian many
years her senior. Her Boston début, as has
been said, was at the National Theatre and she
had been in the company there six years when
the burning of the playhouse made her eligible
for an engagement at the Museum. Here her
connection was continuous, (with the exception
of the season 1861–62 when she supported
Edwin Forrest at the Howard Athenæum)
until her death September 4, 1887. In 1856
she married John Wilson of the Museum company, but, this alliance not proving a happy
one, she was divorced from him ten years later.
It is quite properly as Mrs. Vincent, therefore,
— " dear old Mrs. Vincent," — that this gifted
woman is remembered and honored in Boston.
Up to the very end of her life she kept happily

in the harness. She died, September 4, 1887,
at her home 112 Charles Street; on the preceding Wednesday she had played Kezia Beek-
man in " The Dominie's Daughter! "

Mrs. Vincent's kindness to animals and her
generous charities were famous in the Boston
of a quarter century ago. On one occasion when
all the other members of the Museum company
were assembled, she was found by messengers,
hastily sent out in quest of her, standing in the
midst of a crowd at the corner of Tremont
Row and Pemberton Square, haranguing a
teamster who was driving a lame horse. " Her
fervent denunciations, pointed by her umbrella,"
says Kate Reignolds Winslow,[1] " were scarcely
to be interrupted by the urgent reminder that the
stage was waiting. As she was dragged away
and hurried up the stairs of the Museum, we
heard her panting for breath and brokenly
exclaiming in anything but a tone of penitence:
' Well, I don't care if the stage *is* waiting, and
I don't care for Mr. Keach nor twenty like him.
I won't see a brute driving a horse on three legs
without speaking my mind.' "

This manager, Mr. E. F. Keach, appears to
have been a good deal of a martinet. Yet it was
undoubtedly due to him that the Boston
Museum developed from a mere stage adjunct
of wax figures and curiosities (frequented by

[1] In *Yesterdays with Actors.*

good people who were afraid of the very name,
theatre) to a first rate home of first rate drama.
His "Rules and Regulations" concerning the
conduct of the company, while in the Green
Room, were quite above the standard in other
theatres. They made it clear that the "Green
Room is provided for the quiet and respectable
assemblage of the ladies and gentlemen of the
company," that "conversation there must be
carried on in low tones," and that "smoking
and spirituous liquors would not be allowed
there or in any part of the theatre at any
time." After four years as manager Mr.
Keach was succeeded by R. M. Field, who held
the place until the stock company was discontinued in 1895.

Mrs. Winslow (then Kate Reignolds) was
leading woman in the company beginning with
the first season under Keach (1860–61), and her
vivid account of acting with John Wilkes
Booth, who soon came to play an engagement,
leaves one in no doubt that this man was very
close to insanity even before his affliction was
recognized. "If ever there was an irresponsible
person," she says, "it was this sad-faced,
handsome, passionate boy. As an actor he
had more of the native fire and fury of his great
father than any of his family but he was as
undisciplined on the stage as off. When he
fought it was no stage fight. He told me that

he generally slept smothered in steak and
oysters to cure his own bruises after Richard
the Third, because he necessarily got as good
as he gave, — in fact more, for though an
excellent swordsman, in his blind passion he
constantly cut himself. How he threw me
about! In Othello, when with fiery remorse,
he rushed to the bed of Desdemona after the
murder, I used to hold my breath, lest the bang
his cimeter gave when he threw himself at
me should force me back to life with a shriek."
Once when he and she had been playing " Romeo
and Juliet " the curtain fell on Romeo with a
sprained thumb, and a good deal of long hair
on his sleeve, and with Juliet in rags while
her two white satin shoes were lying in the
corner of the stage. In his last struggle Romeo
had literally shaken his beloved out of her
shoes!

Agnes Robertson was one of the attractions
at the Museum in writing of whom Mrs. Winslow waxes exceedingly enthusiastic. This gifted
young Scotchwoman played for the first time
in the United States (in the season of 1856–57)
at this house and so great was her vogue that
all Boston stood in line to secure tickets. " She
was petted in society, — for women were fascinated by her perhaps even more than men, —
and equally in drawing-rooms and among the
garish adjuncts of the stage there was a bright

purity about her, like the atmosphere of her
own Scotland.

"Opposite the Museum in those days was
Mrs. Mayer's ice-cream saloon, a favorite
meeting place for parties going to the play. A
mob of girls would cluster about the sidewalk
to wait the exit of Agnes Robertson, and the
more favored customers of the shop gathered
at its windows, which Mrs. Mayer would empty
of her showcase to make room for the curious
throng. . . . Often under good Mrs. Vincent's
care, and beneath her ample cloak, the little
form was smuggled past the eager eyes " to her
quarters in the Tremont House. One other
delightful bit about Mrs. Vincent must be
quoted from this book. It is a picture of that
lady among her cats! "Once when a visitor,
who could not abide that 'harmless necessary'
animal, was calling at the house on Charles
Street the door was pushed stealthily open,
after a little space, and a great glossy black
puss, with tail erect and gleaming eyes, slowly
entered the darkened parlor. Soon a second
followed the first, this one with bushy tail,
red eyes and bristling fur. Then came another
and another until there were five. Great was
the visitor's relief when the hostess herself
bustled in calling 'William Warren,' 'Smithy,'
and so on, for all had the names of principal
members of the Museum company!"

But the temptation to linger unduly over the story of the Museum must be resisted. In 1892 the exhibition of curiosities was practically discontinued. In 1896 the wax figures were sold to a travelling manager and the mummies were given to the Boston Art Museum. On April 13, 1900, there occurred a slight fire in the hall of curiosities by which some of the paintings were injured and, in 1903, Margaret Anglin played " Mrs. Dane's Defence " for the benefit of the Vincent Memorial Hospital, this being the last performance held in the old playhouse before it gave way to an office building. " Auld Lang Syne " was sung in the course of the evening and, as the final curtain rang down, the eyes of many a seasoned playgoer were dimmed with tears. For Boston loved its " old Museum " and the associations which clustered around it.

The only one of the really old theatres which survives today, in spirit as well as in truth, is the Boston Theatre. For, unlike the Howard, this house sticks to " the legitimate " for the most part and it is withal a delight to the eye, as its designers intended it should be. William W. Clapp, Jr., to whose *Record of the Boston Stage* (published in 1853) I am indebted for much information about the old theatres, closes his carefully compiled volume with an allusion to the " New Opera House and Theatre now in

process of erection " and the hope that the same
would receive from the public a most generous
support. Whereupon he quotes as follows from
a letter just sent him by Thomas Barry, " The
drama is firmly planted in New England for
good or for evil; you cannot crush it by prejudice or destroy it by misplaced religious enthusiasm. The public can make a theatre a
blessing or a curse. . . . You will have sooner
or later a first class theatre in Boston and, if
properly built and properly conducted, it will
prove a boon to the public and a fortune to the
manager." In many ways these words were
prophetic. For Barry himself soon came over
from New York to establish such a theatre in
Boston and it proved to be quite as successful
as he had said it would.

It was built in this wise: A meeting was
called at the Revere House in 1852 by Joseph
Leonard, the auctioneer, for the purpose of
creating interest in the erection of a new Boston
playhouse. The sum deemed necessary to the
undertaking ($250,000 in blocks of stock sold
at $1,000 a share) was soon secured, an appro-
priate site purchased, the contract let to a
firm of architects who carried out the design
for which H. Noury had won a prize of $500, —
and, on September 11, 1854, the house was
dedicated.

The perfect harmony of proportions attained

in this theatre are a great credit to the period in which the structure was built. For excellent acoustics and symmetry were the aims of those behind the undertaking, not simply accommodation for as many seats as could be crowded into a given space. Alexander Corbett, Jr., who has written entertainingly [1] of this old house, says that " standees," who nowadays often contribute liberally to a theatre's income, were practically unknown when the Boston Theatre was built and that there still existed much of that old prejudice against occupants of the lower floor seats — those whom Hamlet characterizes as " groundlings, caring only for inexplicable dumb show and noise." The balcony, where seats sold for one dollar each, was the place where fashion chose to sit, when it was not occupying a stage box, which then cost six dollars.

The very first folding chairs ever used in a theatre were found here on the opening night and were warmly commended by one of the critics, as " being so ingeniously contrived as to fold up and allow passing and having nicely cushioned backs." Another innovation, which deserved the critic's praise, — though I have yet to find that it got it, — was the substitution of a refreshment counter at which ice-cream, temperance drinks and the like were served.

[1] In *The Bostonian*, vol. I.

for the bar-room on the third tier, which was then a feature of most local playhouses. (The most baneful part of the bar lay not in the drinks served but in the "demi-mondaines" who fluttered about near by.)

The first word spoken on the stage of this new theatre was by John Gilbert, who read an original poem of Thomas W. Parsons, which had won a prize of one hundred dollars. The opening play was Sheridan's "Rivals" and a farce called "The Loan of a Lover" followed. According to the custom of the times, this introduced what are now known as "vaudeville specialties." A feature of the orchestral selections was the playing of the "William Tell" overture, the critics greatly praising this change from the "tinkling polkas" with which most theatre orchestras regaled their patrons. Only five performances a week were given here at first. Then Saturday matinées were inaugurated; but not for several years was there a performance on the eve of the Lord's Day.

During the season 1859–60 the name of the house was changed to the "Boston Academy of Music" and grand opera with Adelina Patti as the prima donna and Brignoli as the tenor introduced. Then (in 1862), under the management of Wyzeman Marshall, the former name was restored. Six years later, in February, 1868, came the memorable production of "The

White Fawn," that marvel of spectacular display which marks the beginning, in this city, of the kind of thing of which " The Black Crook" was the pioneer in New York. The Boston Theatre's chief renown, however, was to come from its association with great acting and great actors, among them Forrest, Edwin Booth, Charlotte Cushman, Rachel, Fechter and Irving.

From 1879 on Henry Clay Barnabee is associated with the history of comic opera at this house, first as a member of the Boston Ideal Opera Company and later (after 1887) as one of the newly formed company long known as the Bostonians.

It was at the Boston Theatre, in 1857, that Edwin Booth first met sweet Mary Devlin, herself then a member of the stock company, whom he soon made his wife; and it was during Booth's engagement here, in the spring of 1865, that the assassination of Lincoln took place at the hands of the tragedian's brother. On that historic evening Mr. Booth was seen in " The Iron Chest " and " Don Cæsar de Bazan," and, without having heard of the sad tragedy, retired for the night at the home of his friend Dr. Orlando Tompkins in Franklin Square, where he was visiting. " On the following morning," writes the son of his host [1] " an old family servant, his colored valet,

[1] In *The History of the Boston Theatre.*

greeted him with, ' Have you heard the news,
Massa Edwin? President Lincoln done been
shot and killed.' ' Great God,' said the horrified
tragedian, ' who did that? ' ' Well,' replied
the negro, ' they done say Massa John did it.' "
It was Dr. Tompkins, then proprietor of the
Boston Theatre, who hastened to New York with
Booth to comfort the grief-stricken mother.
Several seasons passed before Boston again saw
Booth on the stage. Then he became identified,
in the public mind, with that Prince of Denmark
who, like himself, had drunk the bitter water of
affliction.

Another Hamlet who greatly delighted Boston
Theatre patrons was Charles Fechter (pronounced Fayshtair by the person chiefly concerned) who played the rôle here in March,
1870. Clapp pronounces [1] Fechter's love-
making to have been the best he ever saw on
the stage, but he did not at all agree, none the
less, with the foreigner's interpretation of the
Danish prince, and was one day trying to make
his criticisms understood by the actor only to
discover that Fechter really did not know the
meaning of some of the English words upon
which his conception of the part turned! The
prince, said Fechter, did not procrastinate but
pursued his task with vigor. " Do you not
recall," he urged, " the words of Hamlet's

[1] In *Reminiscences of a Dramatic Critic.*

father in the Queen's closet, ' I come to *wet* thy almost blunted purpose? ' It was thus made plain that Fechter had never distinguished ' whet ' from ' wet ' and that he had no notion of the force of ' blunted.' His idea was that the Ghost's declared purpose was to ' *wet* ' *down* and so *reduce* the excessive flame of Hamlet's zeal."

Fechter was financially interested for a time in Selwyn's Theatre, which he renamed the Globe and of which he announced himself " sole manager " September 12, 1870. This house had then been in existence only three years and it survived less than three years longer, burning down May 30, 1873, in the same fire which consumed Chickering's pianoforte warerooms, the Chauncy Hall School and several other buildings in that vicinity. It was, however, soon rebuilt by Arthur Cheney, who kept control of it until, in September, 1877, it passed into the management of John Stetson. To us the house is of interest as the scene, on May 15, 1875, of Charlotte Cushman's farewell appearance in the city of her birth.

Henry Austin Clapp characterizes Charlotte Cushman as " the only actress native to our soil to whom the adjective ' great ' can fitly be applied." By birth, kindred and education she was Bostonian but she played her first part, that of Lady Macbeth, in New Orleans.

Nearly forty years later, when she acted for the
last time at the Globe Theatre in Boston, her
rôle was again — Lady Macbeth. It would be
very interesting to know how far and in what
manner Miss Cushman's early conception of
this great part differed from her later view of it,
but all that we are sure of is that she pleased
the audience, the managers and the members
of the company on both occasions. Clapp
speaks especially of the way in which Miss
Cushman's voice was " saturated with anguish "
in this part during the soliloquy near the opening
of the second scene of the third act: —

> " Nought's had, all's spent,
> Where our desire is got without content:
> 'Tis safer to be that which we destroy
> Than by destruction dwell in doubtful joy."

The words, he says, " were accompanied by the
wringing of her hands; and through the first
couplet, as she gave it, the listener was made
to gaze into the depths of a soul, soon to enter
the night of madness, already enduring the
torments of hell."

Yet *this* Lady Macbeth was a gaunt, stockily-
built woman of nearly sixty in the throes of a
mortal disease! Her return to the stage and to
the readings which marked her later life were
by the advice of her physicians, who thought
she might so bear with less anguish (her mind

being occupied) the inevitable suffering imposed
by her disease.

"I was born a tomboy," is the opening sentence of the autobiographical fragment once
written by Miss Cushman at the request of her
friends. In those days "tomboy" was the
epithet bestowed upon all girls who preferred
games and movement to sewing a seam, in a
quiet chimney corner, and the needle was never
a favorite implement with the great tragedian.
Though Charlotte was an apt scholar the family
circumstances were such that she left school
and began to help towards her support when
she was only thirteen. At this time her home
was in Charlestown, not in the North End,
where she had been born on the site now given
over to a schoolhouse bearing her name. Poverty was her lot for a long time, even after she
had begun to do well in her profession. For
as soon as she had secured a good position at
the Park Theatre, New York, she brought her
mother on from Boston and made her care and
that of the four other children the business of
her life. Then her dearly cherished brother,
Charley, was killed by a fall from a horse she had
given him — a blow from which she never quite
recovered. "The jacket he wore at the time
was always preserved," says Miss Stebbins, her
friend and biographer, " and went with them
from place to place through all her wanderings."

This loss was particularly hard for Charlotte Cushman to bear because hers was an ardently affectionate nature and she had just struggled through " the very hardest thing that can come to a woman." Yet because she had lived through this and once and for all gave over " casting about for the ' counterpart ' " she was able to give her entire self to her work.

In this and in the nobility of her character lies the secret of her success. Moreover, she had enormous courage. The story of her setting forth at twenty-eight, to conquer London, all by herself, is astounding. One very interesting rôle undertaken by Miss Cushman, while in London, — and in this country also, later, — was that of " Romeo " to her sister Susan's " Juliet." This was such a triumph of acting that James Sheridan Knowles, the great dramatist and critic, was completely carried away by it. Of her acting of the passage where Romeo flings himself upon the ground, " taking the measure of an unmade grave," he says: " It was a scene of topmost passion — not simulated passion; no such thing — real, palpably real; the genuine heart-storm was on in its wildest fitfulness of fury, and I listened and gazed and held my breath, while my blood ran hot and cold. I am sure it must have been the case with every one in the house, but I was all absorbed in Romeo till a thunder of applause

JENNY LIND.
Page 289.

ANNIE LOUISE CARY.
Page 296.

COLISEUM IN WHICH THE PEACE JUBILEE OF 1869 WAS HELD.

FITCHBURG STATION, IN THE HALL OF WHICH JENNY LIND GAVE
HER FINAL BOSTON CONCERT.

recalled me to myself." And of her assumption
of the difficult part of Claude Melnotte in
" The Lady of Lyons " Justin McCarthy says:
" I have seen Claude Melnotte played by many
great actors, from Macready to Irving, but
Miss Cushman eclipsed them all. She created
for me the only human, the only possible, and
the only endurable Claude Melnotte I have
ever seen."

It is, however, for her work in Meg Merrilies
that Miss Cushman will be longest remembered.
For this was the most famous and popular of
her efforts and it was, also, the only thing she
did which could deservedly be called a " creation." Scott's character was nothing but the
germ of the part as she played it.

Much of Miss Cushman's life, after she had
made her success, was passed in Rome, where she
had a pleasant home and exercised delightful
hospitality. Theodore Parker was one of the
Bostonians whose last days in the Eternal City
she sought to cheer. Two notes from him give
a pleasant insight into the sweet domestic side
of this great woman:

"MY DEAR MISS CUSHMAN: — Many thanks
for all your favors, — the drive the other day,
the old fashioned chicken pie this day. Alas!
I have no coach, no oven; but as you have
often taken a kindly interest in me, I think

you may like to read some of my latest publications, so I send a couple of little things which
came by mail and are the only copies in Europe."

. . . Another note says, " I thank you heartily
for the great loaf of Indian corn bread. It is
like the song of Zion sung in a strange land and
among the willows. It carries me back to dear
old Boston once more."

To Miss Cushman, as well as to Parker,
Boston was very dear. Three years after the
famous Radical's death she helped dedicate
the Great Organ (November 2, 1863) in the
Music Hall with which his fame is bound up.
Yet the triumph of her career, so far as Boston's
civic festivals go, undoubtedly came when the
schoolhouse which had been built on the site
of her birth and named for her was dedicated.
On this occasion she made what was called her
" maiden speech " to a thousand girls assembled
in the upper hall. She sat radiant upon the
platform, amidst teachers and dignitaries, a
flush of joy illuminating her face, already pale
with the inroads of the insidious cancer which
ended her life in five short years. She said
she had walked those streets as poor as any girl
within the sound of her voice. They knew
something of the niche she filled in the pantheon
of culture and art; but she assured them she

had gained this altitude by unflagging industry, unswerving principle, unfaltering persistence, untiring patience — by giving herself outright to her work; for she ranked painstaking above ability and genius.

Miss Cushman's delight in this school event was profound. In a letter written to a friend in England, we read: "When I went to my native city, where they never believed in me as much as they did elsewhere, I came to have such praise as made my heart satisfied. . . . I was proud, first, that an actress had won this favor; next, that for the first time it had been bestowed upon a woman; and then came the civic pride, in knowing that my townspeople should care that I ever *was* born. Nothing in all my life has so pleased me."

The last winter of Miss Cushman's life was passed at the Parker House in Boston. And there, surrounded by loving friends, she died February 18, 1876. She was buried in Mount Auburn after a funeral service in King's Chapel. From among the many contemporary tributes of pulpit and press I have selected the following by Rev. Henry W. Foote, then the minister at this historic church, because it does justice to the possibilities of the dramatic profession as well as because it memorializes Miss Cushman: "There was a time when the world sneered at the possibility of virtue in dramatic life, and by the sneer, and what went with it, did its worst to make virtue impossible. But it has been given to our generation to show in lives, among which happily our noble townswoman does not stand alone, that a pure spirit can go stainless, as the lady in Milton's ' Comus,' through corruptions."

CHAPTER IX

SOME ARTISTS AND MUSICIANS WHO MADE THE CITY FAMOUS

JUST as Benjamin West had been of immense service to Copley at a crucial point in his (Copley's) career [1] so the Pennsylvanian greatly helped Gilbert Stuart when that gifted young American presented himself, without any kind of introduction, at his London studio and besought his good offices. Gilbert Stuart, generally acknowledged to be our best portrait painter, was born in Rhode Island (in 1755), but inasmuch as he passed the last twenty years of his life in Boston, — where he died, July 27, 1828, — he comes properly within the scope of this book.

Almost in his cradle this born painter began his life work, and by the time he was thirteen he had taught himself so much that he had no difficulty in getting portrait orders which would have enabled him to at least live by his brush. But, just then, Cosmo Alexander, who was in this country on a visit, saw some of his work and was so struck with his talent that he took

[1] See *Old Boston Days and Ways*, p. 190.

him back to England with him, promising to put him there in the way of good instruction. Unhappily, however, Alexander died as soon as he reached home and poor Stuart was left, friendless and penniless, in a strange and hostile land. For two years he struggled manfully to educate himself at Glasgow University and then he returned to America in the hope of finding Fortune once more favorable to his talents. But this was at a time when men's souls were so tried by anxieties that they were not having their portraits painted, and in 1775 Stuart again sailed for England in the last vessel that left Boston harbor before the blockade.

It was at this juncture that he sought out West, who, seeing his promise of genius, taught him gladly and gave him a home in his family. In ten years he had made such progress that he was able to set up a studio for himself. With immediate success, too! No one but Reynolds and Gainsborough charged and received such large prices for their pictures as Stuart at this time commanded.

Then (in 1792) he grew suddenly desirous of seeing his native land again and, abandoning all his old friends, he sailed for New York. Two years there, followed by a sojourn in Philadelphia and another in Washington, intervened before he came to Boston. But when he did come he stayed the rest of his life, as has been said; and in Boston may be found today his greatest work, the famous portrait of Washington, for which, with that of Mrs. Washington, the Athenæum paid $1500 after Stuart's death.

For many years Stuart's home and painting-room was in Washington Place, Fort Hill, where his geniality and charm as a conversationalist drew many sitters, all of whom soon assumed in his presence their most characteristic expressions and so met half way the artist's determination to get a faithful portrait. Washington Allston has said of him that " he seemed to dive into the thoughts of men; for they were made to rise and speak on the surface." His task, as he himself put it, was " copying the works of God and leaving clothes to the tailors and mantua-makers," an interesting variation, surely, from the manner of Copley, who preceded him in the painting of all Boston's " best people."

During the last ten years of Stuart's life Washington Allston was his near neighbor, living and working in a barn on the Prince Estate, near the corner of Pearl and High Streets. Allston was born in South Carolina in 1779 and, after being educated at Newport and at Harvard College, sailed for England in 1801. There and on the Continent he enjoyed a period of study, but the richest years of his life were four which he passed in Rome living on terms of close friendship with Coleridge, Turner, Fenimore Cooper and Irving. He declared that he owed more, intellectually, to Coleridge than to anybody else, and Coleridge, in turn, pronounced him " the first genius produced by the Western world." It was generally conceded that, for two hundred years, no artist's coloring had so closely resembled that of Titian as did Allston's, and there was certainly very much of poetry in the conception of many of his pictures.

Allston's first period of residence in Boston was during the years 1809–10. At this time he married Miss Ann Channing, sister of William Ellery Channing, to whom he had long been engaged, and kept a studio in Court Street, between Brattle Street and Cornhill, where he executed several portraits at good prices. The early death of Mrs. Allston in England was so great a blow to him that for a long time he was nearly frantic with grief; but eventually his mind regained its tone and, in 1818, he again came to Boston believing that he ought now to give his own country the benefit of such talent as he possessed. In 1830 he was married for a second time to a sister of Richard Henry Dana and the next year he built himself a studio in Cambridgeport which was to be his home for the rest of his life. Here he worked, off and on, for years, — until his

death in 1843, indeed, — at the " Belshazzar,"
on which several liberal Bostonians had advanced part of the purchase price of ten thousand dollars demanded for it. Worry over his
inability to complete this work is believed to
have hastened Allston's death. The picture
is now in the Boston Museum of Fine Arts.

The next Boston painter of genius — for
neither Chester Harding nor Joseph Ames, who
were popular portrait painters of the nineteenth
century, deserve this appellation — was William
Morris Hunt, who made his home in our city
from 1862 until his death in 1879. Hunt was
born in Brattleboro, Vermont, in 1824 and he
entered Harvard College in 1840. But he
quitted Cambridge without taking his degree
and, after studying at Düsseldorf and in Cou-
ture's *atelier* in Paris, fell under the spell of
Millet, through whose influence his work grew
notably in depth and power. " When I came
to know Millet," he has said, " I took broader
views of humanity, of the world, of life. His
subjects were real people who had work to do.
. . . He is the only man since the Bible was
written who has expressed things in a Biblical
way." Millet's work is now so highly regarded
that it is interesting to note that this Boston
artist had much to do with bringing to him the
success he deserved, — and that the first hundred dollar bill Millet ever had came from

Martin Brimmer, to whom, through Hunt's good offices, one of the master's pictures was sold.

In 1855 Hunt returned to America and, by his marriage to Miss Louisa Dumeresq Perkins, became a member of Boston's inner circle. What " Hunt said," for he was a great wit, was soon quoted at every dinner-party. His home at this time was on Beacon Street, but he did his painting in a small room at the corner of Summer and Hawley Streets. There he painted his first great portrait, that of Chief Justice Shaw, which now hangs in the Court House at Salem, Massachusetts, and has justly been likened, for its wonderful rendering of character, to the portraits of Velasquez. Hunt had studied sculpture in his youth and there is in this portrait (as well as in that of John A. Andrew, reproduced in this book) much that suggests the sculptor's treatment of his subject. When the Shaw portrait was completed it was exhibited in the gallery of Williams and Everett, and while there, says Helen M. Knowlton, who was a pupil of Hunt and has written a sympathetic life of him, " excited more derision than any other portrait that had even been shown in Boston." Yet after Hammatt Billings had declared it " the greatest portrait that was ever painted in this country " the rule-of-thumb critics were so disconcerted that they quickly subsided. This portrait has in it some of the qualities which have made Sargent's Wertheimer the wonder of our own time.

From the manuscripts of Kate Field Miss Knowlton quotes the following vivid description of Hunt in his studio: "You like real artists and specimens of real art, so come with me to Summer Street, mount to the top of Mercantile Building, pause before the name of Hunt and knock. The door is opened by a tall thin man . . . crowned with a round hat and resembling Titian as painted by himself. You know that you are standing before an original man, before one who answers his own questions. . . . Hunt has genius, not fully developed, perhaps (he calls himself a student), but still genius, and is possessed of all the charming simplicity of character peculiar to it. Cordial in manner and tremendously in earnest while conversing upon real things, you thank the good stars that have led you to one of the elect, one of the few who make life interesting, who furnish the seasoning for the social pudding, a man with whom you can sit down and have a royal good talk, from which you arise exhilarated and refreshed, . . . for William Hunt hates sham in all its forms."

The great fire of 1872 destroyed almost all Hunt's drawings and sketches, — the work of more than twenty years. But he rallied from the blow with characteristic pluck and, five years later, was exhibiting in his new studio at 1 Park Square a very large and varied collection of works done since the fire. In the spring of 1878 he spent some time at Niagara and made several views of the Falls. From this work he was called to fill two large spaces above the windows of the Senate Chamber at Albany, which he did with great success. But his health had not for some years been rugged and he had overtaxed it. The following July he went to the Isles of Shoals to rest under the care of his friends, the Thaxters, and there, in September, the end came. His lifeless body was found floating in a small reservoir among the low hills, having fallen from the adjacent ledge during an attack of the vertigo to which he was subject. Mrs. S. W. Whitman, who was one of Hunt's foremost pupils, wrote of him, " Happily for us his works remain; and to those among whom he lived there remains, also, the glowing remembrance of a nature high, generous and true, — of gifts so noble and of a presence so inspiring that the very memory seems still, even as he seemed, ' a splendor among shadows.' "

What is generally regarded as Hunt's masterpiece, " The Bathers," has just been bought by the Worcester Art Museum for $10,000, the record price for a work of his. The picture represents a group of nude boys disporting themselves in a secluded pool overhung by luxuriant green foliage. The trees, the gray tones of the water, and the flesh tones of the figures, which are partly under water, combine to make a beautiful color scheme while the figure of one lad, who is poised on his companions' shoulders, ready to dive, is a superb piece of modelling.

And now we come to the musicians whom " fond memory recalls " in connection with nineteenth century Boston: Jenny Lind, who was married here, Ole Bull, who had a residence in nearby Cambridge, and Adelaide Phillips, whose early years were passed in Boston and who always called the city " home."

Let us then begin with Jenny Lind, whom Phineas T. Barnum brought to America in 1850 and who seems in every way to have been one of the few among that showman's offerings who was " worth the price of admission." It was a high price, too; $640 was paid in Boston for the first choice of seats at her initial concert in the Old Tremont Temple. Thomas Ryan, to whose *Recollections of An Old Musician* I am indebted for much of my information concerning the concerts of this period, records that he himself paid fifteen dollars apiece for three good seats on this occasion. And when Mlle. Lind gave her final concert in Boston, in the hall of the then just-finished Fitchburg

Depot, one thousand people paid a dollar each for standing room.

Whatever Jenny Lind did as a singer pales before what Barnum accomplished for her as a press agent. Probably a year in advance of the young woman's arrival in America he began to spread broadcast, through the papers of the day, tales of " the Swedish Nightingale," the " musical saint," the " angel of the stage " and the rest. A regular system of short paragraphs and lengthy histories was sent out from his offices and published far and wide, the reason being that he had agreed, without ever having seen or heard Jenny Lind, to pay her $1000 each for one hundred and fifty concerts *in addition to* paying all the expenses of herself, her secretary and her companion. Her pianist was to be given $25,000, her baritone $12,500 and both were to be free of all expense. Before the singer's departure from Europe the entire amount had to be satisfactorily secured and in order to do this — the sum necessary came to $187,000 — Barnum nearly bankrupted himself. No wonder he made it the object of his life to create an overwhelming interest in his " star."

Mlle. Lind's early history was accordingly told and retold: the poverty; the tribulations; the childish singing-days in the streets for coppers; her exquisite voice, which so moved a benevolent lady that she " took her up " and gave her lessons under Garcia; then years of careful training for the opera and preparations for a public début. Finally, all the great capitals of Europe are at Jenny's feet; in one the police were not able to control the crowds who wished to hear her and the infantry had to be called out! Yet, after six years of this, said the press-notices, Jenny Lind came suddenly to the conclusion that she must not longer mingle with theatre folk. Fortuitously, it was mentioned that oratorio was her best medium and that she was now giving away all her money to the poor.

Never before in the world's history had such talent been united with so many virtues and such great benevolence! So skillfully was the public assured of this by Barnum that, when Jenny Lind's steamer arrived in New York, enthusiasm was actually boundless. Twenty thousand people surrounded her hotel until midnight, serenading her with a band of two hundred pieces and hoarsely shouting her name. Not until Barnum had led her out on the balcony to bow her thanks, would the crowd disperse. Mlle. Lind was now a mania just as her manager had meant she should be.

But could she *sing?* you ask. Hear what Thomas Ryan, an accomplished musician, and for many years a member of the famous Mendelssohn Quintet Club of Boston, has to say on

this score: " She deserved all that was claimed
for her, — unmusical nonsensical stories excepted.　Her voice was of extensive range,
reaching easily to D. in alt, — a voice of veiled
quality with something of the essence of a tear
in it.　She had almost unlimited execution,
sang with great earnestness, and did everything
in a highly finished broad style.　Such pieces
as ' On Mighty Pens ' from the *Creation*, and
' I know that My Redeemer Liveth ' she sang
with so devotional a sentiment that she really
seemed like some inspired priestess proclaiming
her faith.　Doubtless many people in Boston
will remember that, when she had reached the
end of the last-named song and made her bow,
Daniel Webster, who was a listener, arose from
his seat in the audience and, with great dignity,
returned the bow.

" Her intonation was perfect.　Benedict had
written for her a very long *cadenza* to fit the end
of a *cavatina* from ' Beatrice de Tenda.'　The
cadenza was sung without accompaniment; it
covered two pages of music paper and was
written in a style suited to an instrumental
concerto.　Towards the end there was a sequence
of ascending and descending *arpeggios* of di-
minished sevenths which flowed into a scale of
trills from a low note to one of her highest;
then, dwelling very long on that note and trilling
on it, she gradually, tranquilly, returned to

the theme of the *cavatina*, when it was perceived that her wonderfully fine musical ear had unerringly guided her through the mazes of the long *cadenza* and brought her to the tonic note of the piece with surprising correctness of intonation. I think she was not overrated when called a ' great singer.' "

As soon as Barnum saw what his " Nightingale " could do he offered to share with her all the proceeds above $5500 a night and pay her her stipulated $1000 a night beside. In this way her receipts from the tour which he managed for her were over $175,000 and his over $530,000. Nearly all her share she gave, as she gave practically all her money, to charity. Yet there was a close approach to a riot, — glass being smashed and many ladies fainting because of the great showman's bad faith, — at the Fitchburg Depot concert, and if " P. T." had not fled by carriage from his quarters at the Revere House and boarded the night train to New York from the suburbs he would have been roughly handled by the indignant mob whose money he had taken for standing room that didn't exist.

The house in quaint Louisburg Square where Jenny Lind married her accompanist, Otto Goldschmidt, is still standing. It was then the home of Samuel G. Ward, a well known Bostonian who was the local agent of Baring

Brothers, the London bankers of that era, and the house with which the " Swedish Nightingale " did her business. In the *Boston Courier* of February 6, 1853, appears this brief notice of the wedding:

" Although St. Valentine's Day has not quite reached us, yet the ' first bird of the season ' has already chosen her mate. The queen of song has committed matrimony. Jenny Lind is Jenny Lind no longer, but Mrs. Goldschmidt. In plain English, the following record was made yesterday on the books of the Boston city registrar:

" ' Married in this city, at the residence of Mr. S. G. Ward, by Rev. Charles Mason, assisted by Rev. Dr. Wainwright of New York, the Swedish consul, Hon. Edward Everett, Mr. and Mrs. T. W. Ward, Mr. N. I. Bowditch, her legal adviser, and other friends, Otto Goldschmidt of Hamburg to Mlle. Jenny Lind of Stockholm, Sweden.'

" Mr. Goldschmidt has attended Jenny as her pianist for many months past. The match has taken everybody by surprise, though we must say that we were struck with something confoundedly arch and roguish in the twinkle of her eye when she sang ' John Anderson, My Jo,' the last time she appeared in public in this city. Such, however, has been the discretion of the parties that it may have been a ' foregone conclusion ' for years. The next song of the nightingale will, of course, be ' Home, Sweet Home.' May she live a thousand years and sing it every day."

For one of her tours Jenny Lind engaged the orchestral services of the Germania Society, an organization which first came to this country in April, 1848, and in which William Schultze was long first violin and Carl Zerrahn first flute. This organization soon put in a whole season in Boston, giving twenty-four Saturday evening concerts and the same number of public rehearsals on Wednesday afternoons. It appears to have been the precursor of the Boston Symphony orchestra which, since 1880, has been generously maintained by Mr. Henry L. Higginson. It was with the Germania that the famous girl violinist, Camilla Urso, of whom a competent critic has said that she was one of the few young wonders who developed into great artists at maturity, travelled as a star.

The red-letter musical event in the Boston of this period was the Peace Jubilee of 1869, organized and conducted by Patrick Sarsfield Gilmore, Carl Zerrahn acting as general musical director, Ole Bull and Carl Rosa playing first violin in an orchestra numbering one thousand pieces(!) the great singer, Parepa-Rosa, doing the soprano solo parts and Adelaide Phillips

the contralto ones. Gilmore had himself been
in the Civil War and the impulse to celebrate
in festive fashion peace and the gathering of
the Southern States back into the fold seems to
have been a genuine one with him. But besides
being a loyal Unionist and a respectable musician he possessed great executive ability and so
was able to inspire a large number of people
with such belief in the success of his undertaking
that they were willing to become its financial
guarantors. Accordingly, a wooden building of
good acoustic properties was erected on or near
the site of the Old Art Museum, — a building
capable of holding *fifty thousand persons*, including a chorus of ten thousand and the
great orchestra already mentioned!

The first question which arises in connection
with this " monster " festival is — where did
the ten thousand trained chorus singers come
from? The answer is " from all over New
England." This was the era of the " Yankee
singing school " and of the so-called " musical
conventions." On these latter occasions famous
oratorios were usually given and young singers
like Annie Louise Cary, — now Mme. Raymond,
— found a favorable opportunity to begin their
solo career. Nearly every oratorio worthy of
mention was thus known, either entire or in
part, to music lovers throughout New England.
And nearly all these people were ready and

CARL AND PAREPA ROSA.
Page 295.

CAMILLA URSO.
Page 295.

ADELAIDE PHILLIPS.
Page 302.

From photographs in the possession of Mrs. Martha Lana Shepard, Boston.

OLE BULL ON HIS FIRST VISIT TO AMERICA.

From a drawing by F. O. C. Darley.

CARL ZERRAHN AS DIRECTOR OF THE PEACE
JUBILEE.

From a photograph in the possession of Mrs

glad, after being carefully drilled by Mr. Zerrahn and his assistants in their home-towns, to come to Boston and help Mr. Gilmore make a Peace Festival. Of course real critics, like John S. Dwight, loathed the whole thing and said so. (Dwight absolutely refused to endorse the Jubilee in the columns of his *Journal of Music* even when requested to do so by Oliver Ditson, his publisher. And he is said to have spent the whole week at Nahant, where the strident echoes of the affair could not reach him.) But several good men had a hand in the celebration none the less: J. K. Paine and Dudley Buck directed their own compositions; Eben Tourjee led, when " Nearer, My God, to Thee " and other hymns were sung, and Julius Eichberg wrote for this occasion his tuneful " To Thee, O Country " which has since become popular.

The most marvellous thing about the whole Festival was that, although it cost $283,000 it paid for itself and showed a balance of nearly ten thousand dollars on the right side of the ledger! This, too, in spite of the fact that real cannon with artillery-men to set them off were used in the national airs, one hundred red-shirted firemen were drafted to bring out the staccato parts of the " Anvil Chorus," and all the professionals were paid for their services. Mrs. Abba Goold Woolson, who went to the

Festival on one of its big days, sent back to the
Concord, N. H., *Monitor* a sprightly account
of this experience by means of which all who
cared to might go with her " into the big tent."
Here are some bits of her article:

"Keeping fast hold of our checks, we walk
down the broad, empty aisle to the balcony's
edge, and look over into the parquet. What
an immense expanse of people and benches
spread below us; what a vast, lofty roof above,
all awave with gay banners! Up there, at the
right, is the organ, and the big drum, large and
thin, towers before it — ' Let Us Have Peace,'
on its head plainly visible. On the left of these
sits the chorus — all men; on the right, a
brighter throng — the women. Faces there
are indistinguishable, of course. It might
be called, indeed, a sea of humanity. . . . Down
again, go our glances, into the parquet. How
quietly the people have poured in; and how
small they look! Among them all we noticed
a large woman, escorted up the aisle. Her
shawl of pale blue crêpe, wrought with white
flowers, her large bonnet, and her breadth
of shoulders make us single her out from
the throng. She turns into her seat; a
glass shows the ruddy face of Mrs. Harrison
Gray Otis, the city's guest. . . . There comes
Gilmore himself forward to his position. How
they applaud him! One glimpse of the red

rose in his coat and his energetic bow, and he has whisked about on his stand, and his white gloves and baton are beating the air. Here comes the music. But we are not stunned. No louder than that? Now it bursts out strong enough. Still we are alive and still able to look about us calmly again when the piece is finished. The voices are full and rich and strong, but blent into strange softness, like the sound from the myriad waves of a distant sea. The Judgment Hymn and Janotti's Grand March, the first original music produced, rouse us more. The house is liberal with applause.

"But now everybody begins to look for Parepa. She seems the chief attraction of the whole festival. They say, around us, that she is to come up the stairway, behind the great drum. All are watching. The applause starts up, there is a gleam of yellow silk, and the queenly woman appears, following her escort down through the narrow aisles to Gilmore's stand. At every step the enthusiastic welcome grows and rolls in a stormy tide to her feet. See, the conquering singer comes! She stands one step below Mr. Gilmore, drops her bouquet, adjusts her music, and is ready. We take note of the gorgeous yellow tunic, deeply flounced with black lace, the light, flowing skirt, and her superb physique, and noble head — when hark! here come the notes, beginning the song from

' Robert.' We wonder that we can hear
them, how sweet, how soft, how clear, yet, too,
how far off! The homage is wild when it is
through. She sails out behind the drum again,
in spite of it all, but it is of no use, she has to
return, amid greater enthusiasm; but only to
bow, she will not sing.

"Now that Anvil Chorus is to come. The
red-shirted firemen, who have been for the
last half hour moving up and down the aisles,
are all in their places, extending back on each
side of the leader, fifty in a row. The music
begins. Their hammers are held in air ready,
but we see no anvils. Clang, comes the stroke,
Gilmore's arms swing alternately up and down,
and they obey them instantly, and cease instantly when he flings them back. Crash, the
guns thunder over our heads. How it starts
us all! The music pours out; the band, drums,
bells and the chorus, the anvils and guns, all
rolling multitudinously, make us wild. Handkerchiefs are in air, waving frantically. Hands
clap and feet stamp, and canes pound the
floor. Still the billows of melody roll on. It is
almost too much to bear. We shiver as with
cold, and feel like bursting into a torrent of
tears. But we wink them back, and keep on
waving fiercely. Over our heads, through the
roof windows, pours the sulphurous smoke from
the guns outside, and the roof shakes and jars.

The plaudits are still more tempestuous when it is through. The proud firemen evidently think themselves the chief element of the success, and they attract all eyes from their picturesque look. It is all gone over again, and the audience seem to wish it might never cease. . . . Those artillerymen out there must be kept busy loading their twelve guns. They are two hundred feet off; yet we wish they were a little farther, for there is a reverberation against the roof, a jar of the building which is not pleasant.

" When the national song is concluded, another storm of plaudits sets in, like that after the Anvil Chorus. All of us are insane again, and this time more so. We can scarcely keep from springing upon our seats and cheering. The men, here and there, do throw up their hats, and all break into an audible — what shall we call it? — not a cheer, but a groan of delight that runs around the house. What a proud moment for Parepa, surely the proudest in her life. As this is her last song, she has taken a chair, and intends to spend the rest of the afternoon with us. Now she is bending over, talking to her husband, Carl Rosa, who sits among the violins on her right. Of course she has to rise and repeat, and now her last note dies away. After that Arbuckle's trumpet, and she applauded him heartily with her white kids.

" ' The Harp that once through Tara's halls '
is sung by everybody and everything there, and
is unspeakably sweet and satisfying. We hope
the soul of Tom Moore is present to hear. But
the audience are now tired of applauding. We
all rise, as requested, at the last, for the Hun-
dredth Psalm, but nobody seems to sing; all
want to hear the chorus.

" Then comes the end. Every note has died
away along the pennoned rafters, and the
breezes only are swaying the sunlit banners. . . ."

The second Jubilee, held in June, 1872, was
to celebrate the World's Peace, — the Franco-
Prussian War being then just over — and the
thing " featured " was the band-work of various
European nations. On this occasion Strauss,
the composer, conducted his own waltzes and
Madame Rudersdorf, a splendid singer of broad,
classic, oratorio style, sang a number of solos.
This Peace Jubilee did *not* pay but left a financial
deficit which the sturdy Boston guarantors
promptly made up with such grace as they could
command.

I have said that Jenny Lind gave away nearly
all the money that she earned while in America.
One favorite form of giving with her was
towards the musical education of young girls
who had talent. Among the beneficiaries of her
kind heart was Adelaide Phillips, who had

already been doing things in a singing way on the Museum stage for some years but who was desirous of pursuing her musical studies further and whom Jenny Lind graciously fitted out with a check for a thousand dollars and a letter of warm recommendation to her own instructor, Emanuel Garcia.

Additional help being given to Miss Phillips by that " grand, upright and square " man, Jonas Chickering, she left home (in 1852) with her father for England, where for two years she studied with Garcia, a brother of the immortal Malibran, and possessed, like his sister, of much magnetism and power. Before returning to the great success which awaited her in Boston Miss Phillips had a triumphal season in Italy, her wonderful voice, sympathetic acting and charming presence uniting to bring her great applause wherever she was heard. But by 1855 she was back in her home city and, the following spring, she appeared with great success in Italian opera in Philadelphia and in New York. Her great rôle at this time was as Azucena in " Il Trovatore," then a new opera, in which Mlle. Fillippi, as she was called, was obliged to create the part. She made this gypsy mother a tragic heroine, just as Charlotte Cushman did with Meg Merrilies, and her rendering of the character has remained the standard ever since.

In oratorio Miss Phillips was no less successful

than on the lyric stage. That was a great
occasion when, on December 30, 1860, she made
her first appearance before the Boston Handel
and Haydn Society in the Messiah. " Her
rendering of the impressive Aria, ' He was
despised,' came not only with artistic power
but from a devotional nature." Miss Phillips'
last appearance with the Handel and Haydn
Society was on November 24, 1878. She then
sang, very appropriately, as it turned out,
Verdi's " Requiem Mass." Two years later,
she purchased the farm in Marshfield with
which her name is now so touchingly associated
and there, in 1882, she died, after a long struggle
— against ill health — to keep up her work
in the Ideal Opera Company, of which she was
an important member. Like Charlotte Cushman, with whom her career has several parallels,
she was buried from King's Chapel, all Boston
agreeing that " her private life was as pure and
blameless as her works were grand and en-
nobling."

Ole Bull, whose widow, a charming American,
still makes her home in Cambridge, was a very
gifted violinist and a highly picturesque figure.
Even in his old age his hair was heavy and
long, and when he had finished playing it
was always in artistic disarray. He was born
in Bergen, Norway, just a hundred years ago,
and he died, at the summer residence he had

there set up, at the ripe age of seventy. Ole
Bull seems to have possessed one quality very
rare among musicians, — real delight in giving
pleasure through his art. " It was not necessary," records Mrs. James T. Fields, " when
he was to give his friends the favor of a visit,
to suggest that he should bring his violin. He
never failed to remember that he could find
his fullest expression through that medium and
when the proper moment arrived was always
ready to contribute his large share to the
pleasure of the time. There was a generosity
about bestowing himself in private for others
which was delightful. He was proud to give
what he possessed. His friends cannot forget
his manner of going and standing with his violin
in the corner of the library, where, drawing up
his fine figure to its full height and throwing
back his head, he would stand silent until he
was prompted to begin." It has been said in all
seriousness that it was an impossibility for
" the heroic Bull " to sit down and play.

CHAPTER X

SOCIAL QUEENS AND THE WORLD THEY RULED

IT is a striking coincidence that three wives of Boston Otises should have been social queens in the real meaning of that word. The first Mrs. Harrison Gray Otis, who was described and pictured in the book preceding this one [1] occupied a prominent place in the republican court circles of her day as well as in Boston; for her husband succeeded Fisher Ames in Congress twenty years before he took up his duties as second Mayor of Boston. By the time Mr. Otis came to occupy the Boston position, indeed, his wife was in rather poor health, so that it was upon his young daughter-in-law, who had been born Emily Marshall, and had married his son, William Foster Otis, that the social duties of his home devolved. Of her charm and exquisite beauty mention was made in the earlier pages of the present volume. She died in the summer of 1836.

Then, speedily, another Mrs. Otis, born Elizabeth Boardman, came to the front in

[1] See *Old Boston Days and Ways*, p. 402.

Boston society. This young woman had been a famous beauty and belle even before she married the young son and namesake of the then Mayor of Boston. She had received the most careful education and the finest culture that the best masters could give, and she had had the advantage of life in one of those Boston homes made luxurious and beautiful by the East India trade. So though the Otis family stood among the highest in the land, it honored itself by an alliance with Elizabeth Boardman.

Very early she was left a widow. And she seems for a time to have fulfilled the lively traditions of that state. According to the gossips of the day she numbered among her admirers men like Daniel Webster and Henry Clay as well as many others of less renown.

Samuel Breck, who was in Mrs. Otis's own set, by birth, appears not to have approved of her at all. One finds among his notes (April 12, 1832) this reference to her: "This lady, a widow and mother of five children and already of a certain age, has been displaying and flirting during the winter in Philadelphia and Washington, giving the tone and assuming the lead. At Mrs. Lloyd's (Breck's Philadelphia sister) she found fault with the rooms; they were too small; she must have spacious parlors; her friends in Boston told her she must go home

and build, and when she does broad and lofty
rooms will gratify her vanity.

" This lady-traveller," continues Breck tartly,
" inherited about one hundred and fifty thousand dollars from her father, and is, for the
rest, a light-hearted woman, not destitute of
wit and smartness, and has been much attended
to by the fashionable circles of our city. She
is a little of a virago, too. It is said that in
Boston she frequently visited on foot in the
evening, always trusting to an Irish servant for
protection on her return home, and of course
declining the escort of the beaux who offered
their services. Some of these were miffed at
her refusal, and one evening waylaid her and
her Irish squire in order to frighten them.
She, seeing a man approach saucily, turned to
the servant. ' John,' said she, ' knock that
man down;' upon which John knocked him
down. This rough hint left her ever after un-
molested." [1]

Boston at this time was much too petty a
place to suit Mrs. Otis, it is clear. She must
have been very glad to sail off to Europe, in
1835, and busy herself there with the education
of her young sons and with her own further
development along congenial lines. She was
absent for about five years and when she came
back, thrilling in every nerve with the joy of

[1] *Recollections of Samuel Breck*, p. 285.

MRS. HARRISON GRAY OTIS.

From the painting by G. P. A. Healy, in the possession of the Bostonian Society.

Page 308.

MRS. JULIA WARD HOWE.

From the bust by Clevenger, in the possession of the Howe family.

Page 310.

life and with desire to make herself felt in her native city, she found that she had quite a task ahead of her. For the social machinery of the time was exceedingly ponderous. And Boston loved its own limitations.

An Englishman who was a resident in the town just before the middle of the nineteenth century has declared that everything essential to the most agreeable society existed there " with one exception and that is the spirit of sociability." Eating was the chief business of all gatherings, and Charles Dickens, who was here in 1842, observed, with thinly-veiled disgust, that at every dinner there was an enormous amount of poultry on the table " and at every supper, at least two mighty bowls of hot stewed oysters, in any one of which a half grown Duke of Clarence might be smothered easily."

The Boston notion of cordial hospitality, in the forties, seems to have been inviting the stranger within their gates to occupy a place in the family pew at church. " I am afraid to say," says Dickens, " how many offers of pews and seats in church were made to us by formal notes of invitation that morning of my arrival (which was on Sunday) . . . but at least as many sittings as would have accommodated a score or two of grown up families! " Not that Bostonians did not know how to be excellent hosts, when the spirit moved, or were

blind to the lack of true hospitality when it
exhibited itself in others. Mrs. Julia Ward
Howe in her delightfully written *Reminiscences* tells with sufficient point of the entertainment she and her husband received at the
hands of the poet Wordsworth. After their
letter of introduction had been presented a
note came inviting them to take tea with the
poet and his family that evening. When they
arrived, however, the sole topic of conversation
was a money loss the Wordsworths had recently
sustained by an investment in American secur-
ities, — and the tea to which they had been
bidden proved to be merely a cup of tea served
without a table. Yet even this meagre hospitality was lavish in comparison with that of
the Bostonian who, in return for the cordial
entertainment that had been offered him and his
while in Europe invited his former hostess to
call at his house on a Sunday evening *after tea*,
at which time his wife and himself would go
with her to church and give her a place in their
pew!

It was such a society as this that Mrs. Harrison Gray Otis attempted to humanize when,
with European *salons* in mind, she threw her
house open every Saturday afternoon and every
Thursday evening to all her set — and many
more. The stirring philanthropic interests of
the day she embraced with ardor, and she soon

proved that, where people of congenial tastes and real mental alertness are met together, there can be true hospitality on slender physical nutriment. For the " mighty bowls of hot stewed oysters " she substituted tea and cakes. And she even served " this and nothing more " at her home at the corner of Mt. Vernon and Joy Streets, during the week when she kept open house in celebration of the opening of the Boston and Montreal road and had President Fillmore and Lord Elgin among her guests! Mrs. Otis dared to be herself — always.

When the spirit moved she even ventured to write a book, thus blandly disregarding those who would place all literary women beyond the pale. *The Barclays of Boston* is interesting reading by reason of its reflection of the social theories of its author. " From the first days of their marriage," it declares, " Mr. and Mrs. Barclay were always at home in the evening, cheerful and happy, and delighted to see pleasant faces around them. This being perfectly understood, and also, from its great rarity, extremely appreciated, there was no lack of visitors. Indeed, no one can exaggerate the value of such a house as theirs had always been in a community where so few are opened in the same way. They conferred a great social blessing on many who, having no ties of kindred, looked upon their fireside as an oasis in the desert;

their house was, also, a resource for strangers; they received all the nobilities who passed through the city, and thereby derived a very signal advantage from foreign intercourse, which does a vast deal, in America, toward rubbing off the dust collected by describing, diurnally, the same circle of opinions and feelings.

" Everything was in daily use in Mrs. Barclay's home; she had no one article of table equipage that was better than another, and this saved a world of trouble, time and temper, the two latter of dominant importance in all households; for, if there is a bit of porcelain that excels another, it is sure never to be forthcoming, in an American establishment, when it is most required. Her dinners were excellent, and served unpretendingly, she having no desire to ape foreign fashions with a few servants, and to adopt the affectation of forcing three waiters to perform the service of thirty. If any shortcomings occurred, they were never perceived, or commented upon, simply because there was no ostentatious pretension.

" Mr. Barclay, being eminently hospitable, invited his friends freely; his wife gave them a gracious welcome, and he a hearty one; and their guests were not confined to the prosperous and those who revelled in luxuries, but embraced poor scholars, artists, and others, to whom a well-appointed repast was a boon indeed, and the charm of social intercourse a greater one still."

It was, however, in the sanitary commission work of the Civil War period that Madame Otis, as she came to be called, contributed what was perhaps the greatest service of her life. But here again she did things in her own way regardless of what " society " might say. For when there was a chance to make five dollars for the Northern cause by selling a kiss to a sailor she sold the kiss. At the beginning of the war she had been asked to take charge of the Evans House, which had been turned over to the city of Boston for the soldiers' use, and she did this, as she did everything, with marked executive ability. Hundreds of thousands of dollars passed through her hands and she herself gave $50,000, as well as all her time, to this fund for the soldiers. It is said that she never missed a day at her post throughout the war, never bought a new gown during that period and usually walked to the office to save cab hire. It was she, too, who, by opening her house for a public reception each Washington's Birthday, drew public attention to the desirability of making that day a national holiday. The honoring of Washington particularly appealed to her and she worked for it in many ways. She helped secure funds for the purchase of Thomas Ball's equestrian statue of Washing-

ton; [1] and for the purchase of Washington's
tomb at Mt. Vernon she gave a ball at the
Boston Theatre, on March 4, 1859, which is
chronicled as being " more splendid in its array
of fair women and brave men, and nobler in its
purpose than anything which has ever preceded
it." This affair netted ten thousand dollars.

It was for the Boston Theatre ball of a year
later, — that given in 1860 to the then Prince
of Wales, the late Edward VII of England, —
that Mrs. Otis's mantua-makers designed for
her the famous gown of old lace and purple
velvet shown in the life-size portrait of her by
George P. A. Healy herewith reproduced.

The first waltz ever danced on an American
floor had for its participants Mrs. Harrison
Gray Otis and Lorenzo Papanti. Since the
annals of Boston society were for years bound
up with the dancing academy of the Papantis,
— father and son, — we may well enough pause
here to consider this man's romantic career.
Scion of a noble house of Colonna, Lorenzo
Papanti, because a younger son, became an
officer in the royal guard of the Duke of Tus-
cany as a means to making his own way in
the world. While in this capacity he committed a political misdemeanor which soon
obliged him to flee his native land in the night.

[1] Characterized by Wendell Phillips as a "riding-master on a
really good horse, heroically staring up Commonwealth Avenue."

PARLOR AT 13 CHESTNUT STREET IN WHICH THE RADICAL
CLUB MET.

MRS. JOHN T. SARGENT, LEADING SPIRIT OF THE RADICAL
CLUB

*From a photograph in the possession of Franklin Haven Sargent,
New York.*

Page 319.

OLD ELM, BOSTON COMMON.

Page 355.

THE BACK BAY FROM THE PUBLIC GARDEN, 1860.

With barely time to get letters of introduction and to take clothing, — in which he did not fail to include his full court regalia, however, — he made his way to the old frigate *Ironsides*, the officers of which, knowing his story, took him aboard as a member of their band. In Boston he presented his letters and for a time eked out a scanty livelihood playing in the orchestra of the Boston Theatre. Then, with the help of his society friends, he founded Papanti's dancing academy. For a long term of years the little assembly room at 23 Tremont Street, opposite the old Boston Museum, was the scene of many juvenile trials and youthful triumphs. For there the two Papantis, father and son, successively taught little slippered feet to glide and not stumble, and awkward but well-meaning Boston youths how to bear themselves with courtly grace. Hundreds of memories centre about the tall spare man who there called out his directions over his violin bow and who was never visible save in the impressive elegance of a dress coat and a well-fitting curly wig.

But though Papanti was teaching Boston's young people to dance, social life was still very simple in the quaint old city. Few people went away in summer, previous to 1850, and those who did strayed not further than Nahant, which Tom Appleton had wittily dubbed "cold roast Boston." Many parts of Boston

were still green with gardens, and in the
softly cool evenings of September people sat
on their front door-steps after the early tea
necessitated by the one o'clock dinner and
perhaps sang together to the accompaniment of
a guitar. On " the Fourth " the leading women
of the city stood on their own house-balconies
and enjoyed the floral processions directed by
Rev. Charles Barnard of what was then the
Warren Street Chapel. Life was simple for the
most part. Girls walked to parties in couples
and young men " saw them home." This was
not a lengthy or involved process. For Boston
was a city every part of which was then within
ten minutes of every other part.

Arlington Street was considered " very far
out." Even as late as 1860 everything relating
to the Back Bay was so new that, for a long
time, Dr. Gannett's church, just beyond the
Public Garden, was referred to as " the Federal
Street Society's new edifice." It was in one
of the grand mansions on Arlington Street
that a reception was held one evening for
Fanny Kemble, to which Mrs. Stowe went in
the simple little black gown which she had worn
on a train-journey made for the purpose of
spending the day with her friend, Mrs. Fields.
Mrs. Kemble was in an elaborate costume of
purple and silver brocade, but Mrs. Stowe's
black stuff gown passed in the crowd all right.

she was in Washington and not Boston at
the time — that Mrs. Howe wrote her " Battle
Hymn."

This house must always be chiefly associated,
however, with Mrs. John T. Sargent and her
assembly of Transcendentalists. Charles
Lamb's remark about the fat woman seated in
the doorway that " it was a shrewd zephyr
that could escape her " had its application to
the person of distinction who could get in —
and out — of Boston without going to the
Radical Club. Not that Mrs. Sargent per-
secuted her lions or tracked them worryingly to
their lairs. Instead she made her house on the
Monday when the Radical Club was meeting
there a resort so intellectually stimulating that
no one wished to escape. The Radical Club
had its origin in the spring of the year '67 in
the growing desire of certain ministers and laymen for larger liberty of faith, fellowship and
communion. It had no formal organization
and its members represented all religious denominations. The Club's first meeting was held
at 17 Chestnut Street, the residence of Rev.
Cyrus Bartol, and for a time it oscillated between
that number and thirteen. But it never went
outside of Chestnut Street and it soon came to
regard the roomy parlor of Mrs. Sargent's
home as its permanent headquarters. Then
it grew in fame and numbers until at its

closing session in 1880,[1] nearly two hundred were present.

A journalist once remarked that the primary distinction of this club was that it survived for years without a kitchen. In other words it had a real reason for being. But it would be difficult to say how much of its success the club owed to Mrs. Sargent and to the gentle stimulus of the home in which it met. One habitué has spoken of the beautiful old harp in the corner of the spacious parlors and, on the wall, the life-size picture of Mr. Sargent's mother playing upon it; of the Gobelin tapestry and other famous relics of Paris's splendor and sorrow during the sad days of 1789. All the furnishings of the old parlors came originally from the Tuileries and were sent over by Col. James Swan, an ancestor of the Sargents, and the close friend and financial agent of the nobility and royalty in France. Two ships were loaded with these furnishings the purpose in sending them being to equip suitable dwelling places in America for many of the nobility who were to escape from France and take temporary harbor here. The plan miscarried and the contents of the first ship found their way, long afterwards, to the parlor of the house on Chestnut Street.

[1] Mrs. Sargent died at the New York residence of her son, Franklin Haven Sargent, May 31, 1904, aged 77.

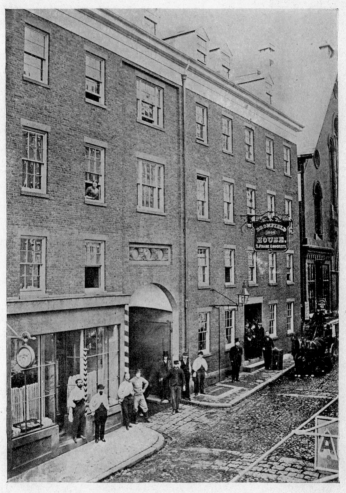

BROMFIELD HOUSE, ABOUT 1860.

Page 333.

OLD RESERVOIR, WHERE STATE HOUSE EXTENSION NOW STANDS.

There they formed the background for the
most extraordinary gatherings ever held in
an American city. Merely to name those who
read papers, contributed to the discussion or
sat quietly listening during the sessions of the
Radical Club would be to call again the roll of
the New England intellectuals. Emerson, who
was quite a regular attendant at the beginning
of the club's career, stopped going as soon as
the meetings were opened to the press because
he had an unconquerable aversion to being
reported. He never could be brought to believe
that interest had anything to do with the desire
to know of the deliberations of the club; he set
it all down to an improper curiosity which
ought to be snubbed instead of humored. But
those who were then reporters became later
very distinguished in literature. Louise Chandler Moulton, whose brilliant accounts of the
club's activities, published in the *New York
Tribune*, did much to increase its fame and
influence, Nora Perry, Grace Greenwood, Frank
Sanborn, Samuel Bowles and Kate Field, all of
whom helped the public to understand what
the club was about. Frank Sanborn's address
on the very modern subject of the newspaper
is delightful reading as sketched in Mrs. Sargent's little volume, *Reminiscences of the Radical Club*. Mostly, however, the topics discussed
were much more abstruse than this.

In 1873 the club gave a reception for Emerson and around the bright wood fire were gathered, among others, Whittier, Longfellow, Wendell Phillips, and the elder Henry James. Occasionally a big memorial festival would be held at the club, as on the occasion when Carl Schurz, Longfellow, James Freeman Clarke and many more assembled at a meeting in honor of Charles Sumner who had just passed away. Many eloquent and incisive things were said; but it is Whittier's quaint remark that gets quoted in connection with the affair, for, upon being asked to add his tribute he replied that he had no skill in speaking and that the idea of saying anything after all those delightful reminiscences reminded him of the dying petition of the captain of the Dumfries rifles, " Don't let the awkward squad fire a salute over my grave."

Even when the club was not in session choice spirits assembled in these famous old parlors. Franklin Haven Sargent of New York has told me of his boyish memories of those childhood days when everybody of distinction in the world of art and literature sought out his sweet mother in her Chestnut Street home: " the Longfellow brothers, so quiet and gentle; Walt Whitman with his shaggy hair and ruddy face, who called me, as did Charlotte Cushman, ' the young Greek.' Miss Cushman was a great friend of my mother's. I remember her as a devoted whist player and tiring to me because I had to wait while she and my parents and William I. Bowditch played cards evenings.

" Kate Field, — strong-minded, — I liked because she was of the theatre; Anna Dickinson, so awfully herself and badly dressed, a great chum of my father's; John Weiss, the nearest to genius of them all except — Emerson — so abstract yet human, sweet and deep. The sight of his regularly failing memory and faculties were painful. Colonel Higginson, gentleman and rhetorician, *par excellence;* my father, of the good old school, above all the gentleman; Mary Mapes Dodge, my mother's closest friend, brimming over with human nature and jokes. . . . One night, to my mother's dismay, the Chinese professor at Harvard stayed, after the others had gone, until 2 A. M.; finally, in desperation, she offered him a cup of tea — and one sip and he was gone — the Chinese convention. — . . . And more than anyone else I remember Wendell Phillips, my father's dearest friend, a wonderful orator and talker whom I revered for the martyrdom he had been through, a fanatic, but the most honest man I ever knew."

Such were some of those whom Mrs. Sargent drew about her fireside at 13 Chestnut Street. Certainly, *she* deserves a place among the social

queens of the period. For she was the only
woman who succeeded, during the most brilliant
phase of Boston's life, in *bringing together and
holding* its picked representatives of both sexes.
And this she seems to have accomplished not
so much by the possession of a brilliant mind as
by virtue of that far greater gift, a warm and
loving woman-heart.

CHAPTER XI

THE OLD TIME HOSTELRIES AND THEIR STAGES

IN the early days of New England [1] the tavern or "ordinary," was very closely connected with the meeting-house. At the time this relation was a necessary one, for it was only by thawing out at a tavern, before and after church, that human nature could prepare for and recover from the long dry sermons given in an unheated meeting-house. Was it because there was so much thought of a fiery hereafter in the religion of long-ago, I wonder, that the setting for devotional exercise was never a warm place? Or was it all merely a quiet arrangement to benefit the tavern-keeper?

Certainly, the discomforts of *staging* benefited the tavern-keeper. And the shrewd Yankees who started our early stage lines were not long in setting up, at convenient intervals along their routes, houses which in fact as well as on their sign-boards dispensed " refreshment for man and beast." Some who are always sighing for " the good old times " like, even in this twentieth century, to linger upon the

[1] See *Among Old New England Inns.*

charms of stage-coach days, the picturesque
driver skilfully controlling his four handsome
horses and heralding his approach by the winding of a bugle, the bustle of interest as the stage
arrived at each new village and the lure of
shady roads with their fascinating vista of
ever-changing horizon. Yet there were many
disagreeable things about staging. Though
Longfellow could spin such " Tales of The Way-
side Inn " as to make us fairly ache for a share
in the life of that hostelry, in prose, he thus
refers to his first acquaintance with the place:
" The stage left Boston about three o'clock in
the morning, reaching the Sudbury Tavern for
breakfast, a considerable portion of the route
being travelled in *total darkness* and without your
having the least idea who your companions
might be! "

Samuel Breck tells us that, early in the
nineteenth century, he was sometimes nine days
going from New York to Boston.[1] Yet Breck
lived to look back on these as " good old times."
For the forced familiarity of the railroad trains
was very distasteful to him. We find him
writing, on July 22, 1835, " This morning at
nine o'clock I took passage in a railroad car
from Boston for Providence. Five or six other
cars were attached to the ' loco ' and uglier

[1] Cf. Journey of Madam Knight in *Among Old New England
Inns.*

TREMONT HOUSE IN 1870.
Page 346.

REVERE HOUSE.
Page 350.

BOWDOIN SQUARE AND FORMER HOME OF FRANCIS PARKMAN.

TRAIN USED IN 1835 ON FIRST TRIP OVER BOSTON AND LOWELL ROAD.

Page 345.

FORT HILL SQUARE IN 1858.

Page 353.

much as possible, in order that the person who was to take the coach might be up and dressed when it reached his door. When the coach arrived there was no light inside and passengers waited until daybreak before they could see who were their fellow passengers."

Even as late as 1835 going to New York by stage was a good deal of an undertaking and for at least a fortnight in advance would be a subject of much conversation on the part of the intending traveller and his friends. Then the adventuring one would go to the stage office at 7 Elm Street, engage a seat for his journey and leave word for the stage to call at his home for him. The following evening at 7.30 the old vehicle would come lumbering up to his door and his trunk would be strapped on the rack behind. This process and the return trip to the office for the mail occupied until 10 P. M. when the stage would really set out on its journey. One who took the trip in the month of February, 1835, has thus described it:

" We left the stage office on time, five passengers on the inside. The route out of the city was through Elm, Hanover, Court, Cambridge and Charles Streets over the Milldam. The Milldam commenced at Arlington Street and ran over what is now called Beacon Street as far as Brookline Avenue. The toll-gate was located about opposite the foot of Clarendon

Street. Then out through Brookline, Brighton and Newton we travelled, stopping at the tavern to change horses, which was done every ten or twelve hours of the journey.

" After riding all night — and a bitter cold night it was and snowing fast — we arrived at the town of Sturbridge on the Worcester turnpike. Here we had breakfast. At this place we changed from wheels to runners. At noon we reached Hartford, Connecticut, and had a good hot dinner. From here the sleighing became poor. Many times during the evening the gentlemen had to get out and walk. Arrived at New Haven for supper — another wild night. We had our breakfast at a tavern on the old Boston Post Road. Every time the stage stopped for a change of horses or for meals the gentlemen went for something in the shape of hot toddy, the price of which was three cents. . . . The price of meals was: breakfast and supper twenty-five cents each — dinner $37\frac{1}{2}$ cents. You could make the latter price by paying a quarter and ninepence, which was twelve and a half cents. Most of the taverns set a good table with plenty of food well cooked.

" On arriving in New York we drove through the Bowery, Chatham Street, Broadway, Cortland Street to the stage house, arriving at noon having been thirty-eight hours on our journey. The fare, including meals, was $17.50. Tired and lame we were, too, when the trip was ended."

How greatly the coming of the railroad facilitated travel to New York is seen by the fact that, in 1839, persons wishing to make the journey could leave Boston for Providence (in all but the winter months) at four o'clock in the afternoon, taking the steamer immediately upon arriving in the Rhode Island city and get into New York at eleven the next morning. The total expense, including supper and stateroom, was now $7.00, a saving of $10.50 over the cost of that trip which, in 1835, made our friend " tired and lame."

The ramifications of the stage coach as a commercial institution were, however, so varied and so numerous that, for a long time, it was quite the custom to talk of the " calamity of railways." The *Boston Traveller* encouraged this cordially, for it was a " stage coach paper," issued on Tuesdays and Fridays (beginning in 1825), for the express purpose of giving all the latest news about stage routes. How large a volume of patronage the stage coach as an institution commanded may be judged from the fact that, in 1832, there were ninety-three lines of stages running out of Boston. Time tables and stage lists were issued by Badger and Porter from 1825 to 1836, and all this time the Eastern Stage Company, a consolidation of stage coach interests, was doing an enormous business in coach-making and blacksmithing as well as in its stages and taverns. Moreover, the taverns in the cities no less than in the country towns were, in many cases, owned by those who controlled stock in the stage lines. One chronicler tells us that " the taverns of Boston were the original business exchanges; they combined the Counting House, the Exchange Office, the Reading-room and the Bank. Each represented a locality.

"To the Lamb Tavern . . . people went ' to see a man from Dedham ' — it was the resort of all from Norfolk County. The old Eastern Stage House in Ann Street was frequented by ' down Easters,' captains of vessels, formerly from the Penobscot and Kennebec; there were to be seen groups of sturdy men seated round an enormous fire-place, chalking down the price of bark and lumber, and shippers bringing in a vagrant tarpaulin to ' sign the articles.' To the Exchange Coffee House resorted the nabobs of Essex County; here those aristocratic eastern towns, Newburyport and Portsmouth, were represented by ship owners and ship builders, merchants of the first class."

The Lamb Tavern here referred to was on the site of the present Adams House and its sign is mentioned as early as 1746 in the books written by foreign visitors to Boston. In later

PHILLIPS BROOKS, AET. 21.
From an ambrotype.
Page 359.

OLD TRINITY CHURCH, SUMMER STREET, ABOUT
1870.
Page 358.

OLD TRINITY CHURCH AFTER THE BOSTON FIRE.
Page 361.

ANOTHER VIEW OF THE FIRE RUINS.

days it was kept by Laban Adams, father of
" Oliver Optic " Adams. Near by, on Hayward
Place, famous today as the resort of Bohemian
diners-out, was another noted inn called the
White Horse.

In the nineteenth century, however, the
unique claim to a picturesque cognomen and
sign-board belonged to the Indian Queen on
Bromfield Street. This was a noted stage tavern
and it was kept - - till 1816 — by Isaac Trask
and afterwards by his widow Nabby. Then it
began to be called the Bromfield House. One
of its landlords was Simeon Boyden, father of
Dwight Boyden, the first landlord of the
Tremont House, and of Frederic Boyden, one
of the early landlords of the Astor House, New
York. Subsequently the Bromfield House was
kept by Preston Shepard (1823) who was, in
turn, followed as a landlord by the Crocketts,
father and son.

Mrs. Kate Gannett Wells has written charmingly [1] of the entertainment which used to be
offered in this picturesque old hostelry:

" In the days of the Crocketts, Col. Selden
Crockett and his son S. Frank Crockett (1844–
1869), its great courtyard was renowned for the
vehicles of all kinds which drove into it from
the suburbs and the city proper. In this yard
was a wonderful well, concerning which Mr.

[1] In the *New England Magazine* of January, 1893.

Sumner, a provision dealer of great local fame for his fresh and salted meats, always declared that ' one bucket of water from Crockett's well made better brine than two buckets of Cochituate.' The hotel also had a cupboard, which answered all the purposes of a bar; for in those days one might as well have a house without a roof as a hotel without a bar; but it was abandoned long before the hotel was closed.

" Mrs. Crockett herself presided over all internal affairs, with a matronly grace and old-fashioned New England order. Neither French dishes nor ' ambiguous entrées ' ever garnished the table. Dinners such as these were given — boiled salt fish with pork scraps, hashed calf's head and dropped eggs, corned beef and cabbage, cottage pudding and cranberry pie! . . . Once New York's Fifth Avenue Hotel was obliged to submit to serving Col. Crockett's original baked beans and brown bread, steaming hot, for a party of Boston merchants, who when in New York, ordered them to be sent on for their Sunday breakfast from the Bromfield House by the Saturday night train, protected by close coverings.

" Col. Crockett often stood at his front door on Bromfield Street welcoming his guests and leading them to the dining room where he carved. He was a man of undeviating honor, true patriotism, and quick kindliness, ' a good man to tie to ' as many a one said who sought his aid. This house was the dinner centre of the old-fashioned Jacksonian Democracy, Franklin Pierce, Caleb Cushing . . . Hon. George O. Hilliard and many others were constantly there; even Governor Andrew said that the best relief he obtained from his duties at the State House was the mid-day dinner at Col. Crockett's. At the farewell dinner, April 7, 1869, when the house was closed forever, B. P. Shillaber wrote an ode called ' The Old Bromfield House ' which was sung to the tune of 'Auld Lang Syne.' "

With the introduction of the " hourlies " several hotels quite near Boston came to be well known, among them the old Norfolk House, which stood on the site of the present Norfolk House in Eliot Square, Roxbury. This was the first public house in the vicinity and it was the terminus of a very profitable line of " busses." Previous to the inception of this enterprise (in 1826) the stage coaches on the various roads running out of Boston had been the only regular means of public conveyance by which a person could get from one part of the city to another or from the city to its immediate suburbs. But in the same year that Brooks Bowman was inspired to set up this service for Roxbury Stephen Wiley established a similar

line to Charlestown and Ebenezer Kimball a
line to East Cambridge. Ere long many such
coaches were plying between Boston and the
suburbs. Boston was connected with South
Boston, then a favorite residential section, by
a single coach which made six trips each day,
Sundays excepted. Its Boston headquarters
were at the Washington Coffee House, which
stood on Washington Street, near Milk Street,
and its route over the Dover Street Bridge.
Men did not use the " hourlies " much, their
principal patrons being women or old and
infirm persons. The fare was twelve and a
half cents each way for a long time, but by 1853
the line to the Norfolk House, of which H.
King was then proprietor, advertised a coach
every seven and a half minutes during week-
days at a fare of six cents.

The " Governor Brooks," an omnibus drawn
by four horses and having seats for eighteen
passengers inside and for six outside, began in
1835 to run regularly from Winnisimmet Ferry
at the foot of Hanover Street to Roxbury,
two and a half hours being allowed for the
round trip and the price of a single passage
being twelve and a half cents. In 1846 Messrs.
Hobbs and Prescott started the Dock Square
and Canton Street line, which was purchased
in 1851 by J. H. Hathorne.

For a long time Cambridge had only half

hour omnibus service with no conveyance
leaving Boston after twelve o'clock at night.
A story is told in this connection which shows
the kindness as well as the shrewdness of
President Walker.[1] He had been attending a
committee meeting of the Historical Society,
held at the house of Chief Justice Shaw on
Mount Vernon Street, and found that he had
only just time to catch the last omnibus out.
Just as he and Rev. George E. Ellis, with whom
he was walking, reached the head of Brattle
Street, the coach's starting-place, the president
said suddenly, " I think I will walk to Cambridge. There may be some young men in the
omnibus who would rather not see me at this
time."

Colonel Higginson has told of sundry narrow
escapes from " nautical eminence " experienced
by him and James Russell Lowell when —
while walking back to Cambridge on dark
nights together, after hearing Emerson lecture
— they would be hailed from the river by
seamen in search of those who could pilot their
craft up the Charles. For there were no lights
across the intervening space and Boston and
Cambridge were then very far apart — at
night. Up to 1856 toll was charged passengers
on this bridge, one cent for those on foot
and " fourpence " for all vehicles. A favorite

[1] President of Harvard 1853–1860.

sport with Harvard students was "running toll."

The Stackpole House, which stood at the corner of Milk and Devonshire Streets, was another famous resort. Originally a private house it was an imposing, Colonial building with a hospitable front hall running through its centre and spacious rooms on each side. It rejoiced in a front yard which contained two gigantic chestnut trees under which, on summer evenings, guests might be seen smoking real Havana cigars at three cents apiece and drinking such beverages as they might prefer at fourpence. A chained bear often disported himself in this yard and now and then a peacock strutted up and down airing his gorgeous tail and giving color to the scene. Other Boston hostelries of the olden days were the Mansion House, the Pearl Street House, the Commercial Coffee House, — where the Exchange Club now is, — Wilde's, Doolittle's and the Elm Street House. Most of these had courtyards paved with cobble stones and were favorite taverns with stage travellers.

At the Marlborough House, which long stood on Washington Street between Bromfield and Winter Streets (and was famous as a temperance hotel), Gen. Lafayette was entertained in 1824 with a banquet at which a distinguished company was present. Nathaniel Rogers was the proprietor here beginning in 1836, and on his parlor wall was this printed regulation: "Family worship to be attended every morning and evening. No intoxicating liquors to be sold or used in the house. No money to be received at the office on the Sabbath nor will any company be received on that day except in cases of necessity. Cold and warm baths are provided here for the accommodation of boarders and a vegetable diet for those who prefer it. The best efforts are promised by the landlord to furnish the table with the products of free labor. Smoking of cigars not allowed on any part of the premises."

This prohibition of liquor, tobacco and the products of slave labor made the Marlborough very popular with the anti-slavery people, most of whom regarded smoking as well as tippling and slave owning as a crime. Which reminds me of a story that Julian Hawthorne [1] tells to illustrate his contention that his uncle, Horace Mann, had a vacuum where his sense of humor should have been. Hawthorne, the romancer, had once admitted in Mann's presence that he occasionally smoked a cigar, whereupon the reformer, greatly excited, said, "Did I understand you to say, Mr. Hawthorne, that you actually use tobacco?"

[1] In *Hawthorne and His Circle*.

" Yes, I smoke a cigar once in a while," was the comfortable reply.

Horace Mann could not keep his seat. He started and paced the room menacingly. His high admiration for Hawthorne's genius and his deep affection for him as a man were obviously greatly shaken by this admission. But the need of being true to his colors at any cost was upon him and he soon said, in an agitated voice: " Then, Mr. Hawthorne, it is my duty to tell you that I no longer have the same respect for you that I have had." With which he turned and strode from the contaminating presence of an occasional smoker.

Among the inns mentioned in Bowen's Boston Guide for 1833 are the Exchange Coffee House, kept by Hart Davenport, with accommodation for one hundred and thirty guests and the price of board and lodging one dollar a day, seven dollars a week, and two hundred and sixty dollars a year. It is stipulated that " annual boarders " shall make express agreements with the proprietor and that all lodgers shall try to be in by eleven o'clock, the " retiring hour." The Commercial Coffee House, on Milk Street near Liberty Square, is referred to as the stopping place of " some Providence and hourly stages " and the City Tavern (Doolittle's) as the point of departure for " Salem, Gloucester and other stages." The Merchants' Hotel, 42

RENFREW BALL IN THE BOSTON THEATRE.

Page 366.

ANCIENT AND HONORABLE ARTILLERY DRILL-
ING ON BRATTLE STREET IN 1858.

THE LATE EDWARD VII. AS HE LOOKED WHEN
VISITING BOSTON IN 1860.

*From a photograph made by command of Queen
Victoria just before the Prince sailed for America.*

Hanover Street, is the headquarters of the "Providence and northward stage," and the Eastern Stage House at 84 Ann Street is the terminus of the line after which it had been named. On Howard Street flourished "Kilburn's (formerly Holland's Coffee House); " at 158 Washington Street the Washington Coffee House, kept by Lewis Boutell; "on Washington Street, opposite Boylston Market, the Lafayette Hotel kept by Mr. S. Haskell; " and on Washington Street, near Essex, the Liberty Tree Tavern of which one G. Cummings appears to have been the proprietor.

The naïve advertisements of some of these houses are quite entertaining. The New England Coffee House was inordinately proud of the fact that it had water on its fourth story "by hydraulic pressure " and that the entire house was lighted by gas. In the *Boston Advertiser* of September 1, 1831, I find a notice of the Julien House, 67 Congress Street, which informs the public that it is kept by "Miss Sarah Hawks and Company " and that "Gentlemen and ladies from the country who are in pursuit of board and pleasant situation will be thankfully received." But the prestige of the stage inn is fading fast now, for six months later (in March, 1831) one comes, in the *Advertiser* files, upon an editorial endorsement of a petition for a railroad to Worcester which has been

signed by H. G. Otis, Joseph Coolidge, Israel
Thorndike, Henry Sargent, Horace Gray, F. J.
Oliver and Robert G. Shaw. This paper was
not particularly dependent upon stage-coach
patronage and, from the very first, heartily
endorsed the enemy. Nathan Hale of the
Advertiser is for this reason often called " the
father of the railroad system of the State."

According to George Glover Crocker, who
has made a special study [1] of the history of
transportation facilities in and about Boston,
the first report to the Massachusetts Legislature in favor of a railroad for passenger traffic
was made in 1827 when it was decided that the
idea was feasible. At this time it was planned
to have a path on each side of the rails, like
the canal tow paths, for the horses who should
convey the cars. Already Gridley Bryant had
in this fashion drawn from the granite quarries
in Quincy to the Neponset River near by the
granite used in the construction of Bunker
Hill Monument. To be sure, there had been
much opposition to the granting of the charter
necessary for the construction of this railroad,
involving as it did the taking of a right of way
by eminent domain. But the patriotic purpose
for which the road was to be used finally caused
the vote in its favor to be carried by a bare
majority.

[1] *From the Stage Coach to the Railroad Train and the Street Car.*

Every step in the development of railroading was opposed by those endowed with " good common sense." Captain Basil Hall, who in 1827 rode by stage coach over the present route of the Boston and Albany railroad, said, " Those Yankees talk of constructing a railroad over this route; as a practical engineer I pronounce it simply impossible." And in the June of that year there appeared in the *Boston Courier* a satirical article from the pen of the editor, Joseph T. Buckingham, which ridiculed the " railroad mania " and declared a line from Boston to Albany to be " as useless as a railroad from Boston to the Moon."

Yet Buckingham himself joined the " fanatics " the next year. Nearly all the editors, indeed, printed congratulatory notices when, on March 17, 1834, the first New England experiment with a locomotive was made on the Boston and Worcester road, then completed as far as Newton. Regular passenger service to this town, with three trains a day in either direction, began on May 16, the trip being made in nineteen minutes and the fare being $37\frac{1}{2}$ cents. When Harriet Martineau visited us, late in 1835, she was able to record " very speedy communication " between Boston and New York by way of Providence, — the distance " being performed in twenty hours by rail-road and steam-boat." The same writer was a good deal impressed by the expenditure of " some thousands of dollars " to clear the tracks of the recently completed Boston and Lowell road from a single fall of snow.

Considerable local interest attaches to the development of this last-named railroad because it connected Boston with the new seat of textile manufacturing founded by a remarkable group of Boston men, prominent among whom were the Lowells, Appletons, Lawrences, Jacksons, Millses, Reads and Lymans. The charter of the Boston and Lowell railroad was obtained through the influence of Daniel Webster and provided that, for thirty years, no road should be built parallel with it. From the start this road was taken rather more seriously than the road to Worcester, whose average speed had been only ten miles an hour and which went so slowly on up-grades that farmers and berry pickers, stationed alongside the rails, could pass their wares to the conductor on the moving train to sell for them in the city.

Four years were required to build the Boston and Lowell road and, on Wednesday, May 27, 1835, its rails were used for the first time. The engine employed was the " Stephenson " and had been built by the Robert Stephenson Company at Newcastle-on-Tyne, England, the previous year. This highly important adjunct of the road was shipped from England to Boston and there taken apart and drawn by canal boat up the old Middlesex Canal to Lowell. On its first trip the twenty-six miles to Boston was made in one hour and seventeen minutes. The cars drawn by this "made in England" engine, were modelled after the stage coach and seated six persons. The conductor, called the captain, rode, without shelter, where the stage driver would have sat and the brakeman rode backwards at a corresponding seat at the other end. The engine had no whistle and there was no cab for the engineer. The particular guardian of the "Stephenson" was named William Robinson and he had been imported from England with the engine. He was an enthusiastic horseman and a good deal of a dandy. Often he would be so busy exercising the fast stepper he stabled in Boston that the train for Lowell would start an hour late! At first there were no baggage cars and no checks, and seats in the forward car, where cinders circulated freely, were somewhat cheaper than further back. For, as Tony Weller pointed out, travelling after an engine was not an unmixed joy.

The stage coach and the tavern had reached the height of their glory together and together they declined. For now an altogether different type of hostelry was required, and in Boston steps had already been taken to meet the new need. By 1828 it had become an actual necessity that the city should have a house for the entertainment of visitors which should not only be spacious but should possess as well dignity and beauty. Accordingly there was erected by subscription the Tremont House, the pioneer first class hotel in America. Peter C. Brooks and David Sears gave ten thousand dollars each to the undertaking, and Harrison Gray Otis, Samuel Appleton, Thomas Handyside Perkins, William Lawrence, Henry Hovey, Samuel Eliot, Josiah Quincy, Edmund Dwight, Robert G. Shaw, John L. Gardiner and Frederick Tudor were among the other well-known Bostonians who contributed liberally to the enterprise. The corner stone was laid July 4, 1828, and the house was opened to the public in October, 1829, its initial event being a subscription dinner over which Mayor Quincy presided. Among the distinguished guests were Judge Joseph Story, Daniel Webster, Peter C. Brooks and Edward Everett, the latter making the occasion notable by his delivery of a witty and remarkably felicitous speech.

" In the erection of this hotel," he then said, " Bostonians have certainly shown that they think the worshipful company of travellers ought to be as well bestowed as circumstances admit. . . . I will, with your leave, propose a toast: ' The memory of Columbus, the father of American travellers, who thought the world too narrow for him, even before he was sure there was any other; who crossed the unknown Atlantic for a trip of pleasure, and discovered a new continent. for his watering place.' "

The first manager of the new hostelry was Dwight Boyden and he belongs at the head of a noteworthy list of men who took great joy in serving the public at this famous old stand. In his day the dining room procedure at the Tremont House was as elaborate as the steps and figures in an old-fashioned minuet. " The waiters," says Benjamin F. Stevens, who wrote the hotel's valedictory, " filed into the upper end of the room where the landlord stood with a long white apron around him, and carving knife and fork in hand; and at the sound of a bell one seized upon a quantity of plates, another knives, a third forks, a fourth a lot of large soup spoons, and a fifth the smaller spoons. At the second sound of the bell they moved into line, and at the third marched with sedate steps behind the chairs of the guests, and simultaneously the bearers of plates, knives, forks and spoons, with a flourish of the hand, placed the different articles upon the table before the guests, and then gracefully stepped back into line ready to carry out their orders. In the meantime, the landlord was carving."

Similar customs were kept up here until the *table d'hôte* system was abolished. And the price of board was only $1.50 a day, $2.00 securing a parlor as well as a bedroom!

The bill of fare for the first dinner in the Tremont House has come down to us and is of decided interest because it is fairly typical of the state " American plan " dinner consumed by our grandfathers. The soups were terrapin and Julien, and terrapin in two forms as well as cod, bass, trout, haddock and blackfish were found in the " first course " (sic). Then for the " second course " came boiled chicken, boiled turkey, boiled mutton and boiled ham together with veal in several forms, chicken salad, and " vol au vent aux Huitres." The roast course included beef, mutton, chicken, duck, partridge, plover, quail, woodcock, mongrel geese and turkey. "Pastry, puddings, jelly, Blancmange and Meringues *a la crême*" made up the " fourth course," while for " dessert " were offered seckle pears and choice grapes.

One interesting custom, which obtained at the Tremont House, in its early days, was that of providing slippers for the guests while their high top boots were being blacked or greased. These, in various hues and sizes, were arranged in a row in the office. On New Year's Day transients were served, free of charge, with all the sherry they could drink and regular boarders with all the egg nog they found it convenient to imbibe.

In June, 1833, when President Andrew Jackson came to Boston to open the new dry-dock in the Charlestown Navy Yard and to celebrate the docking there of *Old Ironsides*, he and his secretaries, as well as Commodore Isaac Hull and Martin Van Buren, then vice-president, put up at the Tremont House. Here, too, Charles Dickens stopped on his first visit to America in 1842; and the house was the headquarters, the previous year, of the Prince De Joinville. In June, 1843, President Tyler and the members of his cabinet were guests here, — the occasion of their visit to Boston being the completion of Bunker Hill Monument. Among the theatrical lights who put up here, while playing in Boston, were Edwin Forrest and William C. Macready. Daniel Webster often stayed here, when he had come up to town from his Marshfield farm, and Mr. Stevens is authority for the statement that " here he wrote some of his undying speeches and orations."

The personality of the man in charge of the Tremont House must have had not a little to do with the enormous success which the hotel attained. Many of the landlords had as fine a sense of the dignity of their calling as have the doctors and lawyers of our own time. Paran Stevens, who was here from 1852–1863, was a born hotel man.

Mr. Stevens had previously had five years at the Revere House. This interesting hostelry is still entertaining guests in Boston. Built in 1847 by a company of gentlemen connected with the Charitable Mechanic Association it was named for Paul Revere who had served that association as first president. The house stands on the site of the dwelling and grounds of Kirk Boott, one of the eminent merchants of old Boston, and father of that Kirk Boott who was connected with early manufacturing in the city of Lawrence. Here Jenny Lind stopped during her memorable Boston season; and Presidents Fillmore, Pierce, Johnson, General (and then President) Grant, General Sherman, General Sheridan, the late King Edward, when Prince of Wales, the Grand Duke Alexis, King Kalakaua, the Emperor Dom Pedro, Christine Nilsson, Parepa Rosa, Adelina Patti and hosts of other well-known people have been its guests. From the balcony in front of one of the large parlor windows speeches have been made by many noted public men in response to the call of the assembled crowds. Another Boston hotel of ancient and honorable history is the United States, whose seal dates back to 1826 and which, though built before the railroad, had the good fortune to have

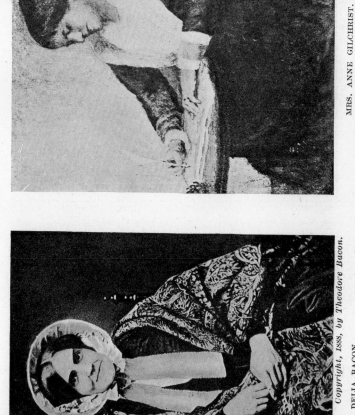

MRS. ANNE GILCHRIST.

*From the painting by her son, Herbert Harlakenden
Gilchrist.*

Page 371.

DELIA BACON.

From a daguerreotype taken in 1853.

Page 375.

OLIVER WENDELL HOLMES IN THE STUDY OF
HIS BEACON STREET HOME.

HOLMES' "THE LONG PATH" FROM JOY TO
BOYLSTON STREET ON BOSTON COMMON.

Page 383

behind it men who foresaw the coming of that change and planned for it. Daniel Webster lived here for a while and it was here that Charles Sumner entertained Dickens.

The American House dates from 1835. It was to this place that Emerson and Whitman adjourned for what Walt describes as " a bully dinner " after the Sage of Concord and the Good Gray Poet had for hours been tramping up and down Boston Common arguing about the wisdom or folly of publishing " Leaves of Grass."

Intimately bound up with the development of hotels and means of transportation is the growth of newspapers and increased facility in mail transmission. As late as 1835 it cost eighteen and three-quarters cents to send a letter of a single sheet from Boston to New York. Necessarily, therefore, newspapers preferred copying from sheets issued in other cities to maintaining their own correspondents in New York and elsewhere. In 1825 Boston had four daily papers, three tri-weekly ones, seven semi-weeklies and fifteen weekly sheets. News gathering then meant actual physical adventure and particularly was this true in the field of marine intelligence.

The first regular marine service in Boston was established by Samuel Topliff, who had been a supercargo in the employment of William

Gray and who was well acquainted with the hazards of the deep. He fully understood, also, how eager merchants are for the earliest possible news of their vessels. As it was only through the news-room (situated at first in the Exchange Coffee House) that merchants could obtain reliable information and so buy stocks intelligently, Mr. Topliff came to be a great power in the community. His accuracy was so well established that his name was frequently forged at the end of dispatches with the hope of enhancing the price of certain commodities and inflating stock values.[1]

A man thus indorsed would not, of course, long remain in another's pay and soon Mr. Topliff became himself proprietor of the reading room and by his marked ability in its conduct developed a business very satisfactory to the merchants and very remunerative to himself. Under him headquarters were removed to the Merchants' Hall building, on the corner of Congress and Water Streets, an admirable site for the reason that the postoffice was then in the same building.

Topliff's news-room was a kind of club as well as an information bureau. It was the headquarters for the merchants who dropped in regularly in the morning before proceeding to their counting-rooms and offices. Besides its

[1] See *Topliff's Travels*, Boston Athenæum, 1903.

" telegraph " (a system of signals operated on Long Island) it maintained two boats, from which Mr. Topliff or his assistant boarded incoming vessels in quest of the latest marine news. The facts thus obtained were recorded for the benefit of subscribers in one of seven books, each devoted to some branch of the subject.

From Merchants' Hall Mr. Topliff moved his headquarters to the Old State House and there his news-room continued to flourish until 1842 when he withdrew from the business. For some years before this he had obtained a good deal of his information by the use of a telescope stationed at the top of his house at 32 Washington Square, Fort Hill.

But just as the stage coach was superseded by the railroad and the tavern by the hotel so this picturesque method of news gathering was swept away when, early in the forties, Samuel Finley Breese Morse,[1] of Charlestown, invented and perfected the electric telegraph. The day of things " modern " was at hand.

[1] See *The Romance of Old New England Roof-Trees.*

CHAPTER XII

THE GREAT BOSTON FIRE

BOSTON had had several destructive fires during the period covered by this book. In 1824 a fire originated near the corner of Charles and Chestnut Streets, spread to Beacon Street and destroyed sixteen buildings, thus inflicting on the city the great loss (for that time) of $150,000. On Fast Day, in 1825, fifty stores valued at a million dollars were burned in Central and Kilby Streets, and in November of the same year ten buildings on Court Street containing many lawyers' offices were destroyed. In May, 1835, there came still another fire which rendered more than one hundred families homeless by the destruction of buildings in Blackstone, Pond and Salem Streets.

The *great* Boston Fire, however, did not come until 1872. It broke out shortly after seven o'clock on Saturday evening, November 9, in the four story granite block at the corner of Summer and Kingston Streets. Ere it was extinguished, it had burned over a space of sixty-five acres destroying property valued at seventy-five million dollars!

This fire is of interest to us not simply because it was a spectacular and impressive conflagration, but also because it utterly changed the aspect of Boston in that district over which it burned. Mr. Harold Murdock has very cleverly brought this fact out in the introduction to his little book, made up of what purport to be "Letters Written by a Gentleman in Boston to His Friend in Paris Describing the Great Fire." He here points out that a member of the Harvard Class of 1872 who might have left Boston immediately after his graduation to return to-day for the first time "would look in vain for the old landmarks and accustomed sights of his boyhood days." Christ Church, Faneuil Hall, the Old State House, The Old South Church, King's Chapel and the Park Street spire he would still find, to be sure. But the Common would have lost its gates and its Old Elm,[1] Tremont Street its far-famed trees planted by coachmaker Paddock, and Summer Street all of that old-time beauty and charm which made it, even in the early seventies, a region to be reverenced.

For Boston in 1872 was still a small city, comparatively, and a quaintly attractive one;

[1] The old elm on Boston Common was the first thing Dean Stanley asked Edward Everett Hale to show him when he visited Boston.

it covered a territory of less than thirty square miles and embraced a population of 250,000. Roxbury had been annexed in 1868, and Dorchester in 1870, but Brighton and West Roxbury were still separate towns. That the city had not yet learned how to deal adequately with a great crisis is, however, shown by what happened when this fire broke out.

To be sure, conditions were untoward. It had been a very rainy day and almost every horse in the city was ill with the strange disease which, for want of a better name, was called "the epizootic." Yet there were four hundred and seventy-five paid men in the Boston fire department — and the scene of the disaster was a centrally located one. The real trouble appears to have been that everybody thought some one else must have given the alarm, with the result that it was not given at all for some time. When the engines arrived upon the scene the fire had already made great headway. And although no wind was stirring it spread rapidly, crossing Summer Street and entering both Devonshire and Otis Streets. It also burned eastward down Summer Street to Church Green and from there went on rapidly to Broad Street and along High and Purchase Streets towards Fort Hill. Thus nearly everything in the territory bounded by Washington Street on the west, Summer Street on the south, the water,

Oliver Street and Liberty Square on the east, and State Street on the north was taken in.

Happily, Fort Hill which, at this time, had been cut away but not built upon, gave the firemen a vantage point of which they made excellent use and from this stand on the one hand and from the Old South Church and the then new Post Office, on the other, an attack was made with such steadiness and pluck that, *on Sunday afternoon*, the flames were effectively quenched. Naturally, however, the city was in a deplorable condition. Thousands upon thousands had seen their property consumed or had been thrown out of employment for they knew not how long, and the terrible excitement of the anxious night and day during which the fire raged had unstrung the nerves of the strongest. The whole community was on the verge of panic, for every vacant space was filled with hastily moved furniture or merchandise and pickpockets and petty thieves wandered to and fro at will. Finding that the police were quite inadequate to cope with the situation, a whole brigade of militia was called out to do active duty (with the Old South for their barracks) and guards were set to patrol the streets at night. Fortunately, these precautions served to prevent any very shocking breach of the peace.

Though the number of dwelling houses which

had been destroyed was comparatively small the loss of income by the stopping of employment was so large that measures of relief had to be organized at once. But the assistance freely and generously offered by the people of other cities was not needed. There was, indeed, a surplus of twenty thousand dollars — of the $341,913.68 collected in Boston itself — to return when the relief committee was dismissed. Fourteen lives were lost in the fire, seven being firemen. For the families of these the relief committee — of which Otis Norcross was treasurer — made permanent provision by placing in the hands of Martin Brimmer, Samuel D. Warren, Avery Plumer, William Endicott, Jr., and George Higginson $81,870.90 in trust. To aid working women and girls nearly seventy thousand dollars was expended in clothing, food, rent, sewing machines and transportation; to families burned out and to other sufferers coal, wood, stoves, furniture, clothing and other necessaries to the amount of nearly seventy-five thousand dollars was expended, while almost twenty thousand dollars was invested in the work of relieving the men who had lost their employment by the fire. The committee seems to have acted with great discretion in all this administering of relief.

Of all the buildings swept away by the fire Trinity Church was perhaps the most pic-

OLD FRANKLIN STREET, SHOWING THE ROOMS OF THE "BOSTON LIBRARY" OVER THE ARCH ON THE RIGHT.   Page 390.

THOMAS GOLD APPLETON, THE FAMOUS BOSTON WIT.

From the painting by Frederic Vinton, in the possession of the Boston Museum of Fine Arts.

Page 382.

THOMAS BAILEY ALDRICH'S HOME AT PONKAPOG.
Page 385.

THOMAS BAILEY ALDRICH'S STUDY, 59 MT. VERNON STREET.
From a photograph by Louis A. Holman.
Page 386.

turesque. Built (in 1829) of stately granite, with a tower of impressive architecture, it was at this time the weekly resort, because of the preaching of the young Phillips Brooks, of a large and varied company of people. Brooks had come here from Philadelphia in 1869, a handsome young bachelor of thirty-three, filled with immense devotion to his work and distinguished by rare powers of eloquence. It was largely through the influence of the Hon. Robert C. Winthrop, long one of the first citizens of Boston, that Brooks had been called to the conservative old parish, but Winthrop's enthusiasm over the young preacher was soon justified by the crowds he drew. From the very beginning of Brooks's incumbency Sexton Dillon had hard work seating the throngs who flocked to listen to him. Vainly did the worthy man strive to meet an emergency so wholly unlike anything he had hitherto known in his long administration. Then he tried to sort the people who presented themselves for admission! " Dillon once came to me in the vestry-room," said Mr. Brooks in speaking of the matter to a friend, " to tell me of a method he had devised to reduce the numbers who sought admittance to the church. 'When a young man and a young woman come together, I separate them,' he explained, and he expected me to approve the fiendish plan."

The journalistic habit of giving space to current church news seems to have dated from these golden days in old Trinity. I find the following description of a Sunday morning there: "The old building seems the fitting place of worship for the solid men of Boston. There is an air of ancient respectability about it. . . . The deep roomy pews, thoughtfully padded, seem adjusted for sleeping, and though seven can sit comfortably in them, if you humbly ask for the fifth seat in some of them, beware of the lofty look and high-bred scorn which seems to say, 'Are not the galleries free to negro servants and strangers? . . . I shall have to let you in, I suppose. Take that prayer-book and keep quiet; service has begun. Don't you see Mr. Brooks?'

"Yes, we do see the Rev. Phillips Brooks, a tall, stout, powerfully built man, with smooth, boyish face and very near-sighted eyes, which nevertheless, by the help of glasses, seem to search you out in whatever dark corner you may be hidden. He is reading the service with a thin voice and rapid, breathless, almost stuttering delivery and yet with a certain impulsive and pleading earnestness that carries even Congregationalists onto their knees, and takes them to the throne of grace."

Brooks felt very keenly the loss of the old church. Plans for the present edifice on Copley

Square were already underway, to be sure, but that he had a great fondness for old Trinity we see from his letters written at the time. " The desolation [of the fire] is bewildering. Old Trinity seemed safe all night, but toward morning the fire swept into her rear and there was no chance. She went at four in the morning. I saw her well afire, inside and out, carried off some books and robes and left her. She went majestically and her great tower stands now as solid as ever, a most picturesque and stately ruin. She died in dignity. I did not know how much I liked the great gloomy old thing till I saw her windows bursting and the flame running along the old high pews."

Yet Phillips Brooks's sermon in Huntington Hall, the following Sunday, was full of an onward and upward sweep, of insistence that life comes through death — the lesson of the fire.

CHAPTER XIII

SOME FAMOUS VISITORS AND THE WAY WE ENTERTAINED THEM

MANY of the famous people who came to Boston for a visit during the period covered by this book have been discussed in connection with the mission which brought them here; and others will, for lack of space, be passed over entirely or merely mentioned. But the visits of Charles Dickens in 1842 and in 1867 call for more detailed attention. His first coming was the sensation of the early half of the nineteenth century. From the day of his arrival in the city press and people vied with each other to do him honor and so great was his vogue that a wit declared him " Fanny Ellslerized," that piquant dancer having been similarly lionized during her stay in Boston. Three days after his arrival in Boston Dickens gave a sitting for the Francis Alexander portrait of himself now owned by Mrs. James T. Fields, and as great a throng attended him from the Tremont House — his headquarters — to the artist's studio at 41 Tremont Row as if he had been Royalty. Dickens has recorded in the

" Boston " chapter of his *American Notes* his impressions of the city and of its institutions during this visit of 1842. The most satisfying passage is that which describes his tour of the Perkins Institution for the Blind in South Boston and his wonder at what had there been done for Laura Bridgman, Dr. Howe's famous pupil.

During Dickens's visit in 1867 he was entertained by Mr. and Mrs. James T. Fields in the charming old house at 148 Charles Street in which Mrs. Fields still lives, surrounded by souvenirs of her many grateful guests. In that pleasant volume, *Biographical Notes and Personal Sketches*, this lady, who was Dickens's hostess on Christmas Eve and who afterwards, that same night, heard him read " the Carol," paints vividly the enthusiasm with which the beloved writer was received by his audience. " The whole house rose and cheered! The people looked at him with gratitude as one who held a candle in a dark way."

It was during this visit that there occurred the famous Walking-Match, posters of which are now dearly prized by American collectors of Dickensiana. Dickens had said that his agent, George Dolby, could outwalk Osgood; but James T. Fields was of the opinion that his partner, Osgood, was the better man. Accordingly, the match was arranged " for two hats a side and the glory of their respective countries " (Dolby was an Englishman, of course).

The time set for the contest was Feb. 29, 1868, and the course was to be over the Mill Dam road to Newton Centre, a route Dickens and Fields had already traversed in preparation for the " event." When the author and publisher went over the ground they became very thirsty, only to find that the stores of the village supplied nothing except a few oranges! They purchased these, however, and sat down on a doorstep to enjoy them. In the " sporting narrative " which Dickens had to write concerning the match (won by Osgood) he indulges in a highly characteristic sentence about this incident:

" Six miles and a half, good measure, from the first tree in the Mill Dam road lies the little village (with no refreshments in it but five oranges and a bottle of blacking) of Newton Centre."

Mr. Dolby, in speaking of the " Great Walking Match," was ever wont to affirm that England must have won had not Mrs. Fields arrived on the scene in her carriage, and, turning around, accompanied Osgood the rest of the walk, plying him the whole time with bread soaked in brandy. All, with the exception of

Osgood, of course, felt that she showed great favoritism in this respect: but she frankly admitted that she would have done the same by the Englishman had she met him coming in first.

To Dickens, as to many another distinguished visitor from abroad, Boston gave a ball; tickets for the function that bears his name brought forty dollars each! Usually, these great balls were given at the Boston Theatre, which was equipped with a floor made in sections and so arranged that it could be fitted on over the parquet seats, thus giving extensive dancing space on a level with the stage. Here were held a number of functions that figure in the social history of the period. The Tigers' Ball, February 28, 1859; the Mount Vernon Ball, March 4, 1859; Firemen's Military and Civic Ball, March 18, 1859; Grand Juvenile Ball, March 23, 1859; National Sailors' Fair, November 7, 1864; and State Military Ball, March 5, 1866. During the war a Fair in Aid of the Sanitary Commission also took place here and many a Bostonian, still living, recalls pleasantly the splendid entertainment and dance given in this place in honor of the Russian Grand Duke Alexis, December 8, 1871.

All these balls, however, pale before the memory of that given to the late Edward VII of England during his visit to Boston in 1860.

This is generally known as the Renfrew ball because it was as Baron Renfrew that the young prince was travelling. Entrance to the city was made by the railroad from Albany and the *Boston Journal* of October 18, 1860, records as an important item of news the fact that the prince was able to take a lunch of " cold ham, tongue and woodcock while the train was in motion! " The prince and his suite entered by the station in Longwood, were greeted by Mayor Lincoln and then made their way, attended by a large military escort, through Roxbury to his quarters in the Revere House. On the following day the young prince — he was then nineteen — attended among other functions a musical festival in Music Hall at which twelve hundred children sang to the accompaniment of an orchestra led by Carl Zerrahn. This the prince pronounced the most thoroughly enjoyable event of his visit.

But it is upon the ball, held Thursday evening, October 18, that chroniclers of the visit are wont to dwell with most unction. The committee in charge of invitations included such imposing personages as Longfellow, Edward Everett and Jared Sparks but lesser people might have been more efficient. The crowd was so great that three ladies fainted on the way to the ball room and one had a fit. Possibly, however, it was the flutter incident to meeting

JAMES PERKINS, WHO GAVE TO THE ATHENÆUM ITS
EARLY HOME ON PEARL STREET.

Page 391.

WILLIAM SMITH SHAW, FIRST LIBRARIAN OF THE
BOSTON ATHENÆUM.

Page 396.

CHARLES SUMNER STAIRCASE IN THE BOSTON ATHENÆUM.
Page 392.

READING ROOM OF THE BOSTON ATHENÆUM ON BEACON STREET.
Page 392.

a young prince, and not the crowd, which was responsible for this; one newspaper observes that " the excitement that agitated the minds of the young ladies as they prepared to enter was very great and betrayed itself in flushed faces, bewildered looks and disarranged gowns." Dr. Samuel A. Green, mayor of Boston in 1882, and for more than fifty years a prominent member of the Massachusetts Historical Society, tells me that the ball came near precipitating a crisis in governmental affairs, which, in its seriousness, was not unlike the etiquette differences between President Washington and Governor Hancock, in 1789. The question of the hour as regards the ball, was, " Who should dance in the first set with the prince?" This strictly social discussion centered around the wife of the governor of the State and the equally worthy helpmeet of the mayor of the city. Which lady should have the honor of being the prince's first partner?

Finally, it was amicably decided that to the wife of the mayor belonged the honors of this occasion inasmuch as the prince was the city's guest particularly. Mrs. Banks was accorded the prince's hand in the second quadrille. The prince did his duty nobly, dancing no less than seventeen times, and all who met him were charmed with his grace and his simple unaffected manners. Four of those

who were his partners are still living in
Boston: Mrs. John Quincy Adams, née Miss
Fanny Crowinshield; Mrs. Greeley S. Curtis,
née Hattie Appleton; Mrs. F. Gordon Dexter,
née Susan Amory; and Mrs. George E. Amory
who was Miss Carrie Bigelow. Among the
throng of girls [1] who would fain have danced with
him but did not was Fanny Carter Ronalds, —
then a bride of a year, — the famous Boston
beauty of the period, who, later, made her home
for many years in London, where she was an
intimate friend of King Edward and of Queen
Alexandra. The news of her death, following
close upon that of the king who was a boy in
1860, comes as this book goes through the
press.

The descriptions of the gowns worn at the
Renfrew ball make very entertaining reading
and I would like to quote several of them, did
space allow. But this, of a literary lady who
appears to have " helped the reporter out " is
too delicious not to be given:

" Miss Martha Haines Buitt, A. M., the
talented and accomplished literary belle of
Norfolk, Va., the author of ' Leisure Moments,'
and the contributor of several highly popular
pieces to the serial publications of the day,

[1] The " female preponderance " must have been appalling on
this occasion. Besides the 1100 tickets admitting *lady* and gentleman, which were sold, there were 525 for *ladies only*.

made an elegant appearance. She was attired in a rich white silk dress, with lace overdress, the body with deep points, the dress looped with mauve imperatrice ribbons, and studied [sic. and how appropriate!] at intervals with enameled flowers of same color, bordered with gold, bertha of lace, ribbon and flowers to correspond with skirt. Hair braided in massive grecian braids and decorated with white flowers and pearls. This dress was an exact fac simile of one worn by the Empress Eugenie on a recent occasion. Miss Buitt had a very elegant bouquet of New York manufacture, from the floral depot of Chevalier & Brower, 523 Broadway, under the St. Nicholas hotel. It represented an imperial star, and was composed of blush rosebuds, tuberoses, heartsease, acanthus and sweet alyssum; it was supported by an elegant silver holder ornamented with a deep white silk fringe. Miss Buitt attracted much attention for her admirable figure, her exquisite costume, and for her graceful movements in the dance."

Dancing lasted until half past four in the morning, supper having been served at midnight in the Melodeon, next door, to which a passage had been cut through for the occasion; but not until three o'clock was there room to waltz comfortably in the huge auditorium. Yet the visitors as well as those who entertained them seemed to find the affair enjoyable and the secretary of the Duke of Newcastle wrote in his published diary of the Boston trip that everything about it "was in better taste than the entertainment of the New Yorkers."

Other foreigners of high degree whom the City of Boston entertained during this period were Louis Napoleon, in 1858; the Chinese embassy in 1868; the Japanese ambassadors in 1872 and Dom Pedro II, Emperor of Brazil, in 1876. The emperor had expressed himself as desirous of receiving private social attentions only from Mrs. Louis Agassiz and Professor Longfellow, but he was anxious to meet Whittier, with whom he had corresponded both in regard to poetry and the emancipation of slaves, and Mrs. Agassiz arranged that they should come together. When they met the emperor would have embraced the poet, Latin fashion, but the diffident Friend shyly avoided the encounter and led the way to a sofa where, for a half hour, the two talked happily.

There is an amusing story connected with Dom Pedro's visit. He went to climb Bunker Hill at six A. M., and, of course, found the keeper abed. That functionary, when roused, was by no means predisposed in favor of his early visitor, particularly when he found the stranger had to borrow fifty cents of his hackman in order to get into the monument. Richard

Frothingham, who lived in Charlestown, happened in at the lodge, two hours later, and, seeing Dom Pedro's signature in the visitors' book, asked the keeper how the emperor looked. Putting on his glasses to examine the handwriting, the faithful guardian of the granite-pile muttered crossly, "Emperor, pooh! that's a dodge; that fellow was only a scapegrace without a cent in his pocket."

Two years after Dom Pedro's visit to America there came to this country, and in due season, to Boston, one foreign visitor who has always greatly interested me. She was Mrs. Anne Gilchrist, friend of the Rossettis, beloved of Walt Whitman and especially interesting to women of our time because she was the first woman publicly to express admiration for that puzzling volume, *Leaves of Grass*.

It was from New England, as we might expect, that the strongest opposition in this country to Whitman's poems came originally. On Boston Common, indeed, were fought out the first skirmishes of the battle afterwards waged so long and so mercilessly against Whitman's book, particularly the "Children of Adam" portion of it. Emerson and Whitman were warm friends at the time of the book's appearance and the Concord philosopher reasoned and remonstrated for hours with the revolutionary Whitman concerning the desira-

bility of omitting some of the poems. Up and
down the mall of Boston Common walked the
two, vigorously discussing the thing. In his
Diary Whitman records that every reason
Emerson advanced for the omission of the poems
in question was sound, every argument un-
answerable.

"Yet," he comments, "I felt down in my soul
the clear and unmistakable conviction to disobey
all and pursue my own way." Which decision he
forthwith expressed to Emerson. That famous
talk on the Common which resulted in Whitman's
adherence to Emerson's own precept, "Insist
on yourself," — as set forth in the essay on
Self Reliance, — occurred May 12, 1863. Six
years later a copy of the resulting volume was
sent to William Rossetti, Dante Gabriel's
brother, and by him lent to Mrs. Gilchrist.
Rossetti knew that this woman, who was his
close friend, had both the heart and the brain
to appreciate Whitman's integrity of purpose,
whether she should or should not admire all
that he had written, but he was somewhat
surprised that she at once accepted Whitman
almost in his entirety, and that with a fervor
such as the poet had never before called forth
from a woman.

"What I, in my heart, believe of Whitman,"
she then wrote, "is that he takes up the thread
where Christ left it; that he inaugurates in

his own person a new phase of religion, a religion which casts out utterly the abjectness of fear, sees the nimbus around every head, knowing that evil, like its prototype, darkness, is not a thing at all, but the absence of a thing — of light. . . . " And of the " Children of Adam " Mrs. Gilchrist made a descriptive phrase that will last for all time when she said: " This is not the heights brought down to the depths, but the depths lifted up level with the sunlit heights that they may become clear and sunlit, too."

To this woman who hastened to send him ardent expression of her faith Whitman's heart almost necessarily went out in warm affection. The letters which passed between the two during the eight years that intervened before Mrs. Gilchrist came to this country constitute one of the most remarkable correspondences of our time. It is to be hoped that they may not much longer be withheld from publication.

Mrs. Gilchrist's headquarters, while in Boston, were at 39 Somerset Street, and she has written that she made more acquaintances during her two months' stay here than during her whole life before. But I have sought in vain for a Boston woman who remembers meeting her. On her way to Boston from Philadelphia, however, Mrs. Gilchrist spent some time in beautiful Northampton, a town which, socially, reminded her of Cranford, but

" Cranford with a difference." For though the
place had its maiden ladies and widows, its
tea parties with " a solitary beau in the centre
like the one white flower in the middle of a
nosegay," she found the Northampton ladies
much more vital than those of Cranford and her
heart went out to them. I once had the pleasure
of meeting two of the ladies who entertained her
in Northampton and they recalled for my benefit
the pleasure they had had in receiving this
guest from England. She was dressed, they said,
in simple black silk, that afternoon she came
from her rooms at the Round Hill House to drink
their tea and present a letter given her by Mon-
cure Conway, whom a cousin of their own had
married. It happened that they had ice-cream
for supper and her naïve pleasure in this dish,
which was then quite a delicacy, especially impressed itself on the mind of her hostess. After
supper Mrs. Gilchrist sang some quaint old
songs very sweetly, and once, when Tennyson
was mentioned as " a great poet," she said
quickly, " Ah, but you have a much greater
one here in Walt Whitman."

In his poem, " Going Somewhere," written
after Mrs. Gilchrist's death in 1885, Whitman
calls this ardent disciple of his his " science
friend," and his " noblest woman-friend." But
the verse itself gives no hint of the great affection which inspired this " memory leaf for her

CHARLES COFFIN JEWETT, FIRST SUPERINTENDENT
OF THE BOSTON PUBLIC LIBRARY.
Page 399.

BATES HALL, READING ROOM IN THE OLD BOSTON
PUBLIC LIBRARY.
Page 399.

JAMES T. FIELDS.
Page 400.

THE OLD TICKNOR AND FIELDS BOOKSTORE, WASH-
INGTON AND SCHOOL STREETS.

dear sake." It is, indeed, Whitman at his very dryest. Which proves that he could be impersonal in treating a subject upon which he felt deeply. His moment of deepest self-revelation seems to have come later when, speaking to Horace Traubel of Rossetti's warm brotherly love for Mrs. Gilchrist, he said, " She was his friend; she was *more* than my friend. I feel like Hamlet when he said forty thousand brothers could not feel what he felt for Ophelia."[1]

Another literary woman who came to Boston during the period we are here considering, — though, in point of years, her visit ante-dated Mrs. Gilchrist's by a whole quarter of a century, — was Miss Delia Bacon, originator of the so-called Baconian theory. In Mrs. John Farrar's *Recollections of Seventy Years* may be found a highly interesting account of this writer's unusual personality and of her sad decline. " She was the first lady whom I ever heard deliver a public lecture and the hall in which she spoke was so crowded that I could not get a seat; but she spoke so well that I felt no fatigue from standing."

This Boston course was so successful that Mrs. Farrar persuaded Miss Bacon to give a series of talks on history in Cambridge and arranged for her a very appreciative class which used to meet in the large parlor of the Brattle

[1] *With Walt Whitman in Camden.*

House. It was after this course had been successfully completed that Miss Bacon first began to talk to her friends about going to England. They encouraged her in the idea, thinking that she could there make a success of her lectures just as she had done here. " But," says Mrs. Farrar, " after talking this up for a time I perceived that I was talking in vain. She had no notion of going to England to teach history; all she wanted to go for was to obtain proof of the truth of her theory, that Shakespeare did not write the plays attributed to him, but that Lord Bacon did. This was sufficient to prevent my ever again encouraging her or talking with her about Shakespeare. The lady whom she was visiting put her copy of his works out of sight, and never allowed herself to converse with her on this, her favorite subject. We considered it dangerous for Miss Bacon to dwell on this fancy, and thought that, if indulged, it might become a monomania, which it subsequently did."

A " Life " of this gentle monomaniac was written in 1888 by Theodore Bacon, her nephew (who has since died), and I think I have never read a sadder book. The little Delia was born, we there learn, February 2, 1811, in a small Ohio town whither her father had gone from Connecticut, to pursue his labors as a missionary. Things did not prosper, however, with the pioneer preacher, so, with his delicate wife and his six little children, he soon journeyed back to Connecticut where, in 1817, he died leaving a very helpless family. Schoolteaching, story-writing and even an attempt at dramatic composition occupied Miss Bacon in the years preceding her success as a lecturer. Her biographer hints at an unhappy love-affair which, coming to her at the mature age of thirty-five, may have had something to do with the unsettling of her mind. By 1853, she could think of nothing but of her Baconian prepossession and she found the burden of her historical lessons an intolerable one.

Emerson was very kind to Miss Bacon from the beginning of his acquaintance with her, about this time, but he never in the least believed in her theory of the authorship of Shakespeare's plays, always referring to it as a " brilliant paradox." From him she was obliged to bear this but she would not bear it from her brother, Dr. Leonard Bacon, a successful and much respected clergyman, and there followed an estrangement between them. The one thing of which she could now think was of England, to which place she sailed May 14, 1853, armed with introductory letters from Emerson to many people of literary prominence. Most of these letters she never used; she was much too occupied with what Carlyle soon

came to call her " tragically quixotic enterprise " to cultivate society. But the Carlyles
were most kind to her and, after her first bold
and brilliant paper had been published, —
through Emerson's good offices, — in the January, 1856, number of *Putnam's Monthly*,
Hawthorne, who was now United States consul
in Liverpool, also aided her, materially as well
as by his friendly sympathy.

Nothing in all Hawthorne's life is more
honorable than the noble generosity and the
unfailing helpfulness which he bestowed on
this forlorn countrywoman of his, whom he
never met but once and who was certainly a
very trying literary aspirant for one of his
nature to deal with. When the lady spoke to
him contemptuously of the " Old Player " he
told her that she really grieved him. Whereupon
she replied, " I am sorry to have hurt your
feelings with my profane allusions to the Earl
of Leicester's groom, a witty fellow enough in
his way. But the person you love and reverence
is not touched by my proceeding. *He* is the
one I am at work for."

Before the two met, the final blow came to
Miss Bacon. Several packets of manuscript,
which she had entrusted to Mr. Emerson for
use in *Putnam's*, were lost in transportation
and in addition the magazine refused to go on
with the serial publication of the work. Miss

Bacon's friends began to urge her by every mail
to come home. But this she absolutely refused
to do. To Hawthorne she wrote, "I *will not
go*. I will open a ' cent shop ' in my House of
Seven Gables first. There is not anything
which is honest that I will not do rather than
put the Atlantic Ocean between me and what
I came to find."

Hawthorne has told in his English note
book of his single visit to Miss Bacon. "I
was ushered up two (and I rather believe
three) pair of stairs" he there records, "into
a parlor somewhat humbly furnished, and told
that Miss Bacon would soon come. There
were a number of books on the table and,
looking into them, I found that every one of
them had some reference, more or less immediate, to her Shakespearian theory, — a
volume of Raleigh's *History of the World*,
a volume of Montaigne, a volume of Lord
Bacon's letters, a volume of Shakespeare's
Plays, and on another table lay a large roll of
manuscript which I presume to have been a
portion of her work. To be sure, there was a
pocket Bible among the books, but everything
else referred to the one despotic idea that had
got possession of her mind. . . . Unquestion-
ably she was a monomaniac; these overmas-
tering ideas about the authorship of Shakespeare's plays, and the deep political philosophy

concealed beneath the surface of them, had completely thrown her off her balance; but, at the same time, they had wonderfully developed her intellect and made her what she could not otherwise have become.

"I had expected (the more shame for me, having no other ground of such expectation than that she was a literary woman) to see a very homely, uncouth, elderly personage and was quite agreeably disappointed by her aspect. She was rather uncommonly tall and had a striking and expressive face, dark hair, dark eyes, which shone with an inward light as soon as she began to speak, and by and by a color came into her cheeks and made her look almost young. . . . I could suppose her to have been handsome and exceedingly attractive once. . . . She assured me that she was perfectly happy and I could well conceive it; for Miss Bacon imagined herself to have received (what is certainly the greatest boon ever assigned to mortals) a high mission in the world with adequate powers for its accomplishment. . . ."

Yet the privations the poor lady suffered while preparing her manuscript for publication were terrible. She lived on the poorest food, was often without the means of having a fire in her chamber, and she told Mrs. Farrar that she wrote a great part of her large octavo

volume sitting up in bed in order to keep
warm.

The introduction which Hawthorne wrote
for the book when it came out is very straight-
forward and very touching. In it he says that
the author " has given nothing less than her
life to the work." And this was literally true.
For scarcely had the monumental *Philosophy
of Shakespeare's Plays Unfolded*, been put between covers when Miss Bacon's mind failed
utterly. Through the good offices of Emerson
and Hawthorne she was then brought back to
her family by a young relative and, after passing some months in a " Retreat " at Hartford,
died in that city of her childhood September
2, 1859. Her best epitaph was pronounced
by Hawthorne where he says, " I know not
why we should hesitate to believe that the
immortal poet may have met her on the threshold of the better world and led her in, reassuring
her with friendly and comfortable words, and
thanking her (yet with a smile of gentle humor
in his eyes at the thought of certain mistaken
speculations) for having interpreted him to
mankind so well."

CHAPTER XIV

BOSTON AS A LITERARY CENTRE

THERE is a stiff-necked reluctance on the part of certain American cities to acknowledge that Boston is or ever has been a literary centre. Even during that golden age when Emerson, Longfellow, Lowell, Holmes and Whittier here sang together; Bancroft, Prescott, Motley and Parkman here wrote history, Garrison, Phillips, Parker and Sumner here preached reform — and Thomas Gold Appleton flitted about from circle to circle, cheering them all with his wit [1] — magazine articles used occasionally to appear questioning Boston's claim to literary distinction!

Emerson was, of course, Boston-born (his early home was on Summer Street near what is now the corner of Chauncy Street), and he occupied a pulpit here as a young man. All his life he came back and forth to the city from his chosen retreat in Concord and he never lost his love for it. Longfellow's relations with Boston were of a much more casual kind.

[1] Emerson called him "the first conversationalist in America."

The lode-star which drew him oftenest to the
city was Father Taylor, whose preaching in
North Square to a devoted company of sailors
seems greatly to have attracted the Cambridge
poet and scholar.

Lowell's closest association with Boston was
about the year 1857, when he became first
editor of the *Atlantic Monthly*, a position which
he held for four years. Holmes, however, whom
Lowell stipulated should be " the first contributor to be engaged " for the new magazine
if he were to accept its editorship, may well be
called the most typical Bostonian that our
modern Athens has ever known. To be sure,
he was born in Cambridge; but almost his
entire life of eighty-five years was spent in
Boston and he was very likely speaking of
himself when he said that for a Bostonian the
State-House is the hub of the solar system.
By reason of this remark as well as because he
is identified with no less than three Boston
streets — besides the " Long Path " which
stretches from Joy Street to Boylston Street on
the Common — there is no danger that his
name will soon cease to be linked with that of the
old town whose very ground he loved. " I
have bored this ancient city through and through
in my daily travels," he makes the Autocrat
say, " until I know it as an old inhabitant of
a Cheshire knows his cheese." For eighteen

years he lived in Montgomery Place, now
Bosworth Street; then from 1859–1871 he made
his home at 164 Charles Street, there writ-
ing, among other things, *the Professor at the
Breakfast Table*, *Elsie Venner* and his fa-
mous poem, "Dorothy Q." And when Charles
Street became too noisy, he moved to 296
Beacon Street, where his study in the rear of
the house overlooked the Charles River to
Cambridge and beyond.

It is hard to realize that Holmes was nearly
fifty years old when, through Lowell's acumen,
he first came into prominence as a literary man.
He has naïvely described his own surprise at
this metamorphosis: "I, who felt myself
outside the charmed circle drawn around the
scholars and poets of Cambridge and Concord,
having given myself to other studies and duties,
wondered somewhat when Mr. Lowell insisted
upon my becoming a contributor. I looked at
the old Portfolio and said to myself: 'Too
late! too late! This tarnished gold will never
brighten, these battered covers will stand no
more wear and tear; close them and leave them
to the spider and the bookworm.' "

But Lowell knew what he was about. He had
been present at many a dinner which Holmes
made brilliant by his wonderful talk and his
occasional poems, and he applied a friendly
pressure to which the little professor cheerily

responded. Already the "first contributor" had christened the new magazine *The Atlantic*, and when his department, The Autocrat of the Breakfast Table, was announced, the success of the venture became assured. To be sure, there were many who did not know what the *nom de plume* meant, and it was a joke, which may also have been a truth, "that the proprietor of a well-known religious weekly assumed the new department to be one given over to cook-book matters!"

Whittier carried a Boston latchkey during the early part of his life. For eight months, in 1829, while he was editing *The Manufacturer* he lived with Rev. William Collier at 30 Federal Street where Garrison also lodged. During the strenuous anti-slavery days he used to stop, while in Boston, at the Marlborough Hotel, of which mention was made in the chapter on the old hostelries, and, later, he was often the guest of Governor Claflin at the spacious house numbered 63 Mt. Vernon Street, which all but adjoins that made famous as the Boston home of Thomas Bailey Aldrich.

It is hard to say whether Aldrich is more intimately associated with Ponkapog, which I assure you is real though many have supposed it to be as fictitious as Puritania, or with this house at 59 Mt. Vernon Street. Since my own memories of him are connected with the latter place we will talk of that, however. Mt. Vernon Street is one of the loveliest spots in the world. Its houses have an air of old-fashioned solidity and of comfort not to be found in any on Boston's " made land," while from the top of the hill, — and Aldrich's house is just at the apex, — one can see the beautiful Charles River, winding lazily into the distance. Some of the homes retain the little blue panes of glass, by passing through which the sun was supposed to acquire even more than its natural salubrity, and in front of the Aldrich house, though it is in the very heart of Boston, is a gay little patch of lawn upon which the sun through the adjacent trees makes quaint arabesques of shade.

To reach the study, which was the heart of the house, one climbed a fascinating flight of winding stairs, — giving glimpses here and there of all kinds of beautiful things, Oriental rugs, pictures and bits of statuary, — or else, entrusting one self to a tiny iron cage, was literally lifted, by a man above and a woman below, — right into the presence of the poet. Aldrich must have been a singularly fair-minded man. He and Whitman never got on — so widely differentiated in temperament were they — and I don't think the younger poet could easily have forgiven the elder for the way in which, one day at Pfaff's, he replied, to his eager, "Oh, Walt, did you know I had a poem in this week's *Home Journal?*" with a nonchalant, "Oh, yes, Tom. They shoved the paper under my door this morning and I heard your little tinkle." Yet on the walls of Aldrich's study, I noticed opposite a portrait of Edwin Booth a photograph of Walt Whitman!

Bancroft and Hawthorne can be more easily connected with the Boston Custom House than with any other institution of the city, for it was while the historian was collector of the Port that he gave Hawthorne that place in the government's service from which the young genius was able to save money enough to buy some stock in Brook Farm. Hawthorne, because of his shy temperament and his poverty, was so obscure as to have been practically unknown in Boston during this period. His son-in-law records that his chief distinction, to the popular eye, at this time, lay in the fact that he was extremely fond of martial music and could generally be found — " a tall shapely figure rendered military by the thick mustache, — following any procession headed by a band! "

The historian Prescott belongs undeniably to Boston. The house at 55 Beacon Street in which he lived from 1845 to 1859 is still standing and is one of the most picturesque of the old homes opposite the Common. Here, he wrote the *History of the Conquest of Peru* and the *History of the Reign of Philip the Second.*

That Boston home of John Lothrop Motley in whose garret he, as a lad, used to play with Wendell Phillips and Tom Appleton, was on Walnut Street, but it is with the houses at 11 Chestnut Street and at 2 Park Street that the later life of the author of the *Rise of the Dutch Republic* is associated. Parkman, too, is identified with Chestnut Street. For nearly thirty years he occupied the house which is there numbered fifty, painstakingly working out, without the use of his eyes, his marvellous series of works dealing with France and England in North America.

One thing which has always helped to make Boston a literary centre — and will continue so to do in spite of the envious elsewhere — is its great library advantages. Colonel Higginson, when writing for *Harper's Magazine* the series of historical articles used by that publication in 1885, had to obtain his books in Boston and Cambridge and have them sent to New York for consultation. The collections at the Harvard College library are easily accessible to Boston literary workers, and the State Library, the Athenæum and the Boston Public Library are rich mines for those who must use many books.

The Boston Athenæum sprang from a magazine, which, like many another young venture of its kind, did not pay, and after six months was abandoned by its projector, Phineas Adams,

CHARLOTTE CUSHMAN.
Page 274.

HENRY CLAY BARNABEE.
Page 271.

JOHN BOYLE O'REILLY.

From a photograph by Chickering, in the possession of Miss Mary Boyle O'Reilly.

Page 403.

ARCHBISHOP WILLIAMS.

From the painting by Frederic Vinton, in the Archiepiscopal Residence, Boston.

Page 403.

a poor Harvard student. Its printers, Monroe & Francis, determined, however, to carry it on, and Rev. William Emerson, the father of Ralph Waldo Emerson, was invited to become its editor. Through him a number of gentlemen and scholars of the day became interested in the magazine, and after binding themselves into a club, continued it under the name *Monthly Anthology and Boston Review.*

There were in all nineteen of these men, and they, it appears, are entitled to be remembered as the founders of the Boston Athenæum. For they soon organized, from the profits of the magazine, and from private subscriptions, the nucleus of the library.

The " Reading Room," as it was originally called, was opened in Joy's Building on Congress Street, Jan. 1, 1807. In February of that same year the subscribers were incorporated as " proprietors of the Boston Athenæum." John Sylvester, William Emerson, William S. Shaw, William Tudor, Jr., Peter O. Thacher and Edmund T. Davis being among the promoters of the undertaking.

The first officers were appointed April 7, 1807, as follows: Hon. Theophilus Parsons, president, Hon. John Davis, vice president, John Lowell, treasurer, William S. Shaw, secretary, Rev. William Emerson, Rev. John T. Kirkland, D. D., Peter Thacher, R. H. Gardiner and Rev. J. S. Buckminster, trustees. To these were added, July 16, Hon. Harrison Gray Otis, Samuel Eliot and James Perkins.

A decided spurt to the new undertaking was given by an article in the *Monthly Anthology* for May, 1807, written by Rev. John T. Kirkland, D. D., president of Harvard College. Soon after this 150 shares at $300 were sold, thus adding what an old writer on the subject has termed " a large number of respectable names " to the corporation. Shares today bring about $400, and are eagerly sought by good Bostonians.

For some time after its inception the Athenæum was the only library of importance accessible in any way to the public. The older " Boston Library," a proprietary institution, which formerly had its quarters in Franklin Street over the arch [hence Arch Street], — moving later to Boylston Place, — was neither so general nor so extensive as the younger institution, and the Public Library was not established for many years, and then only after a plan for making the Athenæum public had failed. But the Anthology Club's institution was much more than a library. Like the original Athenæum in Rome, its purpose was the promotion of literary and scientific studies, and anything tending towards these ends found encouragement there. Its art exhibitions used to bring in a yearly income of from $1000 to $2000, which, with various special funds, was spent judiciously in accessions.

The Athenæum has had many homes. From Congress Street it went to Scollay's Building, in what is today Scollay Square, and in March, 1809, a house was purchased on Tremont Street, on the site of what was until a few years ago the home of the Massachusetts Historical Society.

Here it continued, its collection of books gradually increasing in number until 1822, when it received from James Perkins the noble gift of his mansion house on Pearl Street, to be used as the library's home. At this time it possessed over 17,000 volumes and 10,000 pamphlets.

The rules provided for the free accommodation in the reading room of the governor and his council, the lieutenant-governor and members of the Massachusetts legislature, judges of the supreme courts and courts of the United States, officers and resident graduates of Harvard, Amherst and Williams College, and of the Hanover theological school, the presidents of the American Academy, the historical society, the medical society, the agricultural society, the Salem Athenæum and the East India Marine Society of Salem, as well as clergymen settled in Boston. These last dignitaries were further allowed to take books home.

It is interesting to learn that early habitués
of the Athenæum were greatly shocked by an
innovation which gave to Hannah Adams, the
first American woman to earn her living with
her pen — and a very scanty living it was —
the freedom of the library. This was in Miss
Adams' old age, after she had become deaf as
well as nearly blind. But in spite of her infirm-
ities she retained her keen love of books and
was frequently so lost in the dusty tomes that
she forgot to eat and could not be roused by the
librarian when he departed at noon to satisfy
his healthy man's appetite. He would lock
her up with the books, therefore, only to find
when he returned that she was as unconscious
of him as before. Miss Adams herself seems to
have felt the strangeness of her occupation,
for she laments in her memoirs that circumstances forced her to " do business out of the
female line and so expose herself to the ridicule
of males." The portrait of this first woman
worker has an honored place on the walls of
one of the Athenæum rooms, along with the
pictures of many famous literary men who have
used the library.

The corner-stone of the present building on
Beacon Street was laid in April, 1847, and the
building was completed and occupied in 1849.
The corporation had the good fortune to acquire,
in 1848, a large part of George Washington's

library for the small sum of $4000. These books were in a very good state of preservation, and are now, of course, worth many times the original price paid. Best of all, the Washington library beautifully pieces out the very valuable collection of historical works for which, with works on biography and art, the Athenæum is famous. Another priceless set of books in the Athenæum are those volumes given to King's Chapel in 1698 by William III.

The library is well endowed, having an income-producing fund which amounts to half a million. For many years the American Academy of Arts and Sciences, the oldest literary institution in Boston and the second oldest in America, had its headquarters here, but now these are in the rooms of the Massachusetts Historical Society.

There are in all 1049 stockholders, who, with their families, are privileged to use the library, and may themselves go to the shelves for anything they wish. Students and authors from a distance are always welcome, however, and the courteous attendants succeed admirably in making even casual investigators feel at home in the pleasant old halls, where Tabby the Wise, the Athenæum cat, who seems to have assimilated the quiet air of refinement and culture which pervades the classic old library, sleeps comfortably in a sunny corner, a fit symbol of the unstrenuous life for which this institution stands.

The cat is not the only frequenter of the Athenæum who enjoys cozy naps within its sacred precincts. A number of venerable Bostonians come here every day quite as much, it would seem, for the sake of the soporific as the scholarly properties of the place.

Hawthorne has penned one of his most characteristic, although least known tales, about a good old Boston worthy whom he used to see nodding over his newspaper at the Athenæum. The story is called "The Ghost of Dr. Harris," and was written from Liverpool in 1856 for Mrs. J. P. Heywood, to whom the great romancer had once told it. It tells in Hawthorne's own charming and inimitable style how he saw the old gentleman Harris reading the newspaper in his accustomed place the evening of the day on which the man had passed away! There is one startling sentence which states that the old man was probably reading the very newspaper in which his own death must have been announced. The story was first printed in the *Nineteenth Century* of February, 1900, and has never been added to the works of Hawthorne, though it is in his best vein.

Hawthorne's Concord neighbor, Emerson, used to come to the Athenæum a great deal, even as late as 1875. His daughter, Miss Ellen Emerson, usually accompanied him, carrying his papers and books and her satchel. They would sit by one of the windows overlooking the burying ground and make arrangements as to how they would spend their day in the city. One of the older attendants has strikingly described a conversation between Emerson and Longfellow, carried on as the two great New Englanders stood together overlooking the peaceful cemetery. The author of " Hiawatha," she recalls, was erect and sprightly and smiling as usual, while the transcendentalist, taller in stature, lounged back with his shoulders against a set of *Memoirs of the French Revolution* and regarded his vivacious companion, his strong-cut features beaming with pleasure at the encounter with his long-time friend and sympathizer.

Emerson, this attendant recalls, exemplified in his choice of books his own maxim not to read any publication until it was a year old. But this was, perhaps, necessarily so, inasmuch as he wished always to keep for a long time the books he took out, and recent publications are not permitted to be held for a long period. The record book at the Athenæum in 1867 has down against the Concord scholar Chesterfield's letters, Swedenborg's *Lyra Apostolica*, Huxley, Dryden and Dante. In 1877, which was only five years before his death, Emerson took out Jean Paul's works, Darwin's *Sights and Insights*, Landor's *Famous Women*, Ruskin's *Ethics of the Dust*, Balzac's *Illusions*, Butler's *Year of Consolation*, and *Middlemarch*, as well as Horace.

William F. Poole, who originated Poole's Index, was at one time [1856–68] the librarian of the Athenæum, and it was here that the chief part of the work which has since lightened the labor of so many writers, was done. Others who have served in this capacity are William Smith Shaw, one of the founders (1813–1822); Seth Bass (1825–1846); Charles Folsom, an ex-librarian of Harvard (1847–1856); Charles Ammi Cutter, originator of Cutter's system of classification (1869–1892); William Coolidge Lane, now librarian at Harvard (1893–1897); and Charles Knowles Bolton, the present librarian, appointed in 1898.

About twenty years ago $30,000 was spent in the improvement of the present building, and even then Boston groaned and sputtered because of what was termed the " modernizing " of its favorite literary haunt, involving as it did the loss of the " Charles Sumner staircase " — which occupied one fourth of the building! At intervals one hears that the old stand is to be abandoned and then, again, Boston has convulsions. Just at present, however, the library seems likely to stay on indefinitely in its old brown-front building near the State House.

For a bookish city Boston was astonishingly slow in providing library accommodation for those who needed it most, i. e. for those who could have no share in the rich privileges of the Athenæum. And the idea of a public library emanated, not from a Bostonian at all, but from a Frenchman, Alexandre Vattemare, who was born in Paris near the close of the eighteenth century. Though bred a surgeon Vattemare in middle life became an impersonator. In the course of his professional tourings, the awful waste of books, imperfectly catalogued and glued to their shelves, impressed itself upon him and he determined to devote time, energy and property to " give the intellectual treasures of the cultivated world the same dissemination and equalization which commerce had already given to its material ones." His aim was nothing less than to establish in every quarter of the world " free public libraries and museums ever open to the use of the people." When he came to America, in 1839, he found that he must not only bring books but create free libraries to put them in, but, nothing daunted, he began a vigorous agitation of the whole matter.

At a meeting held in the Masonic Temple

on the evening of May 5, 1841, M. Vattemare first presented his idea. After hearing what "the renowned Frenchman" — he was so styled by Mayor Chapman in his introductory address — had to say, a committee consisting of Dr. Walter Channing, Rev. Ezra S. Gannett, Rev. G. W. Blagden and Charles Francis Adams was appointed to submit plans and estimates for a building. Yet since we were then having one of our periodic "bad times" it was six years more before anything further was done. Then, in 1847, Mayor Quincy (Josiah Quincy Jr.) interested himself in the project and offered five thousand dollars towards a public library on condition that ten thousand dollars additional for the same purpose should be raised. M. Vattemare had meanwhile forwarded fifty valuable volumes which were being stored in the City Hall, and these were soon joined by gifts of books from Edward Everett, Robert C. Winthrop, S. A. Eliot and others, all of which were placed in the City Hall under the care of Edward Capen.

In August, 1850, Mayor Bigelow contributed $1000 towards the library fund, and Edward Everett, persistently advising the erection of a building, Joshua Bates, a native of Boston, — who afterwards became a prominent member of the firm of Baring Brothers, — donated to the city of his birth (in 1852) the handsome sum

of $50,000 for a Public Library. Now at last
the matter was put into definite shape. Steps
were taken to purchase the Wheeler estate
on Boylston Street; in the meantime, the lower
floor of the Adams schoolhouse on Mason Street
was fitted up for library purposes and a board
of trustees and a librarian were elected. The
Mason Street reading room was opened to the
public March 20, 1854, and in May of the same
year the circulation of books for home use began.

The thing in which Vattemare had been
principally interested was a system of international exchanges of volumes concerning the
growth, development and history of each country.
He saw that Boston received nearly one hundred
such works from France and Boston duly gave
back a long list of books to the citizens of Paris.
Meanwhile there continued to arrive from
Mr. Bates a rich accumulation of the higher
class of books. To organize this most important
part of the library and give chief control over
the whole to a skilled hand a city ordinance was
passed (March, 1853) creating the office of
superintendent of the Boston Public Library.
The first incumbent was Charles Coffin Jewett.
Upon his death, January 9, 1868, Justin Winsor
was appointed.

The reading-room and lower hall library of
the building on Boylston Street were opened in
1858, and there, for nearly thirty years, all

Boston was made welcome to a collection of books which constantly increased in variety and value. To facilitate the use of these Arthur Mason Knapp, that " giant among reference librarians " for twenty-four years gave heart, soul and mind in devoted service to the public.

The old Corner Bookstore, and some of the literary clubs and famous literary households of the city, must be mentioned before we leave this subject of Boston as a literary centre. James T. Fields was the *genius loci* at the corner of School and Washington Streets, and hardly a man whose name now forms a part of New England's contribution to literature but has " loafed around " the " Old Corner Book Store," so far as he loafed at all. George William Curtis has said of this institution:

" It was a very remarkable group of men — indeed, it was the first group of really great American authors — which familiarly frequented the corner as the friend of Fields. There had been Bryant and Irving and Cooper and Halleck and Paulding and Willis of New York, but there had been nothing like the New England circle which compelled the world to acknowledge that there was an American literature."

Field's home at 148 Charles Street was similarly a rallying-place and has long been well known for its delightful hospitality to

visiting celebrities. Crowded from entrance to
attic with artistic objects and literary trophies,
this house is still a delight to all so fortunate as
to know it. For, beside its rare books and
the intimate pictures, there are mementoes of
the many famous men and women who have
stayed there for a longer or shorter period. In
one little bedroom, provided with old furniture,
antique engravings and bric-à-brac, have reposed
at different times, as guests, Dickens, Thackeray, Hawthorne, Trollope, Matthew Arnold,
Kingsley, Miss Cushman, and Bayard Taylor.
The late Sarah Orne Jewett made her home
with Mrs. Fields while in Boston.

Of Thackeray, who stayed here in 1850,
Fields tells a delicious story in his *Yesterdays
with Authors*. He gave him a dinner at the
Tremont House and American oysters had been
provided. Thackeray had as yet made the
acquaintance only of the small British species.
A half dozen of the American variety were set
before the Englishman, who looked at them
in some amazement, and then gingerly picked
up the smallest one.

" Try the big one," urged Fields.

" No," was the reply. " It is too much like
the high priest's servant's ear that Peter cut
off."

After some advice as to the proper mode
of procedure, Thackeray achieved his first

American oyster, and he then remarked, " Profoundly grateful. I feel as if I had swallowed a little baby."

Another literary home which was long a centre of intellectual stimulus was that of Mr. and Mrs. Edwin P. Whipple, at 11 Pinckney Street. For thirty years they held "Sunday evenings" of rare hospitality and charm, to which came, among others, the brilliant Rufus Choate, one of the greatest forensic advocates America has ever produced.

For many years the hospitable home of Louise Chandler Moulton at 28 Rutland Square was another happy hunting-ground for authors and visiting celebrities. Her " Fridays " are now perpetuated, in some measure, by the weekly teas, in their rooms at Kensington Chambers, of the Boston Authors' Club, of which Mrs. Moulton was long a valued and devoted member.

Chief in prestige of the literary clubs of the nineteenth century was the Saturday Club, inaugurated about the time the *Atlantic Monthly* was founded. It met on Saturday once a month at two o'clock in the mirror-room at Parker's and among its members were Emerson, Hawthorne, Longfellow, Motley, Whipple, Whittier, Professor Benjamin Pierce, Sumner, R. H. Dana, Dr. Holmes, Governor Andrew, Charles Eliot Norton, Henry James (the elder), Judge Hoar, Chief Justice Gray, Prescott, and later, President Eliot, Howells, Aldrich and Phillips Brooks. Agassiz, who was a great favorite in the club, always insisted on having a huge joint of roast mutton served entire, from which he cut his own slice, requiring the meat to be cooked more and more rare as he got on in years.

Of the Papyrus Club, made up of journalists, authors and painters, John Boyle O'Reilly was long a favorite member and for many years president. It was to O'Reilly, who had a peculiar love for things Egyptian, that the club, organized in 1872, owes its name. At the time of his death in 1890, O'Reilly and Archbishop John J. Williams were joint owners of the *Pilot*, a Roman Catholic paper of wide influence and marked readability. To O'Reilly, who has been called " the most romantic figure in literary Boston," a noble statue now stands on the Back Bay Fens. It is not without significance, I think, that Boston is the only city in the country which has thus honored a purely literary man.

THE END.

INDEX